It Don't Mean A Thing If It Ain't Got That Zing!

It Don't Mean A Thing If It Ain't Got That Zing!

Colin Copperfield

ISBN, paperback: 978-1-80227-262-8
ISBN, ebook: 978-1-80227-263-5

This book is typeset in Times New Roman

This book is dedicated to Robert 'Snitch' Johnson,
to every performer lucky enough to tread the boards *and*
to my darling wife, Kathy, and our dog Crazy Daisy

Overture

Having been born in the arse end of the East End of London, and leaving school with only a 30-yard swimming certificate stolen from a friend, Colin had two possible paths to follow in life: prison, following many of his contemporaries, or show business, following his dad, Wally. Wally, when not employed as a dustman, worked as a 'stooge' (an on-tap straight man and general scapegoat) for visiting comedians at the Theatre Royal, Stratford East. Colin chose the latter as, being a shortarse (if a fairly fit one), he reckoned the 'nick' was "far too butch for a boy of a sensitive nature". He felt that showbiz, with its tall thin men who liked show tunes and who, if not totally gay, certainly helped them out when they were busy, would be a safer bet. (Despite numerous rumours to the contrary, Colin is not Tommy-Two-Ways and doesn't help them out when they are busy. But lots of his friends do, so that's alright then.) After a course of singing lessons with an ex-RAF chap who definitely engaged in extracurricular activities, and dance lessons with a very young, and very gorgeous Arlene Phillips at the Dance Centre in Covent Garden, Col jetéd forth onto the boards and loved every beautiful minute of it. There followed six years in West End shows and twenty-five years with the internationally acclaimed vocal harmony group, 'Wall Street Crash', who performed in over 900 TV shows. Col went on to co-write the Cockney musical 'Paradise Lane', with David Mackay.

These are his tales. There are many more, but these are the ones that, with luck, won't end up with him being arrested, divorced or at the bottom of the Thames wearing concrete booties. Hope you enjoy them....

There really is *no* business like *show* business.

Steve (Perty) Pert

colincopperfield1@gmail.com
www.wallstreetcrash.co.uk

Disclaimer:

To those of a sensitive nature who have difficulty with some of the more colourful expressions in the English language, please steel yourselves for an onslaught. Better still, pour yourself a strong drink or reach for a Camden cornet, and sit back and let the good times roll.

Introduction

Frank Sinatra or a Double Diamond?

There's nothing like a good old fashioned massive decision to be made early on in your career! As it happened, as showbiz choices go, this one was a no-brainer. Yup! We could either appear as Frank Sinatra's support act at New York's prestigious Carnegie Hall, or top the bill at a backdoor dive, the Double Diamond Club in Caerphilly South Wales. Our band's name may have been Wall Street Crash but in America we were completely unknown and supporting Frank Sinatra would have been a huge game changer for the future of the group.

It was Sammy Davis Junior who had raised our hopes of being sprinkled with the Sinatra stardust. We were supporting Sammy at the Victoria Apollo Theatre in London. He was my all-time hero, a singer and dancer and, in my opinion, the best performer ever. I admired him enormously. We had worked with big names before, but we had rarely met any of them. Generally, when the support act performed, half the audience would still be in the bar. They had no idea who you were *and,* what's more, they didn't care. You would come on, do your 30/40 minutes before the interval, after which the main attraction would come on. We were introduced to Shirley Bassey but only after we had toured with her for ages and had been on the Michael Parkinson Show.

We also supported Dean Martin at the Victoria Apollo for ten nights and met him briefly, for one quick photo call after the opening show. It was generally believed that Dean Martin was something of a showbiz lush, and wasn't averse to the occasional extremely large drink. Intriguingly, he had his own tiny private bar installed in the wings adjacent to his stage entrance. We used to come offstage and loiter by his bar in the hope that we would catch him grabbing a quick snifter. But, disappointingly, it didn't happen. He never used the theatre dressing rooms and used to arrive in a chauffeur-driven limo three minutes before he was due to go on. He would enter the theatre through a street pass door, walk past his bar, past us, straight onto the stage and croon ("mock" drunkenly) into his opening number.

- It's knowin' that your door is always open,
  and your path is free to walk". ♪♪

This procedure was reversed at the end of his act. When he came offstage he would saunter past us, pausing momentarily to acknowledge our presence, walk past his bar, out through the pass door, climb into his limo and disappear back to his hotel.

Supporting Lena Horne at the London Palladium was a different kettle of fish. After the first show Lena came straight to our dressing room and insisted that we all go out on the town and get very, very merry, which of course we did. She was a gorgeous down-to-earth lady.

Anyway, we were rehearsing at the Victoria Apollo and our manager Gerry Maxin told us that Mr. Davis would like to meet us. Bloody hell! This was a first. We went to Sammy Davis's dressing room and were introduced.

He said,

- Great to meet you guys. Look, I know what it's like being a support act. Half the audience are still in the bar because they've only come to see the main liner and aren't really interested in you. What I'm going to do tomorrow is this: I will go on first, do three songs then I'll introduce you as my co-stars. That way, all the audience will be there for you.

What a diamond! It was a really generous thing to do, and very much appreciated. So, next night, he went on stage, performed a few numbers …

- ♪♪ Just once in a lifetime,
  A man knows a moment ……. ♪♪

and then..

- Ladies and gentlemen, my co-stars….Wall Street Crash!

We came on. The place was heaving. Fantastic! We did ten nights with my hero at the Apollo. On the last night I was standing by the side of the stage having a natter with Sammy, waiting to go on after him, when he said,

- Colin, it's been great working with you guys. I'm heading back to the States tomorrow and I'm going to have a word with my pal Frank.

FUCKING HELL!

- Ladies and gentlemen, Sammy Davis Junior…

And he walked on stage.

In a state of complete (I'm going to tread the boards with Old Blue Eyes) breathless hysteria, I ran to the back of the stage to find Gerry.

- Gerry, Gerry, Gerry (*gasp gasp*), I've just been talking to Sammy and he's going back to the States and he's going to..have..a word..with his..pal… FRANK.

Ever the sanguine rationalist, he said,

- Colboy, caaalm down, breathe, put your head between your legs (*which, out of interest, I find is my best singing position*). We'll open the champagne when they close the plane doors. Don't hold your breath.

Anyway, a week later, Frank Sinatra's manager rang our Gerry,

- Mr. Sinatra has spoken to Sammy Davis and said that he would like Wall Street Crash to support him for one night only at Carnegie Hall.

TOTALLY FUCKING HELL!!!!!!!!!

This would crack Wall Street Crash in America. We were a glitzy performance band: great-looking girls with legs the length of the M1 motorway, good-looking guys, tall, butch, vast amounts of talent, and……. me. With white tails, flashy choreography, great harmonies, lots of witty banter and all that sort of thing we were PERFECT for the swanky cabaret performance band circuit: Vegas, Caesar's Palace, the Sands, the Las Vegas Hotel, all the big venues, followed by the Oprah Winfrey TV show and the rest, guest appearances at the White House (as opposed to the Shite House - the location of some of our early gigs). THE WORLD WAS OUR LOBSTER!!!

The only stumbling block was that, four months earlier, when we didn't have a lot of work, we had been booked to do a week at the above-mentioned Double Diamond Club in Caerphilly. (Where? You might well ask.) Gerry called the club and explained the situation. He told the guy organising the event that the Carnegie Hall gig would crack the band in America, no question about it.

- Oh no, boyo (*very broad Welsh accent*), you're asking us to let them out. We can't do that. We've done the publicity. We've even put their name up in COLOURED CHALK.

(If your name is up in coloured chalk in South Wales, you've made it. It is a recognition reserved for the likes of Tom Jones, Shirley Bassey, Engelbert Humperdinck, Tony Bennett, and... GOD)

Gerry cajoled Mr. Organising Guy,

- We'll get another group for you. They won't be like Wall Street Crash, but they'll fit the bill.
- No, no, no, we'll take you to court.

Now, if this little setback had occurred a few years earlier, it would have been no problemo. I would simply have got on the blower to Ronnie and Reggie[1], explain that I was a fellow East End backstreet boy trying to make an honest bob in the precarious world of showbiz, and could they possibly see their way clear to sending a few of their boys down to the valleys to 'ave a word and put the frighteners on Mr. OG to 'peacefully' resolve the Frank/Diamond dilemma? Another little request, but it would be great if the away-day coach party to the green, green grass of home could include Albert Donoghue (Reggie's right hand man), Ian Barrie (Ronnie's right hand man) and, just to perk things up a bit, Freddie Foreman (freelance enforcer involved in the gangland demise of Frank 'the mad axeman' Mitchell), a delightful trio who all loved animals and were very kind to their dear old mums. The problem would have been sorted out in approximately one minute and thirty-eight seconds and we would have been on our way, lounging in the front end of a 747, regaled with large glasses of Cristal, all set to hang out with Frank and his massively famous chums. But! Hey ho! Back to reality.

BOLLOCKS! We're up the fuck here. What are we going to do?

At the time, we had our own BBC TV special coming up, a season at the Talk of the Town in Leicester Square, and a lot of prestigious work in the pipeline. We could have been in serious trouble if we had turned down the Double Diamond Club and they sued. With litigation hanging over us, we would probably have never worked in England again. Many people over the years have said, "Why

---

1 The Kray twins were infamous East End gangsters of the 1950s and 60s.

didn't you take the chance? If you'd cracked America you would have made a fortune and would never have needed to work anywhere else in the world." But, being true to our heritage, we decided that wasn't for us. What a bunch of wankers!

So Gerry rang Frank Sinatra's manager and explained the problem: a long-term booking we couldn't get out of.

Frank's manager responded,

- I'll tell you one thing Gerry, you only turn Mr. Sinatra down once.

And so it was. We never went to America and we never worked with Sinatra. We did the week at the Double Diamond Club in Caerphilly. It was like a scene out of the Blues Brothers. All they needed was a net in front of the stage to catch the flying bottles; people were fighting and throwing things at each other (they definitely weren't throwing knickers à la Tom Jones). They couldn't have given a monkey's who was on.

In the 25 years we worked as a group we were only unpaid for two gigs, and that was one of them. The club closed two weeks after we were there. In retrospect, should we have said, "Up your arse Caerphilly", packed our frocks, dancing shoes and make-up bags and gone to America?............ Nah!

How Wall Street Crash Began

In 1979 and 1980 ITV were filming a new series of 'Oh Boy!', a rock 'n roll show that had been very popular in the fifties. Keith Strachan was the musical director and I was one of the in-shot backing singers called 'The Cats and the Kittens'. (The story of what led to this bit of serendipity is told in the next scene: 'Goodbye Dubai'.) Keith approached eight of us with the idea of creating a classy performance group who would combine singing, dancing and acting to produce a vocally rich and original troupe with overt theatrical leanings. It was an ambitious plan. In fact, when we first explained the concept to a group of our friends, they all said, "It's far too big. It will be a financial disaster". So, with a touch of irony, we called the band Wall Street Crash.

We started rehearsals in late 1979 and from the start it was clear that the idea would work. Under Keith's guidance we grew into a group which displayed the breadth of talent that would appeal to a wide range of different audiences and would fill the stage at any large prestigious venue.

The master plan was simple - we would start with a showcase in London which, it was hoped, would lead to offers of work throughout the world. And this is exactly what happened. I don't think any of us at that time dared to hope that anything substantial would come of the venture but we got on well as a creative unit and enjoyed the process of developing new staging ideas. If the group was successful, then great! If not we would go back to being jobbing performers and would definitely be all the richer for the WSC experience.

I think a big part of WSC's success was down to Keith's shrewd choice of group members. An exceptional choreographer, Mary had played the title role in the West End musical 'Irene'. Ricky Piper had lots of quirky off-the-wall song ideas that gave us street cred while still keeping an air of sophistication. Paul and I had worked together in the musical 'Leave Him to Heaven' at the New London Theatre in Drury Lane and had done a lot of improvisational acting under the guidance of the director, Philip Hedley of Stratford E15 fame. Each of us had our own creative ideas and, when we put them together, the mix seemed to work.

Much further down the line it turned out that WSC evolved into having a different focus and appeal in different countries: in the UK we were seen as a slick, up-market cabaret outfit. In Italy and the rest of Europe we were both a cabaret act and a pop group. In Holland we were both of these things and also a cult band - much more theatrically quirky and off-the-wall funny. However, through all of these personas, we maintained the basic WSC format and originality, and we never lost sight of our roots.

The venue was chosen for our first performance. It was 'Country Cousins', just off the Kings Road, when it was at its most trendy. Financial backing came from an unlikely source. One of our members, Jean, had made the acquaintance of a German Baron (Melchior Baron von Schlippenbach), who had been Field Marshal Erwin Rommel's aide de camp at El Alamein in the North African desert in the Second World War. (Schlippi, as he was later known, should have written his autobiography about life on the run from the Nazis and fighting with the French resistance.) While not *really* wealthy, Schlippi appeared to have access to funds. He invested in the group and it turned out to be a very profitable decision for him.

I well remember the first time we met Schlippi. Jean had arranged for us to meet him at a smart restaurant in Chelsea, just opposite Schlippi's posh flat. The purpose of the meeting was to persuade him to invest enough money in WSC to buy costumes, score our musical arrangements and give each of us £50 per week to (just about) live on until, with luck, the venture took off. After the introductions, Schlippi listened intently while Keith outlined the plans for the group.

When Keith had finished Schlippi said,

    - How much money would you need to get started?

Keith said, as we all crossed our fingers,

    - To cover everything, £5,000.

Schlippi left the restaurant and re-appeared ten minutes later clutching a brown envelope crammed with notes.

    - Here is £6,000. I think the group has a good chance of success. If
      you need more, let me know.

We said we couldn't simply take the money and that, to safeguard his investment, it would have to be written into a legal contract. Schlippi used an expression, in his broad German accent, that he would use many times over the following years.

- I tell you friendly. I don't need a contract. You are now my friends and I always trust my friends. If the group is successful you may pay me back in very small amounts and, if success does not come, I will accept my loss and we will always remain friends.

Schlippi, who was not a young man at the time, regained his youth and had the most fantastic time travelling the world with us. The group was immediately successful and his £6,000 was returned within a couple of months, in spite of his resistance. From then on, every so often we would pay him, as if we had a contract, and he would always return it in the form of gifts or smart dinners. He insisted that, because of the fabulous times he had with us, he had received five hundred times more from his initial investment than he ever could have expected. They don't make them like that anymore.

We opened on Tuesday 23rd March, 1980 with a five-night gig. All eight performers, a ten-piece band, and of course, MD Keith Strachan, were crammed onto the tiny stage. The idea was to pack the audience with agents, bookers, promoters, recording company executives - anyone who could make the most of the group's potential. On one of those nights the legendary TV producer, Ernest Maxin, was in the crowd, and he absolutely loved what he saw. Because of him, we found an agent, Gerry, formed a management company, we had our first live gig and made our first TV appearance. Once launched, WSC didn't look back. The group took off like a rocket and zoomed around the artistic constellations for the next quarter of a century. We enjoyed enormous success worldwide. We did countless concerts, produced five albums and twelve singles, garnering many awards for our work and (very importantly) respect from our peers. And, as if that wasn't enough, we also had the time of our lives along the way.

It was our custom to give everyone nicknames so Mary became Marge (after a misspelling in a magazine article) and Paul became Polly (I can't remember why). I became Colboy, probably because they all thought I looked and spoke like a back street car salesman (bloody cheek), Steve Pert became Perty and Mandy became Mand or Brandy Balls. And WSC became known to friends and fans as the Wallies. Over the years twenty vocalists passed through our ranks, but we five were the final line-up for the longest period. Mary, Paul and I were there from the beginning and stayed for the lifetime of the group. And what a lifetime it was!

Having said that, it wouldn't surprise any of us if we got a call next week saying,

- Pack your frocks Wallies, the gigs are back on.

I for one have my frocks ready and waiting by the front door. Bring it on!

Postscript: Keith Strachan had a well-deserved, very successful post-Wall Street Crash career. He was the musical director of many West End shows and was also a talented stage director. During the time Keith was mentoring the Wallies we would spend countless hours in our rehearsal rooms. Sometimes, during a tea break, he would noodle tunes on the piano, often tinkling away at a charming, catchy little ditty that was instantly memorable. One day I asked him what the tune was and he said it was from a musical he had co-written that hadn't taken off. It was called 'Scraps'. I said that, with the right lyrics, it would make a great record because it was such an engaging piece. Not long after he left the Wallies, Keith and his co-writer revamped the song, which became a massive Christmas hit for Cliff Richard - 'Mistletoe and Wine'. Keith also wrote the incidental music for the TV show, 'Who Wants to be a Millionaire', the franchise of which was sold worldwide. Not too shabby a career, eh?

Goodbye Dubai

Well before WSC, from 1973 I worked in five shows in the West End of London. I was twenty-nine. 'Tommy' the musical had closed and, for the first time in six years, I became a 'resting' actor. I love the expression, 'resting' actor. I mean, are we really so exhausted from mincing around the stage for a couple of hours per evening, wearing extremely lightweight make-up, light-as-a-feather custom-made costumes, and generally being so fêted and adored by the audience that we need to 'rest' for three months in a darkened room, lying on an antique chaise longue with a Cinzano Bianco and a copy of 'Who's Who in the Theatre'?

You would have thought that after six years of treading the West End boards, I would have amassed a nice little nest egg of dosh in the bank, enough to relax for a while, have a holiday, take a few dance classes, catch up on all the shows I'd missed and not worry for a while but, for some reason, I was skint! Possibly because of too many well-oiled late nights in Joe Allen's Restaurant, or having too much fun in Macready's Actors' Club, or even too many up-all-nights in the Up all Night Wine Bar on the Fulham Road. Anyway, wherever the hard earned loot had gone I had enjoyed every second of it. So, what to do to make a few bob until the National Theatre and the Royal Shakespeare Company realised I was available and came knocking at my door to disturb me from my very important 'rest'? Any role they might offer would, of course, have to be no more demanding than that of Hamlet's eyebrow plucker, which I would nevertheless approach as a taxing character part involving sixty seconds of enervating Stanislavski-style method acting. Overcome by my exertions I would hike back to the dressing room to watch repeats of 'Drop the Dead Donkey' until the curtain call, when I would be required to perform repeated energy-sapping bowing from the waist along with the other *stars*. As someone once said, "There are no small acting roles, only small actors", and I fitted the bill for both.

But failing that, there was always the good old reliable busking on the Underground with my faithful guitar (more details in Scene 17, The Busker of Love), although London Transport had started to formalise the biz. This was probably due to the fact that the arteries of the tube network had become clogged up by the growing number of 'resting' actors who could just about manage three chords, sing more or less in tune, and had a working knowledge of the Simon and Garfunkel songbook. As a result, you now had to register and be given a designated spot to ply your trade.

Another fill-in option for out-of-work thesps was the 'Singing Telegram', to which I will dedicate a separate story later on. Early one morning after a long day and night of having far too much fun singing telegrams all over London, my girlfriend Yvonne, who was a dancer and a dance teacher at the Italia Conti stage school in Clerkenwell, told me that she had been offered a six-month contract to perform with her dance group at a swish hotel in Dubai and that they were also looking for a boy singer and dancer to join the act. The money was good, we would have smart rooms in the hotel, free food etc and only have to do one show a night. It was coming up to Christmas and I was in a panic about buying prezzies with my limited funds, so this was the perfect get out; I would tell everybody that I would 'do' Christmas for them when I returned to London in June with loads of dosh and a fab suntan to boot. Perfect! We rehearsed the act at Conti's for three weeks. I had rented out my little basement flat in Islington for the six months; one final rehearsal that evening and we were off to the sun on the morning flight. We had a great final run-through and were getting ready to go home when the Entertainments Manager at Conti's came into the room looking very pale and very worried,

- I'm so, so sorry everyone but we have a big problem, the hotel has pulled out of the contract. We don't know why but we think they may have found a less expensive act and have given the gig to them. We're going to sue them for breach of contract. We are so sorry but you won't be going to Dubai tomorrow. .

Oh fuck! Christmas only days away, not much money, and someone moving into my flat on the following afternoon. We were stunned into silence. There was nothing else to do; we slowly got our things together, said our goodbyes, and headed for the door. Then I remembered that Paul was having a farewell party for us at his house in Mill Hill. I rang him and relayed the whole sorry story.

- Well you've got to come to the party, all your friends are here. We'll all have a laugh and worry about it tomorrow. See you soon.

Yvonne said she was far too upset to go to a party and was going home, so I went alone. I arrived to find a huge banner hanging across the front door reading 'Bon Voyage Col', now crossed out and changed to 'Welcome home Col'. We all got absolutely sloshed and I have no recollection of getting home. I woke with a huge hangover and the painful realisation that someone was moving into my flat in a few hours' time. Feeling very guilty I sheepishly rang my intended lodger. Bless her heart! When I explained what had happened she said it wasn't a problem as her boyfriend had asked her to move in with him soon anyway and they had become engaged the day before, so it had worked out well. A huge relief. I fell back into a deep sleep only to be woken by the jarring sound of my phone. It was Paul.

- Hello mate. I was just telling Keith Strachan about your plight and he wants to have a word with you. (Keith and I had worked together on the Rolling Stones musical 'Let the Good Stones Roll' at London's Ambassadors Theatre and he was now the musical director of the TV show 'Oh Boy', on which Paul was one of the in-shot backing singers).

- Hi Col I don't know if you're interested, but one of the singers in the show is having trouble learning the harmony lines and wants out. Paul told me what happened with your Dubai gig. If you don't have anything else lined up, I think you'd fit in with the 'Oh Boy' cast perfectly. I know you can handle the job, so the gig's yours if you're interested.

- Keith at this precise moment if you had offered me a job sweeping the studio floor I would be interested. You're a lifesaver. Thank you.

- Great! We're rehearsing at Cecil Sharp House in Regent's Park. Have a large mug of black coffee and come along as soon as you're ready. Welcome aboard.

There is not one ounce of doubt in my mind that my life has been 60% luck, 25% timing, and 15% talent. This isn't false modesty. I really do believe that's how my life has panned out and I am so very, very grateful for it. This was another chunk of 60% luck kicking in when I really needed it. 'Oh Boy' was a great job: two series for ATV, great fun, lots of fabulous 50s and 60s songs, slick choreography for us in-shot singers, and the chance to work with real stars. It was at the end of that series that Keith had the brilliant idea of putting together a singing, dancing, acting, performance group using the backing singers from the show. He picked those of us whom he thought would gel vocally and in terms of personality, explaining that the idea might or might not work, but it was worth a try. He suggested that we put some ideas together, rehearse, and see how it turned out. And Wall Street Crash was born.

So here's the thing. I really do believe that life is all sliding doors and, as the lovely, and so very much missed, George Michael said,

- Turn a different corner and we never would have met.

If I had gone to Dubai I would never have been a proud member of Wall Street Crash.

Keith, thank you for all the incredible years you gave to so many people for so long. None of it would have happened without you.

But, before we explore how Wall Street Crash blasted onto the scene ..... as Julie Andrews sang in 'Do Re Mi' from 'The Sound of Music', "Let's start at the very beginning...".

But, before we start at the very beginning, I would like to say that this book would never have been written without the help of my gorgeous and adorable friend Ceinwen. We had such fun writing it. I had so much fun living it. And I hope you have fun reading it.

Running Order

The Interval

Colin Copperfield

A Pocketful of Holes

A pocketful of holes didn't bother me at all 'cos I didn't have anything to put in my pockets anyway. Every other kid in the street was the same. In fact, if Mr. Somebody had said, "I'll give £1 to any kid who hasn't got a pocketful of holes", Mr. Somebody would have sauntered off with all of his money intact. But were we having fun playing in the bomb wrecks and devastation of post-war East London? Were we enjoying every bite of our sugar sandwiches (or jam sarnies if we were lucky)? Not arf! Pre-Facebook, Twitter, texting, streaming and all that malarkey, we played all day and half the night on the grimy streets amidst huge, deep, rat-infested holes that were filled with stinking water, holes that once were houses. Our favourite was a bombed-out pub because it had deep cellars full of old beer crates; on a good day we might find a couple of unexploded bottles of booze, which we got down our throats real sharp, no messing.

I was born Colin Satchell in July 1950 in Forest Gate, London E7. (I had no middle name because my parents couldn't afford one!) The 'E' in the postcode is very important, because it means you were born in the East End, and are therefore a Cockney. Now, there is this theory that to be a 'true' Cockney, you have to be born within the sound of Bow Bells. Fair cop guv'nor, if that is the 'official' version. BUT, for my money, if you're an Eastender you're a Cockney, and I'll fight anybody who sez otherwise. (When I say, "I'll fight anyone", I mean anyone less than four feet tall, very out of shape, partially sighted, a great big sissy with preferably only one arm, and paralytically drunk.)

The Second World War had ended five years earlier. Rationing had more or less finished, and life was getting a little easier for everyone. We lived in a tiny two up two down terrace house with an outside toilet. I shared the front upstairs bedroom with my brother Dave, Mum (Ivy) and Dad (Walter or Wally as he was known), all four of us in one tiny room, very cosy. Nan (Alice) had the back upstairs bedroom and a tiny sitting room downstairs. The scullery (kitchen) had a copper (an old tin boiler) which we had to heat up for hours

27

when we had our once-weekly communal tin bath on Sundays: Mum first, then Dad, Dave and then me. You can imagine the colour of the water, and the temperature, after they had all had their turn. (Nan didn't bother, thank God.) She had what's known as a cat's lick, a quick once over with a wet flannel.

Sometimes as a special treat and if Dad was feeling a bit flush he would take us all to West Ham Baths, a large indoor swimming pool on the Romford Road about an hour's walk away. As an added service they provided bath cubicles. The old fashioned baths were so big that Dave and I could almost swim in them. It was luxury! I think it cost about four old pence for a half hour scrub and soak and was a blissful step-up from the old tin bath experience. The baths didn't have working taps. When the water started to cool down, you would shout...

- More hot in number four please!

and the man at the end of the corridor would release more steaming water into your little part of heaven. When your time was up he would pass in a huge fluffy towel and, after a quick dry off, you would put your clobber back on, go out onto the street and back into the real world.

My earliest childhood memory was of my Dad bashing out a sort of tune on the old Joanna ('pianna') in my nan's room. It was a clapped out old upright that Dad had got 'off the dust' (Dad's job as a dustman meant that nearly everything we owned had come off the dust). When I say Dad 'bashed the Joanna', I wasn't joking. He had a style all his own which he called 'vamping', which involved going up and down the keyboard with his right hand while crashing down with his left hand, palms flat, wherever he saw fit (no single notes or proper chords mind you, just a random bash). Anyway it seemed to work OK, and we'd all have a good singsong.

- ♪♪You take the legs off some old table
You take the arms off some old chair..♪♪

When I think back, this is where I did my first professional paid gig! Aged five or six (Dave was three years older), Dad would give bruv and me a week to learn a tune and the words to a current song, which we performed on Friday night after dinner, with Dad bashing out the (err) 'melody' line on the Joanna (no help at all really). If we got all the words and the tune right, he gave us each a penny but, if we buggered it up, he would only give us a halfpenny (an 'a'penny') followed by the other half later than night with the stern-ish warning: "Now you two learn it proper by next week". We really did try to get it right for him and, c'mon...be fair...a paid gig at the age of five!

So here's the thing. How did a little toe-rag from the back streets of the East End (reinvented as Colin Copperfield) come to be standing on stage at the Theatre Royal Drury Lane for the 1982 Royal Command Performance, having just performed with his group 'Wall Street Crash', and about to be presented to HRH Prince Charles and his grandma the Queen Mother?... No mystery! 60% luck, 25% timing and 15% talent.

1. Backstreet Boy

- Call the fire brigade! Call the fire brigade! Nan's caught the bloody
chimney on fire again.

I lost count of the times one of us shouted that, 'cos Nan was '*always*'catching
the bloody chimney on fire, even though Dad used to poke some long brushes
(scored off the dust) up there every now and again. After he'd huffed and
puffed, sworn a lot, and jiggled them around, all the black gunk that was up
the chimney would cascade down into Nan's room, adorning the furniture,
the dog, Nan, the goldfish and us. Despite Dad's gallant efforts, it was pretty
clear that his intervention achieved no improvement in the fire safety of the
chimney, but *was* successful in choking us all and increasing the odds of an
early soot-inhalation death. I never quite worked out if Nan really wanted to
burn the house down (it would have been a big improvement in my opinion),
or if she just liked to see all those butch fireman-blokes screaming up in their
big red fire engine with the bell on the top clanging like mad, leaping out, all
'Towering Inferno' style, leaning their ladder against the house (the weight of
the ladder causing the house to sway slightly), scrambling up onto the roof,
Nan ogling their arses all the way up (she was 105 at the time....she wasn't
really, but even if she had been it wouldn't have stopped her), swishing their
hoses all over the roof whilst shouting out,

- Don't worry Alice , we'll soon 'ave it out *again*.

They all knew her name 'cos they came out at least once a fortnight to battle the
Nan-generated flames, while we, and the other residents of the road, cheered
them on. They also knew 'pyro' Nan would make them a nice cup of rosie after
their heroic efforts.

So...how did Nan keep setting fire to the chimney, you ask? There used to be a
newspaper called 'The News of the World' or 'The *Screws* of the World', as it
was known, because of its gossipy scandals and juicy titbits. The pages were
so huge that you could have wallpapered a small flat with two sheets of it,
and they were also an ideal size for Nan to 'draw' the fire. The art of drawing
the fire consisted of setting the fire as usual with a sheet of 'The Screws', a
few sticks of wood, a little coal on the top, lighting the paper with a Swan
Vesta match, giving it a couple of minutes to get going and voilà: a lovely

roaring fire. However, invariably the roaring bit didn't happen quickly enough for Nan, so she would hold a double sheet of 'The Screws' across the front of the fireplace; the fire behind it would struggle to get oxygen, and this would encourage the flames to surge upwards. It's been a while since I was awarded my PhD in Pure Science and Pyrotechnics from Oxford University, but I think that was the general idea. What of course happened was that the flames flew upwards so fast that they set fire to Nan's 'Screws' and the soot-filled chimney, and 999 was the order of the day, again. We didn't own a phone (Dad hadn't scored one off the dust yet) so we had to choose between knocking next door 'cos they did have one (probably nicked it), or running to the red phone box on the corner of the street. By the time we did this, the flames would be shooting skywards at an alarming rate and the neighbours would be gathering their most precious belongings and considering evacuation, yet again. It was a toss up as to what was more of a danger - wartime bombing or having Nan living in the vicinity. But, thanks to the intervention of our gallant firemen, we all survived Nan's attempts at domestic arson and life went on as normal at 148 Wellington Road. Well, 'normal' in our world anyway.

2. Teddy Bears, No Picnic

One particularly severe winter, when Dad could only find part-time work and
the funds wouldn't stretch to buying coal, Dad bought a little paraffin stove
which we put in the middle of our room and all five of us, including Nan,
would huddle around it. Mum was always trying to make the most of a bad
job, saying,

- Yum yum yum, tonight we're gonna have teddy bears' porridge.

Dave and I would get all excited as Mum put a little saucepan on top of the
paraffin heater, as if we were all going camping. She'd add milk, small chunks
of bread, loads of sugar and heat it 'til it came almost to the boil. Dave and I
would take turns at stirring it and, when the bread was nice and soggy, Mum
would dish it up, claiming authoritatively,

- This is what all the teddy bears in the world have for their dinner.

(There must have been a lot of pissed off teddy bears out there, if this was as
good as it got.)

When things were really bad and we didn't have any money for the electric
meter, we would sit in the dark, secretly wishing that we had enough teddy
bears' porridge left to choke ourselves to death with.

Mum would try her best to lift our spirits,

- Right! Let's have a good old singsong around the fire.

Of course what she really meant *was..*

- Let's have a good old sing song around the paraffin heater,

but I suppose it wouldn't have had quite the same ring to it. Off we'd go,

- ♪ Pack up your troubles in yer old kit bag and smile, smile, smile'
  (none of us was smiling).

- ♪ It's a long way to Tipperary, it's a long way to go (bet they've all
  got *roaring* fucking fires in Tipperary).

- ♪ Keep the home fires burning…. (hang on a minute, Mum! We *are*
  at home and there are no fires burning here).

Did our poverty do us any harm? Well, Dave and I got double pneumonia, Dad got gout in both feet, his left arm and his right testicle, and both of Mum's legs dropped off. No! No *real* harm.

The following winter was even colder and, still with no money about, I think even Mum and Dad couldn't face another winter with all of us huddling and shivering around the paraffin heater, so our faithful old 'Joanna' had to go. We'd sung many a good ditty around her and now she was going to be used for firewood in Nan's fireplace. As we were breaking it up, bashing it with big hammers and throwing the thick strings away, I remember thinking I had never heard it sound so tuneful. No offence, Dad. Anyway, it kept us warm for a few weeks and of course kept the fire brigade busy when Nan set fire to the chimney again, just like the good old days.

At one stage Dad got a two-day job driving what were called 'hospital outpatient cars'. They looked exactly like the old black London cabs and were used to ferry people who were well enough to leave hospital but too unwell to go home on their own. Dad, not one to miss an opportunity now that he had some 'wheels' at his disposal (we never owned a car, probably because even Dad couldn't score one off the dust), decided to make the most of his borrowed transport and 'borrow' some coal. Coal was stored in huge mountains in the railway yard at Stratford station where the big old steam trains would fill up their engines for long journeys. The drivers of the hospital cars wore what looked like chauffeurs' uniforms - smart blue suits and a posh peaked hats. This proved to be the perfect disguise for Dad to blague his way past the security man on the gate. In between hospital journeys one day, Dad nipped over to Stratford, successfully conned his way into the railway yard and filled the car up to the roof with coal. Time was of the essence because not only did Dad have to get his ill-gotten gains back to our house, but he also had to wash the car out, disinfect it (a passing acknowledgment of the need for hygiene, given the usual passengers) then get back to work sharpish. Everything was going to plan. Dave and I were even given the day off school (by Dad) so that we and Mum could be waiting for Dad's coal-thieving, council-owned hospital car to arrive. With outsize shovels that Dad had purloined in the usual way, it was intended that we would decant the 'black gold' out of the now filthy car and into the rat-infested coal cellar that was accessed from the corner of Nan's room. What could possibly go wrong? Never having studied physics (or anything else for that matter) it never occurred to Dad that moving the coal about and shovelling it into a warm car might cause it to combust. What Mum, Dave, I and our terrified neighbours witnessed next was an apocalyptic sight - one never to be forgotten. Travelling at no less than eighty-five miles per hour, Dad's hospital car screeched around the corner into Wellington Road with enough black acrid smoke billowing out of the four open windows to screw up the ozone layer for the next two hundred years. How he managed to continue driving remains a total mystery to this day. He skidded to a halt over the last two hundred feet before falling out of the death wagon coughing up his lungs.

- Quick! (*gasp*) get the bloody (*gasp*), fucking stuff out of the car and (*cough, vomit*) help me (*gasp*) clean the fucking thing (*vomit*) up.

The entire street pitched in, demonstrating the same Dunkirk spirit that helped us win World War Two. Buckets of detergent, jugs of water, hose pipes, brooms, mops, scrubbing brushes, and sacks for the coal that wasn't on fire were rustled up. It was a fiasco. Within fifteen minutes Dad was screeching back up the road with smoke still clinging to his hair, ten minutes late to pick up the next innocent victim who was to be driven home in this still filthy, still smoking, still wringing wet, still stinking.....'health car'.

It's a mystery why Dad was never asked to work on the cars again.

Although Dad wasn't a career 'tea leaf' (thief), he certainly wouldn't pass up the opportunity of 'borrowing' a few non-returnable items if they looked him in the eye. For years, if he wasn't working at the time, he would come home laden with boxes of stuff that *I* knew we couldn't afford, such as expensive wine or fifty tins of prime Yorkshire ham. I was a little confused by this so, one day, I asked him where all the stuff was coming from.

- Son, not that it's any of your beeswax but I gets it off the oysters.

Although I didn't have a clue what 'the oysters' were, I *did* know when not to ask any more questions in case I got a clip 'round the ear. When a new batch of goodies arrived I would say,

- Blimey! They're good Dad, did you get them from the oysters?

- Yes, son, now go and put the kettle on.

One day, When I was a little older I ventured a further interrogation,

- Dad, you know you get all this stuff from the oysters?
- Yes, son.
- What *are* the oysters, Dad?
- The oysters, son, are the people wot 'oist things off the back of lorries.

Suddenly it all made sense, the oysters were hoisters. All Cockney's drop their Hs and Dad's ever so slightly dodgy mates would hoist their booty off or out of anywhere there was something to hoist: factories, shops, warehouses, lorries. Anything that was nickable was hoisted. For thirteen years I had believed that Dad had dubious mates who were of the shellfish variety.

Dad occasionally found weekend work on the market stalls in Petticoat Lane. He worked 'down the lane' on a shoe stall for a man named Morrie. Dad was very fond of him. However his fondness didn't stop Dad, quite by accident of course, arriving home on more than one occasion with a nice pair of ladies' high heels stuffed inside his jacket. Mum loved shoes and was always nagging Dad to 'get her some'. Dad did 'get her some' but, because he couldn't pick and choose the shoes that just happened to fall into his jacket, they were often not quite Mum's size, usually too small. This led to our long-suffering Dad having to totter around the house wearing Mum's high heels until they had stretched enough for her to slip them on to her dainty corn-and-bunion-scarred feet. Although Dad's gesture *seemed* very kind and noble, I was always, even at my tender age, a little concerned that Dad insisted on wearing the shoes for a little longer than the stretching process required. Mum would say, when Dad got home from work and would (all too eagerly) ask,

- Where's yer new bleedin shoes?

- Blimey Wally you've 'ad yer feet in them shoes for weeks nah. When they gunna be ready?

Was my Dad a closet, Cockney, cross-dressing, dustman? Nah! He just would have done anything to keep Mum happy. (Mmmm?)

In the summer months life was much easier, even though we still didn't have any money. We kids would play in the streets all day, only coming home when it got dark. On Sundays we would watch 'Robin Hood' or 'William Tell' or even better, 'The Man from U.N.C.L.E.', a great spoof spy series on the telly.

Actually, we *tried* to watch it, but I think Dad had purloined our set off the dust and there was a reason it had been thrown out. The picture would spin round and round, making it challenging to follow the plot. We boys would take it in turns to try to stop the spinning, a complicated technical process which involved bashing the top of the telly as hard as possible. Of course this approach didn't help at all. It just made the picture spin faster.

Dad had another sneaky trick up his sleeve to avoid parting with all the money we didn't have, and I still can't believe that Dave and I fell for this one. Every Sunday afternoon the ice cream van would drive around the streets selling tempting treats like choc ices and cornets festooned with hundreds and thousands, *or* you could buy a family brick, a big block of vanilla, chocolate ice-cream, or whatever took your fancy, which could be cut into equal sections for all the family to have a slice. There were different ice cream companies: I remember Tonibell, and Rossi's, which was owned by the family of Francis Rossi of rock band Status Quo fame, and Mr Whippy was a big thing too. They all had a different tune to herald their arrival in the street. More often than not, Dave and I wouldn't hear the van pull up as we were busy bashing the shit out of the revolving telly.

I think Dad should have been locked up in Broadmoor Prison on charges of gross cruelty for what he used to do to us. If we ever chanced to hear the enticing jingle, he would assert authoritatively,

> - Oh! What a shame. When they play that tune it means they've run out of ice cream. Never mind, I'll get you one next time.

Bearing in mind Dave and I were in our late thirties at the time you'd have thought we might have rumbled the old sod. But, seriously, being kids we just accepted it and went back to bashing the telly. If Dad did happen to have a couple of bob he would say,

> - Well! It sounds as though they've run out again but you wait here and I'll just go and check.

He would then come back beaming, bearing a selection of ice cream goodies which we would scoff delightedly. Happy days.

You know the expression, 'You can take the boy out of the East End, but you can't take the East End out of the boy'? Well, even later on, when I was a 'sort of' pop star and was hobnobbing with royalty and the rich and the famous, I was always waiting for someone to tap me on the shoulder and say,

- Oi! backstreet boy, get on your bike and go back to where you belong.

A mung bean sandal-wearing, trick cyclist would probably say (in a German accent of course),

- Ah, Liebling, you are clearly suffering from post-traumatic 'not-got-a-pot-to-piss-in, arse-hanging-out-of-your-trousers, pocketful-of-holes, not-the-tin-bath-again' anxiety syndrome. Bollocks! I was just a backstreet boy who could never quite believe his fantastically brilliant luck. Just saying!

3. When Life Guzunder at Christmas

Christmas was always great. Mum and Dad would save a little bit of Christmas money throughout the year. Every Friday the man from the Co-op knocked on the door and they gave him whatever they could afford, pennies usually. He would mark it in his book and on Mum and Dad's little card (a bit like the old building society books). They would build up the savings gradually and cash them in a few weeks before Christmas to buy the prezzies, turkey, veggies etc. Bloody marvellous! Dave and I would try to stay awake as long as we could on Christmas Eve to catch Santa coming into the bedroom with our prezzies. We never managed to stay awake even though, one year, as Mum told us later,

- Me and yer father got ourselves in a right mucking fuddle.

Apparently Dad crept into the dark bedroom in the early hours with the two pillow cases containing our booty (he'd probably been giving Santa's port wine a bit of a seeing to), tripped over the pot, or the 'guzunder' as it was also known because it 'goes under' the bed for night time relief purposes, fell arse over bollocks, bashed his forehead on the floor, staggered up, fell backwards over the guzunder again, bashed the back of his head on the wardrobe door, slipped in the guzunder contents which were now all over the floor, skated out of the bedroom door, knocked over Mum (who was keeping lookout in case we woke up) and both of them fell halfway down the stairs making enough of a racket to wake the dead. Dave and I heard not a thing, and never questioned why, on Christmas Day, Mum and Dad had sticking plasters all over their heads.........

Whilst on the subject of the guzunder and all things related... It was an essential piece of equipment because we only had an outside toilet (or the karzie as Dad called it). If you only needed a pee in the middle of the night the guzunder was the thing for you. However, if things were of a more serious nature, you had to make the perilous, frightening journey to the outside loo: down the stairs, through Nan's room, through the scullery (trying not to bash your head on the tin bath hanging on two nails on the wall), then out into the rat-infested garden. This expedition required two people (preferably SAS trained): the person in desperate need after trying to hold out 'til the relative safety of morning, and someone to ride shotgun. The shotgun carried two very important pieces of equipment: a torch, and a big stick to frighten the rats away, while the needy one threw open the 'lav' door and leapt into the two-foot-square sanctuary. Whilst he/she was inside (Mum screamed all the time she was in there, and had chronic constipation for the rest of her life), Shotgun flashed the torch around, and steeled himself for a ferocious battle, embellished by blood-curdling yelling and rapier-type lunges at the rats who, quite frankly, found the whole thing fabulously entertaining. Then the whole procedure had to be reversed. There was a lot of preparatory shouting and thrusting. On the directive, "NOW!", Needy and Shotgun would leap forth like Butch Cassidy and the Sundance Kid in the final scene of that brilliant film, and dart into the safety of the house where the rats would join them five minutes later and watch 'Wagon Train' with them (from behind the couch).

This procedure was all very well for *our* family, but next door lived Vi and Nell, who definitely 'helped them out when they were busy' but of course none of us realised that at the time, 'coz in those days girls didn't do that sort of thing. Not having the luxury of butch blokes like me, Dad and Dave around, Vi and Nell had to face the 'trial by rat' on their own. One of them, let's say Nell, would put her feet into two metal buckets and glide out of their scullery, sliding and scraping the buckets along the floor (like an early version of 'Dancing on Ice' without the costumes, makeup and music) making as much noise as possible, while Vi dived into the loo. Nell would then stand guard while the rats scampered around the buckets, very frustrated at not being able to feast on her toes. The girl version of Butch and Sundance would then play out.

Dear Reader, you must be thinking (as you lounge on your cosy sofa, a chilled prosecco in one hand and a packet of your favourite kettle crisps in the other, luxuriating in the warmth of your safe, non-rat-infested *maison,*

- Oh, what an exciting life I've missed out on.........

One more guzunder story. Dave and I occasionally had a row (a 'bull and a cow' in Cockney speak). One night at bedtime it all kicked off, probably over something earth shatteringly important like who sucked the last bit of chocolate off the last Malteser. I think I was about four and Dave would have been seven. There was a lot of jumping up and down on the bed and whacking each other with pillows (Mum and Dad always put the machetes and the Kalashnikovs away at bedtime). I think Bruv was getting the upper hand, so drastic measures needed to be taken. Like the fully trained Ninja that I was, I dived under the bed, and reached for my secret weapon, the Mark One, Long Range, Intercontinental Ballistic Guzunder, jumped back onto the bed and whacked Dave over the head as hard as I could, with the heavy ceramic bowl. Bosh! Bruv keeled over a treat, and I stood tall, (3' 2") *the victor* and king of all I possessed (a broken yoyo and a half-sucked toffee). Unfortunately, my elation was short-lived as I started to feel very damp around the head area. The considerable contents of the Mark One were now soaking my hair, dripping down my face, into my eyes, my ears, and everywhere else for that matter. Dave looked up through the stars he was still seeing and, despite a lump the size of Mount Etna on his head, claimed victory. Bugger!

To continue....... On Christmas night, we all went over to Uncle John and Aunty Alice's...and again, this is where the seeds of music were being sown. Uncle John was a *brilliant* banjo player. By day, he was a crane driver in Silvertown Docks (which had been heavily bombed during the war) but after work he would have a quick wash in the sink, a bit of dinner, change his strides (trousers) and then go out busking in and around the East End pubs with his brother Bill, also a brilliant banjo player. They became quite famous and had photos and write-ups in the local papers. I remember sitting on the steps outside the pub with a packet of crisps and a lemonade, listening to John and Bill bringing the house down. Maybe it's just my romantic memory, but I swear those banjos were louder than a Led Zeppelin concert. At the end of the evening the punters would form a conga line and dance up and down the street, with John and Bill still giving it max. I was mesmerised......

Anyway, back to Christmas night at Alice and John's. All the relatives would arrive with contributions for the evening: hams, turkeys, pickled onions, gherkins and sides of beef (probably nicked off the back of the butcher's lorry). All the booze and food would be laid out on the kitchen table, the carpets would be rolled up, the banjos would be tuned, and the entertainment would begin. Everyone danced so hard to John and Bill's music that the floorboards were heaving. It's a miracle we didn't all crash through to the coal cellar below. This would go on till five or six in the morning when we would all roll home, get some kip and then do the whole thing again on Boxing night......What a fantastic time we had! There were often crowds of people standing outside in the street, dancing and singing along.

Uncle John gave me a couple of lessons on the banjo and, many years later, I bought a brand new one for myself on hire purchase or the 'never-never' as it was called. It was my pride and joy. It slept on the bed with me and my dog, Prince. I was singing with a group at the time. One night we were packing up after a gig and left some kit outside the club while we went back to fetch the rest to load it into the van. When we came back out, someone had nicked two of the guitars and my microphone and stand. We had another gig a couple of nights later, so I had to sell my banjo to buy another microphone and stand. My lovely banjo was the first new thing I'd ever had. It broke my heart to hand it over to the man in the shop. The next gig went well though, and I toasted my lost banjo with love and a warm beer.

4. Mum and Dad, a Brief History ('cos it's a good story)

Dad was of Irish descent and Mum had French ancestry, though I don't ever recall Dad Irish jigging on his way to work, or Mum can-canning around the scullery but, indubitablement, je suis un Cockney-Irish-froglegs mélange. Mum and Dad met while walking with friends in West Ham Park. They courted for three months before the Second World War broke out, when Dad joined the Royal Engineers. Because he had worked briefly on the docks as a stevedore loading and unloading ships, as a soldier he was also tasked with loading and unloading ammunition ships. His regiment, along with many others, was due to embark overseas. At that time, because of tight wartime security, they had no idea where they were going, but they did know they would be gone for some considerable time and were told to make arrangements with their families. Dad was *actually* sailing to take part in the evacuation of Nazi-occupied Norway.

He thought it would be a good idea (just in case there was a bullet out there with his name on it) to get married so that, if the bullet found its mark, at least Mum would get a war pension. So Dad got down on one knee and proposed to Mum in West Ham Park, and then went off on his troop train to Scotland while Mum followed in a 'civvy' train. They stayed in a bed and breakfast and slept in a little alcove in the wall with just a curtain across the front. Dad wrote a song for Mum called,

- ♪ 'It's only a hole in the wall, but there's plenty of room for us all'. ♪

Mum used to sing it for us when we were nippers and remind us,

- Ya farva (*father*) wrote that!

They got married on a special licence on the Sunday and early on Monday morning she waved Dad's troop ship off to war. She didn't wave him back till four years later. After Norway he served all over the place, in Italy and North Africa. Anywhere there was fighting, Dad was there, although I bet he spent more time ducking and diving than he did ducking the bullets.

Mum worked at Yardley's cosmetic factory in Stratford E15. (The site was demolished to build the 2012 Olympic stadium.) She was a packer and checker, packing the perfumes, bath cubes, talcum powder and soaps, and making sure that they were all up to par. She was a voracious reader and she told us that she would often read for the whole hour it took to walk from Stratford to Forest Gate. Sometimes she would be so engrossed in her book that she would walk through an air raid, oblivious to the bombs dropping all around her. When she miraculously reached home, Nan would say,

- Blimey, Ivy, why didn't you get yourself down a shelter?
- Ya know what, Mum? If one of them bombs has got my name on it, it'll find me anyway.

I don't know what books Mum was reading, but they must have been pretty riveting.

She had one really close call. Mum was sauntering through an air raid with her nose in a book as usual. She had just turned into Wellington Road, when she heard a different kind of roar coming from behind her. She spun around to see a German fighter plane actually flying at rooftop height with the guns on its wings blazing. Mum dived into the front porch of a house as the bullets traced along the pavement she had just been walking on. The bullets whizzed past the porch and the plane shot off up into the sky. She said the plane was so low that she could clearly see the pilot's face.

Nan and Mum had a very special dog called Peggy, an Alsatian. Peggy either had a sixth sense or the most incredible hearing because, fifteen minutes before an air raid warning sounded, she would prick up her ears, run to the Anderson shelter at the end of our garden, jump in and bark like crazy until everyone joined her and was safe - well, as safe as you could be. If a bomb had landed on or near them it was pretty certain that they'd have had their chips. Still on red alert, ten minutes before the all-clear, Peggy would jump out and run back to the house. She was always the first into the shelter and the first out. Nobody could ever explain her extraordinary ability.

One night there was an intense raid that lasted for hours. When it seemed as though it was over, Nan said,

- C'mon, I know they haven't sounded the all-clear yet, but I'm starvin'. Let's go.

As they stood up Peggy barred the door and barked at them, refusing to let them out. They hesitated and, at that precise moment, a parachute bomb landed on the roof of the house next door. The roof caught fire and shrapnel rained down onto our garden. If Peggy hadn't stopped them, Nan and Mum would certainly have been killed.

Nan's husband, my grandfather Tom, was killed in 1939, at the beginning of the war. He was a painter and decorator and was pushing the cart that held his paints and working materials when a bus turning a corner at Stratford Broadway drove straight into him. The inquest was held at Stratford Town Hall during an air raid. The raid was so intense that the coroner, Nan and Mum had to shelter under a big wooden table. Nan was awarded a meagre £100 by the bus company for the loss of her husband, the breadwinner of the family. In those days working class people didn't have the knowledge or the money to challenge the authorities.

In spite of this tragedy, I think Mum had a pretty good war; she would go out dancing as often as she could, sometimes three or four times a week and, as she 'fessed' up to me later, did quite a lot of flirting with the American servicemen who were, as it was said at the time, 'over-paid, over-sexed and over here'. As a result, Mum got more than her fair share of nylon stockings, chocolate and fags, of which the Yanks seemed to have an endless supply. Good on you Mum, happy days!

When Dad eventually did get home, it wasn't all hunky-dory with him and Mum. They had only known each other for three months before their four-year separation and, although he only talked about his war days with humour, I think Dad had seen some things he would have preferred to forget. After a few months, they ended up in a divorce court in front of a wise and wonderful judge who talked them out of going through with it. He reminded them that they had been apart for a very long time in trying, stressful and dangerous circumstances. It was his firm belief that, if they gave it some time, and both worked on it, they could have a long, happy life together. Which they did.... for the next sixty years.

Mum, apart from looking after Dad, Dave, Nan and me would occasionally take part-time work. I remember one job she had which especially delighted us kids. In the next road there was a confectionery factory that specialised in seaside rock candy of all shapes and sizes. For a few weeks when Mum clocked off work for the day she would accidentally on purpose drop a few 'samples' into her large handbag. We would run home from school and wait eagerly by the front door. Mum would tease us by saying,

- Not 'til you've 'ad your tea.

A slice of bread and jam didn't take long to polish off. Mum would empty the booty onto the kitchen table and Dave and I would pounce on the sugar mountain like vultures. When Dad came home from work he would invariably say,

- Ivy, I 'ope you ain't been givin' the saucepans (saucepan lids = kids) loads of sweets again.

- No, just a few Wally.

Yeah right! One day, Mum came home from the factory and declared,

- That's it! I'm not goin' back there no more.

- Aw Mum, why?

- Because I was watching the guv'nor standing over the great big vats of rock mixture. He's had a terrible cold all week and his nose was dripping into the mixture and he was stirring it in. Sorry boys, but that's it for me.

Blimey! That was the last time Dave and I ate seaside rock. Just as well. If Mum had worked there any longer, not only would our teeth have fallen out, but we would have been even more hyperactive and troublesome than we were already.

5. Dave and the Magic Egg

Perhaps because of the rationing which was still in place, Dave was very underweight when he was born. For years Mum took him to Great Ormond Street Children's Hospital in central London and she would occasionally take me along as well. We had to keep changing buses and it seemed like a never-ending journey. Once there Dave was put through all sorts of tests but nothing seemed to help. Our doctor suggested a spell in a convalescent home by the sea in the hope that a healthier environment and fresh air might help - East London was still littered with open sewers from the bombing. And so, one Sunday, without telling me, Dad took Dave on the train to Brighton. Dave must have been about six and had no idea where he was going or why. He was there for three months. He told me later that it was the worst time of his life and that he never recovered from the feeling of abandonment. Suddenly he was without his parents and baby brother and he didn't know how long he was going to stay there. Dad would visit him every Sunday but decided that it would be too upsetting for Dave if he saw me and Mum and then have to say goodbye. So on Sundays the three of us would catch the train to Brighton. Mum and I would hide behind the sea wall opposite the home and watch Dad collect Dave and take him out for a few hours for an ice cream and to play on the beach. Once they had gone one way, we would go the other way and do the same thing. Dave had no idea we were there.

He always insisted that those three months didn't do him one bit of good. All he had felt was rejection, although he told me recently that he also knew that Mum and Dad, though sometimes misguided, tried to do the right thing for him, and that their hearts were in the right place. The day he came home was brilliant and we played for hours.

You'll be pleased to hear there's a funny side to this story. In the 1950s the government wanted to encourage the population to eat more eggs; they were cheap to produce and full of protein. They ran a TV advertising campaign starring Tony Hancock ('Go to work on an egg'). Every fresh egg of the highest standard had a little blue lion printed on the side. Dad had the wizard idea of buying our own chicken and to keep it in a nice coop in the garden with lots of space to run around and lay healthy eggs. These eggs would be even better than the ones with the little lion on the side, and they would be reserved for Dave to build him up.

Our Nan was the kindest person in the world, but she had her quirks. At first Doris, the chicken, was laying beautifully and there would be a lovely warm egg waiting for Mum to collect every morning. However, Mum started to notice that there was no morning egg but, if she returned five minutes later, an egg had appeared. It would be stone cold. This was a mystery! Mum became suspicious so, one morning, around about laying time, she hid behind a bush in the garden opposite the chicken coop. Lo and behold, Doris duly laid her egg and then Nan appeared, furtively scurrying out to the coop bearing another egg which she exchanged for the one Doris had just laid. Mum waited until Nan had returned to the house and went to investigate. On picking up the egg Mum couldn't believe it; it had a little lion printed on the side.

That night she told Dad the story of 'Egg-gate'. At first he was hopping mad but they couldn't help but see the funny side. It was such a mad thing to do. The next day Mum followed the same plan and waited for the phantom egg thief to appear. Sure enough thirty seconds after Doris had performed Nan rushed out with her replacement egg. Mum waited until the coast was clear, retrieved the egg and went into Nan's room where Nan was sitting innocently reading the News of the World, upside down.

Mum said,

- 'Ere Mum did you know we've got the cleverest chicken in the world?

- Oh yeah, why's that Ivy?

- Well, not only does Doris lay eggs, but she stamps a little lion on them at the same time.

Without looking up, Nan said,

- Isn't it amazing what chickens can do nowadays?

Apart from that little episode Nan couldn't have been kinder, or lovelier to Dave. In fact, one day when Dave was crying because he didn't want to go to Great Ormond Street yet again, Nan said to Mum,

- Why don't you leave him alone? OK, he's not the biggest boy in the world but he'll do alright in life if you just let him get on with it.

Through his tears, Dave said,

> - Nan's right Mum, I'm not going anymore.

And he didn't. He turned into a cracking little footballer, nippy and as strong as an ox. For a while he even played for West Ham United's youth team. Good on yer, Bruv.

Anyway, *enough* about them and more about *me*.

6. An Audience Reacts! I like this Feeling

On Sunday afternoons, we used to go to Sunday School. None of us was remotely religious, but Sundays were always boring so, for a couple of hours, we would rock up at the church hall and listen to the vicar telling some meaningful stories. All joking aside, some of those stories were really great. Then we'd be given a glass of lemonade and a piece of cake, and off we'd go in search of more skulduggery. In this unlikeliest of places, another performing seed was planted.

One Sunday the teacher told me there was to be a big meeting of all the churches in the area. One child was to represent each church and give a reading to the whole congregation. I was asked if I would like to represent our church and read a couple of parables. All my mates thought this would be a good laugh and a chance to meet some girls from different areas (we must have been about eight or nine, so I don't know what we thought we were going to do with them). Anyway, I really put my heart and soul into learning the pieces I was to read and, over the weeks, I could feel the adrenalin starting to kick in. On the Sunday of the meeting, I couldn't believe how many people had congregated in the church, probably about four hundred (that's about three hundred and ninety-seven more than I had at some of my later professional gigs before I became a 'sort of' pop star!). My turn came. I was surprised that I didn't feel nervous, just excited. One of the parables had some amusing lines in it and, as I read it, the audience was laughing in all the right places. This was a real shock as I wasn't expecting any response at all. I had thought I would just do my bit, go back to my seat, and that would be that. But this was a bloody marvellous feeling. They were all enjoying what I was doing, and what do all performers want? Exactly that. This was another one of those moments.

7. The 'Bad Boy' Years

Mum and Dad had paid for me to have clarinet lessons. There was a performer called Acker Bilk who had had a big hit playing 'Stranger on the Shore' on the clarinet. He wore a bowler hat and a waistcoat...and, consequently, so did I. I would sit on the stairs (for better acoustics), playing 'Stranger on The Shore' over and over and driving the neighbours barmy.

Then a film came out called 'Some People' about a group of rockers, and that was it, Acker was history for me, and so was the clarinet. I wanted to be a rocker and play the guitar. Now about thirteen years old, I bought an imitation leather jacket and, with some mates, started a band. We never played any gigs, but we practised a lot.

Then, as was the norm in our 'manor', I got in with a bad crowd which involved quite a bit of fighting other gangs. I hated it, and never got the buzz that the others seemed to get when we went off to Bethnal Green or Canning Town to find 'their boys' so that we could all beat the shit out of each other. It was like 'West Side Story' without the fab songs. We were also doing a lot of nicking. There was a sweet shop not far from where I lived, the owner of which was a really nasty sod. Misery Guts, we called him. He would whack the kids around the head for doing nothing, just for hanging around coveting the sweets they couldn't afford. One day I was in the shop with my mate, 'Big Len' (Big Len was 6' 3" when he was twelve years old, hence the 'Big'), and we were on the nick. BL distracted MG while I shoved as many sweets and fags up my jumper as possible. (I would have shoved them in my pockets, if it weren't for the holes in them.) MG sussed us out, started to holler, and chased us out of the shop and down the street. BL, with his long legs, was really legging it, but I was starting to flag a bit because the sweets were falling out of my jumper and I kept stopping to pick them up. MG was gaining on me and it looked like I was done for, but BL looked around, assessed the situation, ran back, and biffed MG right on the nose. Bosh! MG was down and out. *Good! That's for all the kids* you've *bashed, you spiteful old bugger.*

Around this time, BL and I got done for nicking a motorbike. Well, let's be fair. When I say *we* nicked a motorbike, it went more like this. He had knocked on my door and declared,

- I just found a motorbike,

like he would often knock on my door and say,

- I just found 200 cartons of fags in that tobacconist shop (the one where the window had considerately been left just open enough for them to be found).

When we went to court, the judge at least had a sense of humour and summed up with the following remarks:

- When the two offenders were arrested, the big lad was sitting on the motorcycle laughing, while the little chap was pushing him up a very steep hill. I would only advise you Colin, if you intend to pursue a future career in crime, *and* are tempted to steal another motorcycle, perhaps it would be a smarter move on your part to claim the sitting option.

But BL was a good bloke and always had my back when things were going tits up and getting a bit nasty. We were both already on a conditional discharge for finding the motorbike and fighting with some gang or other, and the court sent us both to an attendance centre (one step away from Borstal, a young offenders' prison). This was meant as a short sharp shock. That place, and my girlfriend Marilyn's intervention, saved me.

- Col, this isn't you! Concentrate on your singing, get away from all this trouble, otherwise you'll end up with the rest of your mates, behind bars.

Mal, wherever you are now, thank you from the bottom of my heart.

Big Len served in the Merchant Navy for a few years but died, tragically young, while running a pub on the island of Jersey.

Phweeeeeew. Thank God the bad boy stuff is out of the way. Mal was right! It wasn't me. Back to the fun stuff...

8. Dad Left Holding the Baby

Dad had now elevated his employment status and was a trained ambulance man (paramedic in today's terms.) No more OTD for us. Bugger! We had all helped him with his studying, taking it in turns to quiz him on anatomy, slings, bandages, resuscitation, etc. and he passed his exams first time with flying colours. He didn't really talk about the job much, if at all. So one day when I got home from school (correction: when I got home from bunking off school), Mum proudly showed us The Stratford Express, a newspaper that covered the news and events over a large area of the East End.

- Look wot ya farva's been up to!

There, on the front page, was a big picture of *our* dad, in his ambulance uniform, smiling his head off, posing with a new-born baby on a red London bus.

Here's the story. Dad was coming home from work on the bus as usual when suddenly an expectant mother went into labour. Dad swung into action and delivered the baby right there and then on the bus (I don't remember any of us quizzing him on bus-baby-deliveries). The press got hold of the story and organised a photo shoot with Dad and the baby on the bus, telling the whole story in great detail, and making Dad a local hero. We all waited for him to arrive home and were sitting around the kitchen table trying to act as normal when he strolled in, his usual cheery self,

- Evening luv, wot's for tea?

(To Cockneys lunch was dinner, dinner was tea and breakfast was nothing because we never got any.)

Dad sat down and Mum pointed at the paper,

- What's all this then?

Dad glanced at his own beaming face, smiled, and carried on levering a burnt sausage into his mouth.

- Well? Why didn't you tell us you was bein' Doctor bleedin' Kildare on the 178 bus?

Dad crunched a bit more of the inedible sausage,

- I forgot.

He forgot? I mean, you forget your sandwiches, you forget your keys. You don't forget delivering a baby on a 178 bus! Dad, now being a bit more forthcoming, filled us in,

- Yeah! It was last Tuesday. You remember love, I was late getting home, and you'd burnt the sausages.

Now, if that had been me, I would have taken a full page advert in the Sunday Times with photos of me with the baby, as well as its parents, aunts, uncles, extended family, the head of paediatrics at the Chelsea and Westminster Hospital, the London Fire Brigade, Kate Middleton, the head of MI5 and the Queen. He forgot?!

9. The Big Bang Theory

I had a physically active childhood. There was no sitting at the computer for hours on end. We were always daring each other to do risky and frankly stupid things, like climbing up the side of high rise buildings using only the drain pipes and the overhangs on the balconies to grip onto, sometimes right up to the tenth floor. Or, on less adventurous days, running full pelt, taking off and diving over high security fences that were topped with barbed wire, forward rolling on the other side, jumping up and then out-running the Alsatian guard dogs who were desperate to bite a large chunk out of our arses. We were pretty fit.

Keith Ridgeway lived in a pub that was run by his parents. In the back garden there was an oak tree which must have been hundreds of years old. It was massive. We 'found' some really thick ropes and built a Tarzan course by attaching the ropes to the thicker branches and we would spend hours swinging through the upper canopy of the tree, letting go of one rope, diving through the air and catching another, trapeze-artist-style. Dangerous, but great fun.

Another life-threatening jape of ours was 'fireworks'. On and around the 5th of November, fireworks would be sold in shops, not the wimpy fireworks you get today that are all fizz and fizzle; these were fuck-off big buggers with a huge bang! We bought or 'found' as many bangers as we could (explosives so punchy that they could have been used to scare the shit out of the terrorists during the storming of the Iranian Embassy siege). We would then go over to Wanstead Flats, a huge area of forests and fields where courting couples went at night to 'ave it off' in their cars. Sometimes there would be as many as thirty or forty cars, rocking and rolling around with the goings-on inside. We used to wait till the windows were steamed up then each pick a car, creep up on it under cover of darkness, place a banger up the exhaust pipe and, on our team leader's secret whistle, light the blue touch paper and run like fuck. Five seconds later, massive deafening *bang bang bangs* would go off all over the place, scaring the in-car shaggers senseless. Erections now collapsed, they would rev up their engines and try to hunt us down, headlights flashing across the Flats, cars crashing into each other in the dark, and the girls screaming their heads off. Bloody marvellous! (The boys in those cars may well have suffered from erectile dysfunction for the rest of their lives). Of course, it never occurred to any of us that we could have blown the car and its occupants to smithereens if the petrol tank had ignited.

S.E.X.

While we're on the subject of s.e.x., we were never short of somewhere to take a bird for a bunk up because we had so many derelict buildings and bomb-damaged wastelands with old wrecked cars and vans at our disposal. Our unedifying Jack-the-lad conversation at the time would have gone something like this.

- Ere!, I got a bunk up off that Mary Sprigget in tha back a' that bombed out jam dahn at the rec yesterdee, yeah! I gave 'er a right seein' to. Bet she tells all 'er muckers wot a huge fuckin' todger I got, and they'll be gaggin' fa me ta give 'em a large portion.

Translation:

- Attention! I partook of sexual intercourse with Mary Sprigget on the rear seat of that fire-damaged car at the location of the bomb site yesterday. It's quite possible that she will alert all her chums to the fact that I have a larger than normal sized member, and it's more than likely that I will receive enquiries as to whether I may be able to accommodate an allotted number of ladies and provide the same service in the not-too-distant future.

10. Judo and a Few Crap Jobs

One day a new teacher arrived at my school to teach us judo. I think he had worked as an unarmed combat instructor to the troops during the war. He looked *slightly* Oriental and had a name that sounded convincingly Japanese (Sushi Origami Kamikaze or something similar), but I think he came from Scunthorpe. I was hooked from the very first minute, and joined other judo clubs so that I could train in the evenings and at weekends. This fitness routine was a massive help to me later when I was training to be a professional dancer. Balance, agility and gymnastic skills made up for my lack of formal dance training, no question about it. I left school at the age of fourteen[2], running through the doors as fast as my little legs would carry me.

There was a weekly music paper at the time called 'The Melody Maker'. The back pages had auditions for groups and ads from bands looking for singers, guitarists, drummers and so on. I would scan the pages and go along and try my luck. I *was* lucky, and sang with a few amateur and semi-pro bands. It was good training. At this time, to make ends meet, I had a succession of dead end jobs: a ladder factory, fixing hundreds of rungs to ladders every hour; a welding factory, spot welding metal struts to lamp shades; a paint factory, spraying chair legs; a trainee motor mechanic on the Mile End Road, sodding up people's cars. One day I was servicing a Mini; I'd changed the oil filter and drained the oil and lowered the car lift back to the ground. I knew Minis took eight pints of oil but I was feeling a bit weary that day having been up all night at a gig in Birmingham. I was filling the car with oil and it seemed to be taking ages, but I kept pouring, and pouring. Suddenly I noticed that my boots felt a bit damp; I looked down, and I was standing in a pool of about twenty pints of oil. I'd forgotten to replace the sump plug and the oil was going straight through. There's no question about it, I was the wrong man for that job, and probably any job they might have thrown at me.

Then a mate spotted an ad for 'Trainee Hairdressers' in a West End Salon. Not 'arf, we thought, we'll 'ave some of that. All that 'posh totty' at our disposal just for putting a few rollers in, doing a bit of backcombing and swishing a

---

2 The school leaving age was 15 at the time. I decided to do the Duke of Edinburgh award scheme because you were allowed to leave school a little before your 15th birthday. That's how desperate I was.

hairdryer around. It hadn't done Vidal Sassoon[3] any harm, that's for sure, and he was a backstreet boy. I got the gig but my mate didn't, and I started work in Mark Ramon's Hair Salon in High Street, Kensington. Mark's *real* name was something like Arthur Farnsbarn and he was from somewhere in the East End. He would welcome his uptown, well-to-do clients,

- Ah!, Lady Crunchbucket, how deeelightful to see you, and looking absolutely deeevine as always and, if I may say so, younger than ever, and oh!, you've brought darling little Pinkypoo, *the most* adorable, cutest, cuddliest, squishiest little Peekineeze in the world. Please take a seat and I'll have you shampooed at once, if not sooner.

He would then dash into the staffroom and say, in a broad Cockney accent,

- Oi! Col, move yer bleedin' arse, and give that old bird's barnet a once-over will ya? And don't let that fucking dog piss on the floor. Coming, Lady Crunchbucket!

I was singing with a group at the time which often meant driving back from a gig through the night. I would be dropped off outside the salon and Mark would get really pissed off,

- Don't park that bloody old wreck outside my salon. This is High Street Ken, *not* Bethnal fucking Green fucking High Street.

My hairdressing career *however*, was mercifully short-lived. But, praise the Lord, the magic world of showbiz was just around the corner.

---

3 Vidal Sassoon CBE was born to Jewish parents in 1928 in West London and lived in Shepherds Bush. He grew up in extreme poverty and spent seven years in an orphanage. He left school at 14 and found low paid, usually manual work, during the war. His ambition was to become a professional footballer but his mother had other ideas and found him a job as an apprentice hairdresser. Not only did he charm the female clientele but was an innovative cutter, creating the 'Greek Goddess' and other close-cut geometric hairstyles. Vidal found world-wide fame and was the go-to hairdresser for a vast array of film stars and celebrities (Mia Farrow, Goldie Hawn, Mary Quant, Natasha Kinski).

Colin Copperfield

Showbiz

My lifelong fascination with the wonderful, magical world of showbiz, and my instant attraction to the buzz of performing, began on holiday in Southend (Sarfend if you're a Cockney), a holiday town on the coast of Essex. I was six or seven years old and, with my Mum, Dad and brother, I was watching a carnival procession travelling along the promenade. There were lots of coloured floats, each one with a different theme or performer: jugglers, acrobats, beauty queens, bands, actors and all sorts of wonderful entertainment. And then it happened! On one of the floats were two rock'n'roll jive dancers, a boy and a girl aged about sixteen, twisting and twirling, the girl being thrown in the air and then through the boy's legs. They were dressed in white: the girl in a white flared dress, socks and pumps, the boy in white jeans, shirt and pumps. They were having so much fun and the crowd was clapping and yelling. I stood mesmerised. I wanted to be up on that float with them, 'showing off' with every fibre of my body.

That moment is as clear as yesterday, and was definitely the start of my lifelong passion for performing.

Some of the following stories are from my acting days and some from when I had my own cabaret act, while others are from musicals I was in. Then, my long career with Wall Street Crash. They are not in chronological order. It seemed more fun to simply dip in and out of the stories, and mix them up a bit. There are a fair number of Wall Street Crash stories but, then again, after doing it for twenty-five years, I guess there would be.

Scene One: Curtain Call with Dame Vera

Wall Street Crash were performing in a big TV show in Amsterdam. It was going out Europe-wide and was called 'The Night of a Hundred Stars'. There were some twenty or thirty big acts, but only two English acts: Wall Street Crash and Vera Lynn. She was the big star of the night. The Dutch loved the English.

The director was an English guy called Norman Maen. At the afternoon rehearsal he told us how he wanted us to do the curtain call,

- Once you have all finished your acts, the orchestra will begin the play-off music. I want you all to come on from both sides of the stage, meet in the middle in one long line with Dame Vera centre-stage. Wall Street Crash will stand on either side of Dame Vera, then Sacha Distel, Johnnie Halliday, and the rest of the line-up. I want you all to walk forward to the front of the stage. You are to take your cue from Dame Vera and all bow to the front together. Then you are to turn to stage left and make a long slow bow towards the royal box where Queen Beatrix of the Netherlands will be sitting. You will then turn back to face the audience again and, following Dame Vera, take another bow to the front. With everyone still facing the audience, you will reverse to the back of the stage. Dame Vera will then walk forward on her own and take a final bow. She will return to the line-up and the curtains will close.

Live television. Nothing complicated. What could possibly go wrong?

On the night everything went well. It came to the finale. The band struck up. The cameras were focused on us. We all bowed to the front, then to Queen Beatrix, followed by one more bow to the front. We all reversed to the back of the stage and Vera Lynn walked forward.........and so did Marge from Wall Street Crash! The two of them, standing centre-stage...together.

Now, Marge was our choreographer and should have had some idea of what was going on, but she seemed blissfully unaware of what she was doing. Vera gave Marge a look as if to say, "Who on earth are you?" They both reversed back and Marge took her place next to me.

I whispered,

- What the bloody hell were you doing dear?

- I don't know what came over me. I was miles away. (*With 20 million viewers? Really? I mean there's laid back, and there's laid back.*) I was thinking about what bar we would go to afterwards for a drink. (*Wot a pro.*)

The curtains closed. The rest of the artists were doubled over with laughter. Vera Lynn …...and Marge: the stars of the show! We weren't well known in Europe at the time. The 20 million viewers must have thought, 'Why is that random girl from that group taking a bow alone with Dame Vera Lynn?'

I have no idea if the footage still exists but Marge getting it so spectacularly wrong in such a public way made the night all the more magical.

A postscript:

Karen, a very pretty girl from up north was part of the group at the time. She had a great voice and was a vision to look at, but she had a mouth like a soldier: "Fookin' this, fookin' that"….

- What time's this fookin' plane takin' off? ….I can't eat this fooking shit...Who's that tosser screeching his tits off in the next fookin' dressing room? (*Peter Gabriel*).

We had a couple of rehearsals with the orchestra in the afternoon. The bass guitarist wasn't great but it was a live show and all the music acts were in the same boat, so you just had to go with the flow and hope for the best. But when we came offstage after the live show Karen was going on about him like a woman possessed.

- What the fookin' 'ell was the fookin' bass player doing? He was fookin' useless.

There was a knock at the door. I was wearing boxer shorts, just about to jump in the shower. I opened the door. Karen was still raving on,

- Fookin' useless wanker... I've got more musicality in my left tit than that fookin' tosser's got in his whole fookin' body.

It was Dame Vera at the door. She said,

- Hello, I thought I would introduce myself to the other British act in the show.

- Oh, do come in Dame Vera,

I said, trying to look cool in my Snoopy boxers.

In the background:

- I am going to get his fookin' guitar and shove it so far up his fookin' arse he'll have to tune it through his fookin' ears.

Dame Vera raised her eyebrows. She had entertained the troops all through World War Two often singing from the back of an army lorry just a bullet's distance from the front line, raising the morale of thousands of British and Commonwealth soldiers, often with just a beat up old upright piano for accompaniment. She had been in the thick of danger, had seen the severely wounded and held their hand to comfort them in their time of need. At that moment, she was the mother that many of them would never see again. Her song: 'There'll be Bluebirds Over the White Cliffs of Dover' had given hope to so many, both overseas and at home. She was a proper Dame and a legend and now, after all that, she was face to face with Karen who wanted to stick the fookin' bass player's fooking guitar up his fookin' arse.

She gave me a quizzical look and a slightly strained half smile and, as she reversed out of the door, she said very gently,

- OK! I'll pop back later.

That was the last we ever saw of Dame Vera. Good old Karen! Classy bird. I think she's working as an elocution teacher for the Diplomatic Corps now.

Vera Lynn passed away on 18th June 2020 at the grand old age of 103. Who knows, Dame Vera, maybe someday we'll meet again?.

Scene Two: Behind the Couch with Val

Wall Street Crash were doing the Val Doonican Christmas Show, which was going out live. We were on with the Nolan Sisters and Howard Keel who was in 'Dallas' at the time and had been in many musical films like 'Oklahoma'. He was a tall, good looking guy with a massive voice. We were on set at the Shepherd's Bush Television Theatre. The stage was set up like a Christmas party, as if we were in someone's sitting room. There were three couches. We were on one, the Nolan Sisters on another and Val was on the middle couch. We did a song with Val, the Nolan Sisters sang with Val, and then Val performed on his own. Howard Keel came on a bit later and did a song with Val and then we all did a song together.

At the afternoon rehearsal we were given drinks that looked like wine but were simply coloured water. Coloured water! We 'sort of' pop stars don't drink coloured water. I had a quick word in the stage manager's BBC-indoctrinated ear,

- This evening we will have proper drinks, won't we?

He looked at me, aghast,

- No, no, no, this is the BBC. You don't have alcohol onstage at the BBC. You can all have a drink at the party afterwards in the green room but there will be no alcohol onstage.

Not good news! What sort of a jolly Christmas party was this going to be? I mentioned our little problem to the guys who came up with a plan,

- Sod this. Let's go over the road and get one of those wine boxes. We'll hide it somewhere and ditch the coloured water. I know! We'll put it behind Val's couch and, when the Nolan Sisters are singing, we'll top up our glasses. It will be a much better party atmosphere and no one will notice.

So we went across Shepherd's Bush Green, found a friendly off licence and bought a box of Chateau Buisson de Berger[4], which cost around £1.50 for five gallons. When there was a break in rehearsals I hid it behind Val's couch,

---

4 Translation: Shepherd's Bush

under a throw. I thought, "Sod it. I'll have a little tipple while I'm here." (Just to ensure it was worth all the dosh that we'd shelled out on it). I had just put my thumb on the tap, plastic beaker at the ready, when I heard an unmistakable resounding Irish voice,

- And what would be going on here then?

Oh fuck! It was Val, and I had been caught red bloody wine handed. I would be thrown off the show and banned from the BBC. The death throes of my career flashed before my eyes.

Maybe some serious grovelling would help,

- I'm so sorry, Val. It's just that they've given us these horrible coloured drinks and I thought maybe we'd get a box of wine and top up our glasses during the show, just to give it a bit of welly, Val.
- Bloody right too, Col. Give us another glass and let's start now.
- I've only got this old plastic one, Val.
- We'll share it, Col.

So, there was I with Val Doonican, a massive star, both of us behind the couch like a pair of drunken old reprobates, drinking gut-rot wine from a shared plastic tumbler. And we did that throughout the show. He'd sing a song and when the camera cut to the Nolans we'd top up Val's plastic beaker from the box. Even Howard Keel got in on the act when he twigged what we were up to and had a quick slurp behind the couch while Val was singing. Another top up Howard? He didn't look too impressed with the quality of the grape but, as he hadn't chipped in, beggars can't be choosers can they? Nobody ever knew, and the show went off without a hitch.

Val Doonican was a lovely down-to-earth guy. We worked with him a few times after that and he was always a real pleasure to be with. God bless you, and Merry Christmas up there in heaven. Cheers Val.

Scene Three: Cilla Black and a Bucket

I was in Brighton filming a commercial with Cilla Black for Cadbury's Dairy Milk chocolate. The square had been roped off, which meant that the public could watch the filming but were out of camera shot. I was playing a postman. Cilla Black would sing,

- ♪ Well, you give a little grin when you pop the chocolate in,
  It's Cadbury's Dairy Milk.

I was to walk up as the postman, Cilla would pop a piece of chocolate into my mouth, and I would do some (*Mmmm!*) delicious chocolate acting. She would then skip off down the road and I would go on my way with my postman's bag over my shoulder. Simple.

Because we were outside we had to do take after take - either the lighting wasn't right or there were traffic sounds, and so on. There must have been about 2,000 people watching the filming. We were at take 137. I had eaten more bars of chocolate than I could count and was starting to turn various shades of green. Cilla said to me,

- Are you alright?

- Not really, I've eaten so much of this chocolate I'm going to throw up in a minute.

So Cilla called over to Bobby, her husband, who was also her manager, and said,

- Col's eaten so much chocolate that he's feeling really queasy.

Bobby spoke to the director. He was an evil old queen.

- You may need to do more takes, but Col can't keep on eating this chocolate.

- Well, what can I do dear? The lighting, traffic noise and so on...

I said I could probably manage a few more takes but not many more. So Bobby came up with an idea.

    - We'll get a bucket. Don't swallow the chocolate and you can spit it out when you've done the shot.

Off we go.

    - Take 138 ladies and gentlemen. And action...

I minced along in my postman's kit, Cilla popped the chocolate into my mouth and I pretended to chew it. End of scene. Cut! I spat the chocolate into the bucket, and 2,000 people applauded like mad.

That's the commercial they should have broadcast!!

Scene Four: Throat Sweets and Giggles

My agent was able to get me a commercial for Rowntrees' Tunes, the throat lozenge, as they wanted someone who could do judo. As I had done several years of judo training and was a brown belt, I got the gig. I had always been working whenever they were holding the gradings, as they were called, so I had never been able to fit in the time to achieve my black belt. There were hundreds of guys at the audition but the two main parts were given to me and a guy called John Morenno. For the filming I was directed to walk through the door of a dojo[5], obviously blocked up with a heavy cold (me not the door). John came up to me in his judo gear and said,

- 'ere! You need Tunes.
- Tunes?

With that he put his arm around my shoulders, led me off to the dressing room and gave me a Tunes lozenge to suck while I put on my judo outfit. The next shot showed the two of us on a judo mat, with a lot of judo aficionados standing behind us looking on. I threw him over my shoulder using a double-handed throw. It is quite an impressive throw. He landed heavily on the mat and lay there winded. I bowed to him and said,

- Tuuuunes!!

He looked both aghast and impressed by the throw. The voiceover announced, "Tunes, make you breathe more easily". End of the commercial.

We were filming the first shot of me walking through the door and John saying his line. When filming commercials, there is invariably something wrong, usually the lighting or sound. We had done about seventy takes with poor old John having to crash to the floor every time, and we both started to get the giggles. Because it is an expensive process, all of the Rowntree executives were there watching. The director came over to me and John, and said,

- Look guys we got the shot that we wanted on the second take but all of the Rowntrees' suits are here and they want to see where their half a million quid's going, so we're going to do a few more takes so that it looks harder than it is. That should impress them. But *stop fucking giggling*!

---

5 A martial arts studio

This made us feel like laughing even more. Shit! What to do? This could go on all night. I came up with a cunning plan. I went back out through the doors.

- Stand by studio, Take 78, and......action.

I walked through the door, bunged up with my cold, and John came over,

- 'ere, you need Tunes.

To which I replied,

- Tunes, they're fucking useless.

And with that we both fell about, and so did all of the camera crew and the makeup ladies. The suits were not amused but my cunning plan worked. It was the only way I could get it out of our system so that we wouldn't carry on corpsing.[6] We did the rest of the takes without a hitch. The director came up to me afterwards and said,

- That was totally out of order but thank God you did it, or we would have been filming for the next seven hours.

"Tuuunes" is all I have to say to that. The commercial was screened for about three years and, as I was on *repeat fees*, I was paid every time it was shown. That was a nice little earner. Lovely jubbly.

The next time you're bored out of your brains, Google 'Tunes Judo' and check out my breathtaking performance for which an Oscar should have been awarded (or at least a mention in dispatches).

---

6 Theatre-speak for laughing uncontrollably. The expression is thought to originate from the gravediggers' scene in Shakespeare's tragedy *Hamlet*. As the gravediggers were burying the corpse of the newly-deceased Ophelia, the actress playing the role got the giggles. Once this happens you are invariably doomed, probably because of the heightened tension of the situation; only on very rare occasions are you able to control yourself and get back on track. More often than not, because corpsing is a highly contagious disease, you tend to take your fellow actors along with you until one of your shambolic mob is grown-up enough to get a grip. Unfortunately, on more than one occasion I have lapsed, including one spectacular occasion during the run of 'Leave Him to Heaven' at the New London Theatre in Drury Lane when a single meaningless and benign cough from an audience member sent me into 'corpse hell'. It was a very long speech and 'corpse hell' started at the beginning of it. I was helpless. I eventually threw myself down onto the stage and rolled around, hoping that the audience would think that I had had an aneurysm and had gone mad. It didn't help. My fellow thesps, realising that I was about to do myself some serious damage, tried to improvise us out of the scene (which only made me laugh even more). We were rescued by a premature blackout from an on-the-ball stage manager. That corpse should have rated a mention in the Guinness Book of Records as it went on seemingly forever. And I should have been permanently blackballed by the actors' union, Equity - and shot at dawn.

Scene Five: Roger's Coat

This was again with Wall Street Crash when we were doing the Michael Parkinson Show. The show was massive and at the pinnacle of its viewing figures. On that night, we were the only guests along with Roger Moore. We did five songs on the show, unheard of before or since. It all went well and there was, as usual, a party afterwards in the green room.[7] I was flagging so I sat down, enjoying my wine, my sarnies and my crisps. Roger Moore was hovering around with the director, the sound crew and the makeup ladies, all having a bit of a party. After about an hour Roger came over to me and said,

- Terribly sorry old chap, can I have my coat?

I thought,

- Cheeky bugger! He can't possibly think I'm a cloakroom attendant. I mean, he's just watched me prance around for an hour, giving it my all and being totally fabulous. Really Rog, get over your 007 self. I'm a 'sort of' fucking pop star, y'know. OK, so you've minced around in a couple of films with your toy guns, snogging all that hot totty, but I do a real job mate! I have to (almost) sing in tune and (vaguely) get the steps right *and* I've done a bit of acting you know, Moory. You must have seen my 'Tunes' throat lozenge commercial. They showed it all the time *and* I got *repeat fees*. I bet you didn't get those for 'The Man with the Golden One-Eyed Trouser Snake'. No! I didn't think so, you...you...you...... tall good looking person, you.

But of course I said,

- I'm sure you can Roger, where is it?

- You've been sitting on it for the past hour, dear boy.

---

7 The 'green room' gets its name from Elizabethan times when plays were usually set on the village green and the stage would be painted green. Most probably during the rehearsals for one of Bill Shakespeare's earlier works, the bloke painting the stage must have had some green left over and, rather than waste it, or nick it to paint his thatched cottage, thought, "Bollocks! I'll just use it up and give a lick of paint to the room next to the stage where all those luvvies hang out before they go on stage to show off." Thereafter the room next to any stage, TV or film studio was named thus.

It was a lovely cashmere coat, and I'd been dropping my crisps all over it, and probably my wine as well.

I said,

- I'm so sorry Roger. I didn't realise.

- No problem at all dear boy, as long as it kept your bum nice and warm.

I always liked Roger: lovely man, unpretentious, not up his own arse, marvellous actor, too.

- Here's your coat, Mr. Moore. Can I carry your bags to the car, sir?

I bet he couldn't believe he'd had such a talented arse sitting on his £250,000 cashmere coat.

As a tag, after that night on the Michael Parkinson Show with Roger Moore, the phone didn't stop ringing for Wall Street Crash for the next four years. So Michael Parkinson was directly responsible for cracking Wall Street Crash in England. Bless your heart Michael.

Scene Six: Peter Ustinov. UNICEF. Madrid Eh?

We felt honoured to be asked to perform in a Eurovision TV concert for UNICEF which was going out live from a huge amphitheatre in Madrid. It was a multinational show with top performers from all over Europe. Peter Ustinov was asked to compère the show as he is fluently multilingual. At the afternoon rehearsal Peter said he would do a short interview with us before introducing our first number; he asked which one of us he should talk to, and was there anything in particular we would like to promote? As a rule we took it in turns to do this sort of thing and that night it was Polly's turn. Polly suggested that he could mention the release of our new album, and that we had a new TV series about to air in Italy. Peter thought this was a good idea and said he would see us later when the cameras were rolling.

The show was lengthy and we had great fun watching the other acts from our vantage point on a circular balcony outside our dressing room high up in the theatre. At one point Sacha Distel, who had the dressing room next to ours, was leaning on the rail with us enjoying watching a famous Spanish flamenco guitar player giving his all. It is not widely known that Sacha was a brilliant jazz guitarist, rated alongside performers like Django Reinhardt, one of the all-time jazz guitar greats. (Sacha also wrote the beautiful song 'It's the good life' which has been covered by many singers.) Sacha was waxing lyrical about the flamenco player's technique when Polly turned to him and uttered the immortal words,

  - So, do you play the guitar then, Sash?

Now first of all it is probably accurate to assume that nobody, not even his mum, has ever called Sacha 'Sash' and, secondly, Mr Distel's guitar playing is off the planet. As I slipped away to the safety of our dressing room, crimson with embarrassment and hoping beyond hope that Sacha didn't think that I had anything remotely to do with this musical heathen, I heard Mr. Incredibly Talented Distel say very gently,

  - Yes, I play a little.

Only to hear Polly respond,

  - Nice one, Sash.

71

The time for our performance arrived and we joined Peter on the stage for our pre-act interview live in front of millions of people. It all started well with Peter saying,

> - Ladies and gentlemen, mesdames et messieurs, damas y caballeros, signore e signore, meine damen und herren, senhoras e senhores, and so on, please welcome from London, England, Wall Street Crash.

He then proceeded to interview Polly in Spanish which, unfortunately, Polly cannot speak. He's not bad at French and, when pissed, has a stab at Italian but Spanish, he *no comprendo*. Peter didn't give an inch and continued asking questions, to which Polly clearly had no answers. At one point he did say,

> - Sorry, Peter, but my Spanish is a bit rusty.

This made no impression at all on the indomitable Mr. Ustinov, who cruised on undeterred. Now Polly may not know that Sacha Distel can play more than three chords on the guitar but he did know he was in deep shit and that this was going out live in front of a Eurovision audience of millions. Any other living soul would have crumbled. However, Polly, who has always been known for having more front than Harrods, gave up trying to fight the situation and just stood there grinning inanely until Peter finally said in English,

> - Ladies and gentlemen, Wall Street Crash.

And we were mercifully back into safe territory.

Sometime later we were appearing again on the Michael Parkinson Show and so was Peter Ustinov. He laughingly admitted to stitching us up like kippers. What a wag, eh?

Scene Seven: Bonkers with Bob Monkhouse

During one of my, fortunately brief, periods of being a resting actor I was chatting to a mate who was working as an extra to tide him over until something more substantial came along. He said the money wasn't bad, you got free food and most of the time you would be sitting around doing bugger all. You could catch up on your correspondence, maybe do your tax return (considering that 90% of professional actors are unemployed at any given time, for most this is a pretty quick process), or just hang around nattering with your fellow resting thesps about the good old days of repertory when you rehearsed one play during the day and performed another in the evening for an almost non-existent salary but a wealth of acting experience. All the greats had done their time in rep; Michael Caine and that generation of great actors all agree that it was the rep experience that gave them the tools that later proved invaluable in their careers.

Norm gave me the number of his extras agency saying,

- Give it a whirl and if it's not for you give it the swerve.

I sent the agency my details and a 10 by 8 photo and hoped that, if any work came my way, my 'proper' agent wouldn't find out that I was moonlighting, as 'proper' actors didn't work as extras. The phone rang the next day; I was offered work on a new comedy series for ATV, starring Bob Monkhouse and an American act called the Hudson Brothers. One of the brothers, Bill Hudson, was married to Goldie Hawn at the time and they later had a daughter, Kate Hudson, who now has a very successful film acting career.

I pitched up early the following day at Elstree studios in Borehamwood and took my place with the other extras on the set of a show called 'Bonkers'. There were about twenty of us and, as Norm had quite rightly said, there wasn't much to do. We spent most of the morning dressing the set, or sitting around while the director, Bob, and the Hudsons argued about what was funny and what wasn't. From what I could gather Bob didn't think much of it was funny at all.

The set for the sketch they were working on consisted of a large scaffolding structure. The action (or lack of it) seemed to be based on the Pink Panther film idea of Bob being a sort of bumbling Inspector Clouseau character, while the

Hudsons were the villains trying to kill him off. Bob was to wander around the scaffolding in search of clues to some crime or other and, in turn, each of the three brothers would attack him, Kato-style. A domino effect of disasters would ensue and, being an unarmed combat expert, he would deftly throw each of them around the set in a comedy slapstick fight scene scenario. If one of the villains was about to hit him with a plank of wood, Bob would bend over to pick something up, the villain would lose his balance and fall over him, Bob would stand up and catapult his head back against the villain's nose; the second villain would then grab Bob, who would pick him up and, using his signature judo move, Morote Seoi Nage - a double-handed shoulder throw (the one I used in the tunes advert for which, you may recall, I received *repeat fees*) - toss him onto the villain with the damaged nose and, when the third villain lunged for him, Bob would deftly chuck him off the scaffolding. There was only one problem. Clearly none of them, the director, Bob or the brothers had the first clue about unarmed combat.

I was minding my own business, trying to solve the Sun newspaper 'Easy Crossword for Thick Twats', when a God Almighty argument kicked off up on the scaffold. Bob was not happy with the way the sketch was progressing and it looked as though there might be a real punch up at any moment. In desperation, the director screamed down to the studio floor,

- Does *anybody* here know anything about martial arts?

Brow furrowed, I had got to the clue 'What animal has four legs, whiskers and goes meow, three letters?' Relieved that at last I knew one of the clues, I was filling in d-o-g when I heard the exasperated director's plea. I looked around me. There was silence and much shaking of heads. I chirped up, in a falsetto voice,

- I do!

- Who said that?

The pissed-off director was scanning the studio twenty feet below him with the sort of relief you might see on the face of a man who had been waiting for the blade of the guillotine to fall and who suddenly realised that the mechanism was jammed. He had had a last-minute reprieve.

- I did. I trained in judo, karate and unarmed combat.

All eyes were now on *me*. Did these mere mortals realise that at that precise moment I was ATV's answer to Bruce Lee?

- What's your name, sir?

Fucking hell! They've already given me a knighthood and I haven't even left my chair.

- Colin (*formerly known as 'that short-arsed extra over there reading the Sun'*).
- Colin please come up and join us.

(I might do later, if I feel like it, but at the moment I'm busy doing the crossword, so bog off. d-o-g)

- I'm on my way, sir. (*My voice was already two octaves lower, in anticipation of my new incarnation as the King of Kung Fu.*)

I ascended the scaffolding like a prowling tiger, the sinews of my lithe body taut and ready for action, pausing only slightly as my Cuban heel got caught in the hem of my flared loon pants. I was *the* man.

It took me eight seconds to climb up the scaffolding, using the circus skills developed in my youth on the tree in Keith Ridgeway's back garden, to be introduced to my new best friends/pupils: BD (big director) Bob, and the Hudsons. I completed the round of hand-shaking, squeezing their hands just a little harder than was necessary to prove what a tough martial arts dude I was, maintaining my vice-like grip for rather too long while treating them to my famous (just improvised) Claude van Damme-is-a-big-girl's-blouse stare, and only releasing my grip when their eyes welled with tears of pain.

- Hi, I'm Col. (*My new butch basso profundo voice working a treat until....*)

In a super cool manner, I casually leant against a rung of the scaffold, my elbow slipped and I just managed to prevent an ignominious fall to the studio floor by grabbing the cuff of Bob's Yves Saint Laurent sweatshirt. Composing myself, I swished my lethal hand weapons around in a many-times-practised Kata move (a Karate sequence) but realised that I was now scaring the shit out of everyone, including myself. I eased back a little, softening my war face to a slightly more benign, if a little droopy-lipped, smile.

75

Having got all of the fake showmanship shit out of the way, I asked BD what he wanted me to do. He explained his (fabulously original) Pink Panther idea. I was about to describe the throws I thought would look the most impressive and require the minimum of technique, and to explain that we would need crash mats for the boys to land on after Bob had thrown them off the structure when, from out of nowhere with a Superman-type swooosh, a very official clipboard-clutching vision appeared amidst us. He explained that he was the extras union representative and that, before we went any further, we should discuss my new fee as 'fight/stunt director' which would be considerably more than my previous measly (but all the food you could eat) extra's fee.

This could never happen today as now, quite rightly, the stunt and fight profession is tightly-controlled and highly respected. BD told the union man that money wasn't a problem, to sort it out with the producer and my agent, and to fuck off and let him get on with directing. The union man fucked off with another superhero swooosh and I explained my ideas to BD, Bob and the boys. If we were to complete the shots impressively, and more importantly safely, we would need a good two hours' rehearsal to block and teach the sequences of moves so that he could get the whole thing in one continuous shot, which would flow much better on film. BD told me to take all the time I needed and to let him know when we would be ready to start shooting.

By this stage, I had become very popular with the rest of the extras as we would most probably have to go into overtime and their fees would increase dramatically for standing around doing sod all. Because we took time to rehearse the stunts, the shoot went really well and BD, Bob, the Hudson Boys and my extras buddies were all very happy.

That evening my new extras agent rang to say that my fee had increased substantially and that the director was over the moon with what he had in the can. They would like to develop the idea and would I be available for more work doing the same thing on 'Bonkers'? I said, "Great! Keep me posted." The following morning my proper agent called with an audition time for the following day for a new musical called 'Let the Good Stones Roll' about the Rolling Stones. I did the audition, got the gig, and that was the end of my fight directing career.

I think it was that good old 60% luck thing kicking in again.

Scene Eight: Oh, I Do Like to be Beside the Seaside

It was my first audition for the summer season of a theatre show in Great Yarmouth. I had been singing with various bands and groups when my singing teacher suggested that I try to get into the theatre. I knew nothing about the theatre apart from going to see my dad performing as a stooge for visiting comedians at the Theatre Royal Stratford (East) when I was knee high to a grasshopper - well, actually about the same height I am now. He told me that there were open auditions for summer seasons being held at the Prince of Wales Theatre in London and suggested I give it a try. In those days, in the 70s, summer seasons used to last for three or four months, so it was good work.

The next day I went along to the theatre. One of the numbers I was singing with the show band I was working with was a song called 'Love me Tonight' by Tom Jones. It was number one in the charts: ♪♪ "I know that it's late and I really must leave you alone…"

I took along my music and gave it to the pianist who was on the stage and asked him if he knew it. He didn't. Before my audition, I had been standing at the side of the stage listening to the other singers. The other guys had sung show songs like, 'My boy Bill, he'll be tall and tough as a tree..' and 'O…♪… klahoma where the wind comes sweeping down the plains'. I didn't know any of those songs. I had only worked in bands. I was singing the intro of the song to the pianist just to give us both a fighting chance when, from deep in the auditorium, came a piss-elegant voice,

- Can we get on with this please? We have a lot of people to see, you know.

So I said to the pianist,

- Just go for it and I'll sing along.

He started playing the intro and I sang,

- Well I know that it's late… ♪♪

And Mr Piss-elegant's voice barked from the back,

- Thank you!

I didn't know what that meant (possibly, "Thank you, it's great to have an auditionee who isn't warbling the usual shit from Carousel or Oklahoma."), so I carried on singing,

- ...and I really must leave you alone.. 🎵
- Thank you! (Mr P-E again, this time rather abruptly)

So I stopped singing. The pianist gave me my music and a sympathetic look, and I walked offstage to the sound of my own dejected footsteps, as some bloke barged passed me in an excited rush to regale Mr. P-E with a wanky song from 'Hello Dolly'.

I rang my singing teacher, Freddie, and he asked how I got on.

- Terrible. I started singing and they said, "Thank you very much." And that was it.
- What did you sing?
- 'Love me Tonight', the Tom Jones song.
- No, no, no, Col, you twazzock. This is the theatre, a different thing entirely! Come around here now.

Freddie taught at the Maurice Berman School of modern pop singing in Baker Street. I followed his advice and went round to see him.

- Learn this song: 'On a Wonderful Day Like Today'. Go back tomorrow. They won't remember you (*bloody cheek!*) 'cos you were only on the stage for about a minute.

So he taught me the song:

- On a wonderful day like today 🎵
  I defy any cloud to appear in the sky
  Dare any rain drop to plop in my eye
  On a wonderful day like today

I went back the next day and gave the music to the pianist.

- Do you know this?
- Yeah, of course, much better than that pop crap you came in with yesterday (*well, **he** remembered me anyway!*).

From the back of the auditorium (*Here she goes again, dear! Definitely a friend of Dorothy's*),

- Can we get on with it please? We have a lot of people to see today, you know.

The pianist started up. Giving it some right welly I launched into....

- ♪♪ On a wonderful day like today
     I defy any cloud to...

- Thank you very much! (*So much for my new incarnation as a star of musicals!*)

She-who-must-be-obeyed minced down to the front of the stage.

- Would you like to go to Great Yarmouth for four months with Harry Worth and Bert Weedon?
- What!!?..... Lovely! Thank you very much!

So off I went to Great Yarmouth for four months, and bloody *great* it was too. I lived in a caravan on the beach with my friend Pete, who was also a singer in the show. Our code name for the caravan was 'T-Triple-S (The Seaside Shag Shed). We had the most marvellous time. Pete and I were the young performers in the show. There were two other boy singers who 'helped them out when they were busy', and twenty young, nubile unattached girl dancers. That's not to mention all of the gorgeous girls who were on their two-week holiday without their parents. Life was very depressing indeed. Sometimes the 'action' in TTS was such that, if it had obeyed the laws of physics, it should have rolled into the sea. We bought a tandem bike. Every night after the show we would go to a few bars, get some falling-down water down our throats and then, as dawn was breaking, and singing at the tops of our voices, we would pedal our trusty tandem precariously along the seafront for half an hour, back to our caravan. One night after chatting up two girls, and having partaken of rather too much amber nectar, we cycled all the way back to TTS with the girls perched on our two handlebars, singing Beatles songs and swerving all over the road. It was a minor miracle that we made it back without being arrested or suffering a worse fate.

We used to have all-night barbecues on the beach with the singers and dancers from our show, with Harry Worth doing his brilliant ventriloquist routine and Bert Weedon[8] playing his fantastic guitar all night for us. The performers from the other three summer shows would pop along for a right old knees-up on the beach. On the Wellington Pier next to us was the cast from the 'Carry On' films, Sid James and the gang, and Leslie Crowther on the next pier to that. Bloody marvellous! I was nineteen years old and loving every single wonderful minute of my fantastic life.

During these seasons, it was the custom for all of the shows to get together and do something for charity. That year it was decided that we would have a light-hearted inter-show cricket match in the local park, with the celebrities making up the two teams. The aim was simply to have an entertaining afternoon and raise quite a few bob for good causes. Well! We were all in the pavilion with the referee, picking pairs of names out of a hat to decide who would bat and who bowl. Sid James was picked to be the first to bat, a good call as he was a major celebrity and the crowd would go bonkers when he came out. Great! And first to bowl to Sid, from the Britannia Pier show, Colin Copperfield. Silence. It was my first theatre show, I was a singer in the chorus and nobody apart from my show mob knew who I was. Never mind, off we go....

- Ladies and gentlemen, from The Wellington Pier show and the fantastic Carry On Films, the rogue you've all come to know and love, give a big hand for Mr. Sid James...
- Hooooooooooorah!

As predicted the crowd went wild. Out came Sid, swishing his bat round his head,

- Hooooooooorah! We want Sid. We want Sid.

He ran around the pitch soaking up the adoration,

- We love you Sid, oh yes we do. ♪♪

He played up to his audience brilliantly, milking it for all he was worth. Good man, Sid.

---

8 Bert Weedon wrote the series of Teach Yourself Guitar books called 'Play in a Day', which every musician from the Beatles to the Stones credited for getting them on the right track.

- And now from the Britannia Pier show...Colin Copperfield..

For the second time in half an hour I realised I was 'Mr.-who-the-bloody-hell-is-Colin Copperfield'. I knew nothing about the game of cricket and asked Pete if he could give me some pointers on the correct way to bowl. Helpfully, and clearly with a lifetime's experience behind him, he suggested, " Just run as fast as you can and chuck the fucking thing". I ran out, ball in hand, to a rapturous...nothing,...well, a few kind people managed a half-hearted, "Yay".

But, I'm a pro..... To the deafening sound of *silence* I took up where Sid left off. I ran around the pitch tossing my ball in the air (the moment was slightly spoiled when I failed to catch it as it came down). Sid was at the wicket waiting for Mr. Nobody to stop farting around and get on with it. RIGHT! I'll show you lot wot a backstreet boy can do when his back's against the wall. Hang on to your hat Sid, here I come...

The world went into slow motion. I started my run, increasing my speed ... faster, faster. Someone in the throng shouted, "G'wan my son!" (probably my agent). That small sliver of encouragement gave me all the strength I needed..... Whooosh the ball left my sweaty hand and arced gracefully through the balmy summer Sunday afternoon air. My God!!! It was heading straight for Sid at an alarming rate. This was beyond my wildest dreams....whooosh straight past Sid's bat...whooosh straight into the bloody wicket...whoosh up in the air go the stumps...whooosh up in the air go the bails. Fucking Nora!!! I've only just gone and bowled out Sid (star of stage and screen) James... My high pitched scream of

- Yeeeessssssssssss',

and the triumphant sound of my pumping fist in the air was, for a brief moment, the only sound in that vast, gladiatorial arena..............

BAD MOVE.....The crowd had come to see Sid and the other 'proper' celebrities putting on a show, not to see him bowled out on the first ball by some short-arsed nobody. As the umpire reluctantly called "out" (looking at me with more poison than a vat of Russian novichok), the crowd erupted..

- No!...No!..No!

But the deed was done, and so was I. I had stolen his thunder.[9] Off Sid slunk. I slunk after him. We walked in silence to the pavilion. Once inside, out of sight of the baying crowd, I started to say,

- Sid I'm so sorry, I just got carried away...

But Sid cut me short...

- You... fucking.... stupid.... WANKER . (Accurate, but a little over the top I thought.)

These people have paid good money to see me give them a performance. They have come here to be entertained by me. And you....you....you, you stupid prat, bowl me OUT. Talk about stealing a chap's thunder, you monumental tit.

The air was still blue when an announcement came over the tannoy.

- Ladies and gentlemen, the referee has decided to overrule the decision of the umpire and to give Mr. James a second innings. Would you all agree with this decision?

Too fucking right they would!

- Yes! Yes! YES!, came the answer from the drooling Sidites.

Sid looked at me and shook my hand,

- Sorry I shouted at you mate. No hard feelings. Enjoy the rest of the season.

I couldn't resist it...

- No probs Sid. Want me to bowl?

He called me a wanker again, though this time with a smile, and went off to woo his adoring crowd.

---

9 This brings to mind another of my favourite luvvy expressions. In the 18th century, a playwright by the name of John Dennis came up with a novel method for creating the sound of thunder to be used in one of his plays. This involved hitting large tin sheets together backstage. While the audience loved the realistic sound effects, the play flopped and was replaced by 'Macbeth'. When that production used his technique, Dennis was enraged and is purported to have said: "How these rascals use me. They will not have my play and yet they steal my thunder."

Scene Nine: A Life on the Ocean Waves

I was performing in panto in Coventry with Ted Rogers the comedian and presenter of the long running TV show '321'. During a break between the matinée and the evening performance I was chatting to Loretta, one of the dancers. She asked if I had any work lined up when the show's run was over. I had nothing else planned so she suggested that I audition for a director and choreographer named Geoff Ferris who was looking for performers who could sing, dance and act, to work on the cruise ships. Geoff had been a very successful dancer and had worked in many West End shows, including being one of the original cast of 'Oliver'. He later became Cameron Mackintosh's right hand man, overseeing many of his shows around the world. Loretta had worked with Geoff and thought I would fit in with the way that he worked. She kindly said she would give him a ring and put in a good word for me. The shipboard shows were produced by a larger-than-life, very tall American named Vic Ogley, who lived in Scotland in Drumtochty Castle.

I did my audition for Geoff a couple of weeks later, singing a few songs and doing the dance steps he had choreographed for the shows. Not only did I think that *he* was brilliant, but luckily he thought I was the right guy for the job, and said that Vic would send me the contract for a three-week rehearsal period, followed by three months on the high seas cruising around the Mediterranean on a ship called the Northern Star. I was twenty years old and had never been anywhere more exotic than Southend-on-Sea and Great Yarmouth.

Vic called and, in a very broad American accent, said,

- Good to have you onboard, Colin, your contract is in the post.

The not-so-good news was that I now had three months to find some work to see me through until rehearsals began. I got a few gigs singing in pubs and worked as a hod carrier (lugging loads of bricks up buildings for the bricklayers), bloody hard work for a nipper. But work was scarce and, by the time I had to get my passport, I was almost skint. The passport office was in central London and I only had enough money for the passport and my train fare one way. I decided I would go there on the train and then walk home. I queued up for quite a while but I got the magic document. It took me five and a half hours to walk home, but all the way I was thinking,

- Not long now and I'll be in rehearsals, then off on a luxury ship to have the time of my life.

So the long and winding road home didn't seem too bad at all. The next day the phone rang and I heard the unmistakable voice of Vic Ogley,

- Colin, we have a problem.

- Fuck, I thought, That's my loverly job up the spout.

But Vic continued,

- Colin, one of our other ships, the Andes, has had problems with one of the entertainers and he wants to leave the ship. We still have one more month-long cruise around the West Indies to complete, to honour our contract. I've spoken to Geoff and he thinks he could rehearse you into the shows pretty quickly. Are you available to start rehearsals tomorrow?

(*Not fucking many am I available to start rehearsals tomorrow. I walked for five and a half bleedin' hours yesterday to get my passport. Bring it on Vic.*)

I started my crash course with Geoff the next day in a grotty rehearsal room in Shepherds Bush. (Years later I would rehearse in the same still-grotty room with Wall Street Crash.) Blimey, there was a lot to learn. The shows were one and a half hour versions of well-known musicals: 'Guys and Dolls', 'West Side Story', 'The Sound of Music' and some I'd never even heard of like 'The Student Prince' and 'The King and I'. The current company had been doing these shows for three months and had had the luxury of four weeks to learn the routines. I was sailing with Geoff from Southampton in three days' time, and my first show, with fifteen singers and dancers I had never met, would take place on the night I boarded the ship. Shit!

Geoff and I boarded the Andes. I couldn't believe how big it was. After hurried introductory hellos and hand-shakes we started a run through of the programme for that evening. It was an Ivor Novello show. *Who?* I had a duet to sing called 'We'll gather lilacs in the spring ' with a lovely girl called Ollie Shaw, who was an East Ender from Buckhurst Hill. Yippeeeee, one of my own. I was so under-rehearsed that Geoff said to the company,

- Look, you'll all just have to guide Col through it, gently push him in the right direction and cover for him wherever you can, because there's no way he's had time to learn the whole show.

Good man Geoff. Show time came and I was bricking it. With a lot of pushing and shoving I was just about coping, getting most of the songs and the steps more or less right, and then came my big number with Ollie. After a bell note (one single note) from the trombone player, I sang my first line:

- We'll gather lillocks in the spring again.

For some reason, I was having trouble pronouncing the word lilacs. It kept coming out as 'lillocks'. Geoff kept asking,

- What the fuck are lillocks?

That proved to be the least of my problems at that precise moment. How this duet worked was: I would sing a line, then Ollie would repeat part of the line after me, and this would continue throughout the entire song. So! Off I go....

Me:

- We'll gather lillocks in the spring again.

Ollie:

- We'll gather lilacs.

That first line was the only one I got right through the whole song. My next line was meant to be,

- And walk together down an English lane.

Instead, me:

- And see a dog climb up a tree again.

Ollie:

- Tree again

The next line was meant to be,

- Until our hearts have learned to sing again.

Me:

> - I'll hear a bell go tingaling again.

Ollie:

> - tingaling.

And the correct line:

> - And we'll come home once more.

Instead, me:

> - And I must shut that door.

Ollie:

> - Shut that door.

We went through the whole song like that, with Ollie, bless her heart, repeating, with her beautiful soprano voice every bit of nonsense that came out of my mouth. I will never forget the look of sheer horror in her eyes as I bluffed my way through that song. When, thank God, the show finished, and we were all safely backstage, Ollie was laughing so much she almost lost control of her bladder. This poor girl had performed in seven West End shows until, just when she really didn't need it, she got me. As it turned out, most of the clientele were in their later years, and every single one of them knew all the words to the song by heart. The next day, on the deck, passengers were stopping me and saying,

> - By Jove old boy, cracking show last night, never heard that version of 'Lilacs' before though.

I replied,

> - Well Ivor Novello wrote a couple of different versions of that song and we thought, as it was the last cruise, we would honour him by singing one of his earlier versions.

And I kept a straight face!

Every day I rehearsed with Geoff and the company, and performed in a new show nearly every night. I don't wish to blow my own foghorn here (well I do a bit), but I did ten different musicals in fourteen nights, four of which I'd never heard of. That's got to be a first, hasn't it? C'mon give an old trouper a bit of applause, eh!

The Andes was a very old ship; in fact, this was her farewell voyage. She had also served valiantly throughout the Second World War as a troop carrier, and was *the* most beautiful vessel. She had magnificent oak staircases and oak four poster beds. There were tea dance with cucumber sandwiches and Earl Grey tea on the deck every afternoon, accompanied by a tuxedo-garbed pianist playing a white grand piano. And, as if this wasn't elegant enough, you could order lobster and chips in your cabin at 3.30 in the morning and it would arrive within ten minutes. Those were the days. When we sailed back into Southampton harbour, many of the crew lining the decks were sobbing their hearts out as they had served on her for most of their lives. It was incredibly sad and very moving.

So, back in Blighty, I soon started rehearsals for the Northern Star with a new company of performers. Having been through my baptism of fire on the Andes I was feeling much more confident and was looking forward to it. My new company were the most fantastic bunch to work with, much younger, all about my age, and very talented. The rehearsals flew by, with loads of laughing and joking and, before you could say "I haven't got to sing 'We'll gather lillocks in the spring' *ever* again", we were on the Star. Not only were we doing great new musicals, but we also had our own cabaret spots and loads of other opportunities. I became the keep-fit instructor and my regular morning classes on the deck with the sun shining, the sea rolling, and tons of young, lovely girls leaping about to the music with me, were the dog's bollocks.

STOP! Let's just assess the situation for a minute, OK? I was twenty years old, single, not bad looking; flares and stack heel boots were still in fashion so, when I put some elevator lifts inside them, I was at least 6' 7" tall. I was on stage every night showing off in the shows and cabarets, I had my own love shack (cabin) *and* I was getting paid for it! Tickle me tangerines and call me Nora, a life on the ocean waves for me, boys. Go large.

Scene Ten: You Dance with Lola

When I boarded the Andes, I had no idea about anything nautical. For example, I didn't know that, under threat of being made to walk the plank, you never call a ship a boat; every crew bar on every ship is called the Pig and Whistle; walls are bulkheads; the ship's police are Masters at Arms; the left side of the ship is port, the right side is starboard; the front is the bow and the back is the stern; and the kitchen is the galley. Because ships generally have quite a large contingent of men who 'help them out when they are busy', there are quite a few theatrical terms (known as Polari) thrown into the mix as well. A 'palone' is a girl, an 'omi' is a man, an 'omi-palone' is a gay man, 'varda' means look, 'carts' are men's privates, 'lallies' are legs, 'bona' is good, 'naff' is bad, your 'latty' is your cabin, 'drag' is dressing up as a girl, 'dragging back to your latty' is taking someone to your cabin, 'Aunt Nell' is to listen, 'polari' is to speak, 'frocks' are clothes, 'nanti' is don't, 'eek' is face and 'riah' is hair. Every sentence ends with 'dear'. For instance if you said,

- Varda the carts on the bona omi, dear. Naff eek but worth dragging back to the latty. Nanti polari to the palones though, dear.

The rough translation would be "Look at the crotch on that lovely bloke. Ugly face, but worth dragging back to the cabin. Don't tell the girls though."

The late-night cocktail lounge singer and keyboard player, Barry St David, whose real name was Billy Yarrow but was known off-stage as Yana Yarrow, came from Yorkshire. He was as gay as a party hat. He said to me,

- Cora (everyone was given a girl's name and I became Cora Copperfield), tonight's drag night at the Pig and Whistle. Put on a bona frock dear, and I'll take you down.

I didn't have the first idea what he was talking about but thought I should agree, just to be polite.

- I'll knock on your latty after the show dear, about 11.45.

- OK, great,

I meekly answered.

At 11.45 she knocked on my latty and I opened the door to a sight I shall never forget until the day I die. There stood Yana in full drag: her hair (riah) piled into a one-foot-high blonde bouffant on top of her head, a gold lamé dress (frock), six inch heels, and more tasteless jewellery than a Soho tart.

- C'mon Cora, let's go dear. (*I know where I want to go: back home to my mum and dad!*)
- Bona Yana, lead the way dear,

I said lamely, trying to get into the camp shipboard spirit of things.

Off we went, leaving the safety of the passenger area, down increasingly tatty stairways, deck after deck, into the bowels of the ship, until I could hear thumping music: Shirley Bassey's 'Big Spender' at 50,000 decibels. We entered a world I never could have believed existed - the gaudiest, campest, most tasteless discotheque you could imagine, crammed to the bulkheads with men wearing more drag than Danny la Rue on acid, bumping and grinding and trying not to fall over in their ludicrously high heels. Now I *really do* want my mummy!

Yana was screeching and hollering her tits off to all her palone friends,

- This is Cora, dears, the new girl. She's just come on board. Let's show her how we party, dears.

With that, the biggest and tallest man I had ever seen in my life, approximately 6 feet 7 tall, and 6 feet 7 wide, wearing full drag, sashayed up to me and ordered, in a booming voice,

- You dance with Lola.

It was not a question or an invitation, it was a command. Before I could say, "Launch the fucking lifeboat, I'm off dears", Lola escorted me onto the dance floor and, enveloping me in her muscle-bound arms, swept me into a seductive tango. The crowd whooped and hollered as we swept across the dance floor like Fred Astaire and Ginger Rogers (only with Ginger leading). She tossed and turned me, dropped me backwards over her arm so that my head hit the deck, glided with me across the room at 130mph, and lifted me up above her head, twirling me around in never-ending circles until I was drunk with giddiness and about to throw up. After an eternity the song ended and Lola, ever the gentlewoman, escorted me back to Yana who screeched,

- Didn't I tell you dear what a fun time we'd have?

I finally managed to excuse myself and crawled up the fifty-nine decks to the safety of my latty. I kept thinking of that line from 'Sweet Charity', 'If my friends could see me now'.

The postscript to the story:

The next day we docked in Barbados. We had a great day on Paradise Beach drinking rum punches, dancing to a steel band and swimming in a turquoise sea. When it came time to board the launch which would take us back to the ship, a swell had blown up and the sea had become very choppy. The crew members who were helping the passengers onto the launches were concerned as it was becoming dangerous. As we were entertainment staff not passengers, we were the last to board. By then the swell was lifting the launch several feet into the air, and then down again with a terrifying hollow thump. My buddies just managed to jump aboard. I was the last to go. As the wave lifted the boat and I jumped, I felt a very strong hand grab my wrist just as I was about to fall between the launch and the sea wall, and a muscular tattooed arm pulled me over the side of the launch to safety. I was an inch away from being crushed and drowned. I looked up to thank the crewman who had just saved my life. He smiled and said,

- You dance with Lola.

Lola, whose real name was Lawrence, and I became lifelong friends and stayed in touch for many years after our seafaring days were over. I later found out that Lola had been an airborne warrior with the elite British parachute regiment whose motto was 'utrinque paratus', ready for anything. Lola had a Pegasus tattoo on his forearm, inscribed with the para logo. He had served with distinction in skirmishes around the world but had given it all up to be a Merchant Navy sailor, where crossdressing was more the order of the day. He cut a fine figure in a frock but, on that occasion, I was grateful for the muscle!

Thanks again for saving my life, Lola. I'll dance the tango with you any time you want.

Scene Eleven: High Jinx on the High Seas

The day I boarded the Star, I met two of the loveliest blokes in the world. They weren't in the shows but they performed in their own cabaret spots and ran everything else: the discos, the bingo, the spotlights for the shows and the deck sports. They were from Birmingham and their names were Robert and David Johnson but, for some reason I can't remember, they became known as Snitch and Snatch. We became the three cavaliers, and inseparable. We laughed and shagged ourselves stupid for three months solid. There was one cruise that was overbooked so we were told that the entertainers would have to share cabins. (We had been allocated passenger cabins, whereas other cruise lines gave the entertainers crew cabins, but the Shaw Savill Line treated us well). So Snitch, Snatch, a dancer called Nick and I agreed to share for the next cruise. We were allocated cabin B20. (I believe that, after we left the ship, a plaque was mounted on the door in our honour, commemorating the shenanigans B20 witnessed. Snatch still has the key to B20, to this very day.) The problem was that communal living was going to severely cramp our style with the ladies. A lot of the young girls on these cruises were sharing cabins with their mums and dads, so having our own love shack was paramount. The cabin we were given had four bunk beds, not ideal for four lads on night time manoeuvres. We got around this small hiccup in the innovative way that nineteen and twenty year olds do: 'love tents'. If all four of us had 'pulled', the bed cover from the top bunk was lowered down over the bottom bunk like a curtain, so the proceedings in the lower bunks weren't visible, hence love tents. However, the two studs in the upper bunks *were* visible to each other, so they just had to get on with it, and get on with it they did! For those of you with queasy stomachs, please close your eyes now, and try not to imagine the sight and sound of eight people 'at it' in a smallish love shack, rolling around on the Mediterranean Sea.

After a couple of weeks of networking we got to know the officers in the purser's office really well. (The purser's office is the administrative centre of the ship. They allocate cabins, organise shore excursions and are also the financial hub of the floating city.) After Snitch, Snatch and I had plied them with our wily charms, the pursers were all too happy to assist us in our lady-chasing hedonistic lifestyle. They would give us the heads-up as to which cabins were occupied by the unattached young ladies and, on the second day of any given cruise, the three of us would put on our best bib and tucker and do the rounds, knocking on their cabin doors, introducing ourselves as members of the entertainment staff and inviting them to the 'travelling alone cocktail party' later that evening. This gave us a massive advantage over the handsome young deck officers who looked irresistible in their poncy pristine white 'Officer and a Gentleman' uniforms. Quite frankly, this was war and any underhand tactics we could employ to get one over on these sailor boys was a huge result for us skirt-chasing thespians.

Snitch, Snatch and I would then spend hours swotting up on the girls' names so that, when they arrived at the cocktail party, we were primed and ready for action. Looking dashing and debonair, with our white tuxedos enhancing our deep suntans (as I'm writing this I'm getting excited all over again), we would greet them with,

- Hi! Susan, Jilly and Jenny, welcome to the party, you all look beautiful. Would you like some champagne?

And we were out of the traps and off and running. When the cocktail party was winding down and we had stunned them with our unbelievable wit and charm, we would home in on the girls we fancied the most and invite them to the disco where we would impress the hell out of them with our finely-tuned, best John Travolta moves (the three of us were revoltingly smooth). Then, if the gods of the oceans were with us, we would hear the call of the love shacks beckoning us home. Yippeeee.

Each cruise usually lasted two weeks. In between cruises, we had a very quick one day turnaround in Southampton docks, our home port. As the passengers from one cruise were disembarking down the rear gangway the passengers for the next cruise were embarking up the front gangway. After a couple of cruises the Johnson boys and I had established a slick modus operandi. By the last three days of each trip we would usually have found three lovely girls who we were 'going steady' with, so we would curtail our philandering ways and have a lovely relaxing time *just* with them. On disembarkation day the three of us would be at the gangway bidding farewell to our 'steadies'. This would involve protestations of undying love and treasured moments never to be forgotten, and toadying phrases like 'You have been a chapter in my life' and 'Go slowly, come back quickly'. (Dear Reader, if you wish to 'take five' for a vomit break I totally understand.) But hey! we were young, for God's sake. The loves of our lives would board the waiting coaches, we would wave and wave until they were out of sight and then, clutching our broken hearts, run like crazy along the deck to the forward gangway to spot the new talent coming on board. Shallow or wot?

Scene Twelve: Burial at Sea (Farewell, Old Friends)

When I had joined the Andes a year previously I was so low on funds that I didn't have many clothes, and certainly no *smart* clothes, apart from my cabaret outfit. My entire wardrobe consisted of one pair of worn-out trousers, one pair of worn-out jeans, two worn-out shirts, a couple of halfway decent t-shirts, a pair of Dad's old army shorts with 'Property of Her Majesty's Armed Forces' printed on them (quite fashionable now, but extremely embarrassing then), one pair of wrong size flip flops (nicked), one pair of Cuban-heeled boots (bird pulling: for the use of) and my pride and joy, my bespoke cabaret outfit, black jacket, trousers and waistcoat, white shirt with frill down the front (à la Tom Jones at the time) and a bow tie so big that if the ship had sunk it would have kept me afloat for weeks. I muddled my way through until I received my first wages, then upgraded my wardrobe to fit my posh new lifestyle. With regard to my Cuban-heeled boots, I had become very attached to my old faithfuls; they had seen me through some rough times and many good times and I was loath to part with them, even though they had seen better days and were in truth ready for the knacker's yard. When I joined the Star they were still a key part of my wardrobe and essential to what I loosely regarded as my 'look'.

In the cabin next to mine lived Fred, a singer and dancer. Fred was as gay as the crocuses in spring and had the campest wit imaginable. For one riotous party in my latty, when we had tried to break all records for squeezing people in, I had festooned my quarters with birthday balloons and all sorts of colourful decorations which I had never quite got around to taking down. One morning Fred minced in to borrow something or other and uttered the immortal words,

- Really, Cora dear! How much longer are you going to live in this fucking Christmas cracker?

But back to my boots. Snitch and Snatch had named them 'Col's EPs', short for 'Col's ever populars' because I wore them on every occasion possible. A couple of times, when hung over and lacking sleep, I even sunbathed on deck wearing only my shorts and the EPs.

Fred would often comment,

- Well Cora! Who got lucky last night, dear? I heard all the giggling and then the familiar sound of zip, zip, crash, crash as the EPs hit the deck. Bona dear!

We were docked in Tangiers when Snitch and Snatch, looking very grave, asked to have a word with me in private.

- Col! We're sorry to have to tell you but the EPs have got to go. We know it will break your heart but to be quite frank they are letting down the side. They are an embarrassment to us seafaring gigolos. Steel yourself! The time has come. Tonight at sunset you have been officially requested to bring the EPs to the forward promenade deck where we will commit them to the waves with full military honours. They will spend the rest of their days lounging in Davy Jones' Wardrobe, having a well-deserved rest. Be brave Col! See you, and the EPs, at eight o'clock sharp.

I spent the rest of the day in a state of near terminal depression but, in my heart of hearts, I knew they were right. The time *had* come.

At the stroke of eight I opened the promenade deck door. There, before my eyes, stood the entire ship's crew. The captain was flanked by all twenty-five officers and other ranks, dressed in their ceremonial white uniforms. The Union Jack was lying on top of the plank that would be lifted to slide the EPs into the drink, consigned to their watery grave. A lone bugler stood to attention, ready to play the haunting 'last post'. The burial party was suitably sombre. I tuned into the gravitas of the situation and adopted an appropriately funereal expression. Terry, our drummer, had brought his snare drum and started playing a slow military march and I began my solemn walk through the corridor of mourners. Sailors and entertainers stood to attention, their heads bowed. My slow march seemed to last a lifetime. Eventually I stood before the medal-bedecked Captain O'Connell. Palms up, he held out his hands to take the EPs. I passed them to him and he bowed his head respectfully. He began his eulogy.

- Friends, officers, thespians lend me your ears. I come to bury Col's EPs, not to wear them. Many have been the occasions when these world-renowned boots have carried out their duty with the highest degree of valour and altruism. They have been unzipped in the most perilous of circumstances and have fulfilled all of their missions with exemplary courage. There have been boots before, and there will be boots again, but there will never in the annals of footwear be boots like Col's EPs. Before they leave for their final resting place please join me now in singing the National Anthem in honour of Col's EPs.

Accompanied by the portable electric organ, and to the tune of "God Save the Queen", the mourners sang,

♪♪

- God bless Col's EP boots
  Hailed from their East End roots
  God Bless Col's boots.
  They have pulled many girls
  Their stories rich as pearls
  Now as our flag unfurls
  God rest Col's bo-o-o-ts. ♪♪

The lone bugler played the Last Post. As the plank was lifted, my old faithfuls slipped gracefully from beneath the Union Jack into the azure Mediterranean Sea. A minute's silence was observed. Then Captain O'Connell requested,

- Three cheers for Col's EPs. Hip Hip Hooray. Hip Hip Hooray. Hip Hip Hooray.

The officers threw their caps into the air. Waitresses appeared as if by magic with silver trays laden with canapés and crystal glasses brimming with champagne. And a happy, but fittingly poignant celebration was had by all.

Farewell old friends. Thanks for the memories. I loved you with my heart and 'sole'.

Scene Thirteen: Sister Act

On our final cruise I was tipped off by Chris the purser that three lovely sisters were on board with their parents, and that the three of them were sharing a cabin of their own on a different deck to Mum and Dad. Whizzzz! The love antenna was activated. As was our usual practice, Snitch, Snatch and I dutifully knocked on their cabin door to invite them to the travelling alone cocktail party. I was instantly smitten by all three of them. Caroline 18, Pippa 20 and Melanie 23. At the party I couldn't believe my luck. The Johnson boys immediately latched onto two lovely girls from Liverpool so I spent the evening (with flirt factor cranked up to overload) chatting to the sisters who (clearly deaf and blind) seemed to think I was a hoot. The officer sailor boys tried to muscle in but I was too well established by that stage to give the handsome, Richard Gere look-alike bastards a chance. Lots of disco dancing followed, with me throwing down shapes that should have left me in traction in Southampton General Hospital for months. By 4.30am the girls were starting to flag a little. So, under the bitter, drooling eyes of the Gere boys (I gave them a 'you losers' wink as I chasséd smugly past them) and, being a gentleman if not an officer, I escorted les girls to their cabin. En route Caroline gave my hand a quick surreptitious but meaningful squeeze. And Pippa gave my bum an undercover pinch. At their cabin I planted a quick peck on their six cheeks, wished them sweet dreams and went on my way. As I reached the lift I heard gentle footsteps behind me and turned to see a shoeless Melanie running toward me. She put her finger to her lips to hush me then removed her finger and replaced it with my lips. In an instant she was gone BUT it was the start of many things to come.

On a ship of that size, especially if you are au-fait with its topography, you can pretty much engineer it so that you can stay as incognito as you wish. Over the course of the next heady week, life with the three sisters was very interesting to say the least (possible details in next book[10]). But, by week two, Caroline and Melanie were dating two of the Richard Gere boys, both great blokes as it happens. Snitch and Snatch were with the two Scouser (Liverpool) girls and I was having a fantastic time with the gorgeous, funny, sexy, divine

---

10 Once the danger of lawsuits and potential death threats from the sisters has been carefully assessed and eliminated by my legal team.

and unforgettable Pippa. Our last gangway goodbyes were, despite all of our youthful, laddish bravado, rather poignant. As the five of us waved off the five of them, we realised that a chapter in our lives really was over. I never saw Pippa again but we stayed in touch for a couple of years. Then, as is the way in life, we eventually lost contact. Wherever you are Pip, thanks for making my last cruise on the Star absolutely, amazingly perfect.

Those three months flew by far too quickly. Truth to tell, there is a whole book that could be written about those three magical summer months in 1971. Maybe another time, eh? If you buy this one for your friends and family, well maybe not the kids eh!, that one could be next. Go on, spoil them.

I really missed Snitch and Snatch after the cruises. They went back to Birmingham where Snitch/Robert went to work with his father in their very successful chain of jewellery shops, Rex Johnson and Sons. Snatch/David joined the West End Musical 'Tom Brown's School Days', and was very good in it too, before he also gave up showbiz and went to work in the jewellery business with Robert. Whenever Wall Street Crash was appearing in Birmingham, at the Night Out or other clubs, we would have riotous reunions with lots of hysterical reminiscences about the summer of 1971. Very sadly Robert passed away, far too young, in January 2002 he was only 52. Polly, who had also become firm friends with Snitch and Snatch, visited him with me just before he died. Saying goodbye to him for the last time broke my heart.

In my life I have been fortunate to have met some incredibly lovely, loyal, genuine people. Robert and David Johnson are without a shadow of doubt right at the very top of that list.

Scene Fourteen: Gabby to the Rescue

The Christmas and New Year of '71/'72 passed with the pantomime 'Cinderella' in Liverpool with Barbara Windsor and Vince Hill. There was a very camp actress in the show named Gabby Vargas, playing the wicked witch of the west. She wore tons of very thick black eye makeup, had a huge bouffant hairdo, outrageous clothes and had a very theatrically-camp speaking voice. (I'm talking about off-stage here; what she wore as the wicked witch was mild in comparison.) One night after the show Gabby asked,

- What are you doing tonight, dear?
- No plans Gabby.
- Well dear we must go out on the town and get outrageously pissed.

Which we did.

At about three in the morning, very sloshed and rolling down the street singing selections from 'Oklahoma' and 'My Fair Lady' at the tops of our voices, we realised we were lost. Finding ourselves in a markedly seedy area, sobriety and panic were starting to kick in. Suddenly, appearing out of nowhere, in front of us appeared a gang of fifteen or so very aggressive-looking Scouser lads. They stopped in their tracks, aghast at the unearthly sight that met them. There was Gabby, 6'3" and dressed up like a Christmas tree, mascara running down her face and her left tit hanging out of her outrageous frock, bright pink hair standing on end, and as pissed as a fart. And next to her, trying to hold her up, is short-arsed twat - me.

- Wot the fooking hell we got 'ere then lads?

(Wot you got 'ere lads is two theatricals shitting themselves.) I mutely accepted that this was the end of our lives and was offering up a silent prayer to that great God of Thespians in the sky, when Gabby leapt forward and falsettoed in the campest voice I've ever heard,

- Don't harm us you lovely darlings, we're actresses and our faces are our fortunes!

For ten seconds there was silence as the earth stopped turning, then they all started laughing.

- Well fooking hell, have you ever seen the likes of this?,

grunted their butch gorilla-like leader.

Gabby shrieked,

- Help us darlings! We're lost babes in the woods.
- C'mon, said butch boy, we'll see you home.

So, with that, all seventeen of us, now arm in arm, skipped down the street singing,

- Oh-oh-oh-klahoma where the wind comes sweeping down the plain.

Pheeeeew!

Scene Fifteen: A whirlwind romance. And a hurricane

After the panto I went on tour with 'The Wonderful World of the Musical', choreographed and directed by Geoff Ferris. On this tour I met Lesley Duff a singer/dancer/actress, and we fell *madly* in love. At the end of the tour Lesley was going onto my old ship the Northern Star and I was sailing on the Ocean Monarch. It was horrible. We had to part for three months, only meeting briefly for one day when the Star was berthed in Tangiers and the Monarch was in Gibraltar. Les flew over and we had just five or six hours together; it was heartbreak all over again when she left. When the summer cruise season ended, Les joined me on the Monarch and, on the 5th November 1972, we sailed for Australia (known as deep sea cruising). We had a one-year contract to do two- and three-week cruises out of Sydney, visiting the Fiji Islands, Singapore, Hong Kong and countless other beautiful places. Again, as well as the shows, we were involved in all forms of passenger entertainment, a bit like Butlins' Redcoats but with eighteen fathoms of water beneath us. Les ran the charm school and taught makeup, and once again I took the keep fit classes. On the Star I had also done a couple of children's shows, which I hated. Don't get me wrong, I like kids, went to school with them. But entertaining a bunch of them for an hour and a half? Forget it! Janice, the entertainment coordinator, delivered the bad news that I had to do the kids' shows for the whole year. Begging, crying, bribing her with vast amounts of money got me nowhere. I was doomed. The UK kids weren't too bad, but I could tell the Aussie kids were going to be a different kettle of fish. I used to sing a song called 'Little White Bull', made famous by Tommy Steele, about a timid bull who grows to be the bravest bull in the world and beats all the matadors. I chose this song because it had answer lines for the kids to repeat back to me. I would sing 'Once upon a time there was a little white bull', and the kids would answer 'little white bull'. The very first show I did for the Aussie kids, I could see they were going to be trouble. They were scruffy little buggers, aged from four to eight years old, with demonic glints in their eyes. I did my usual welcome,

- Hi kids, my name's Uncle Colin and we're gonna have lots of fun this morning.

I continued with a bit more warm up crap to try and get the little sods on my side, and then explained how we would sing "Little White Bull" together. They all looked at me like I was the most boring fucker on God's green earth.

- And here we go kids, after four. Ah one, ah two, ah three, ah one, two, three, four... ♪ Once upon a time there was a little white bull.

A kid who must have been all of six years old was sitting cross legged in the front row. He looked me straight in the eye and said, in a very loud voice, "Wanker", and you know what? I had to agree with him.

The two-week cruises followed roughly the same pattern. We would sail from Sydney across the Tasman Sea to Wellington or Auckland in New Zealand, and then around the Fiji Islands. It was often pretty rough for the two days it took to cross the Tasman, force six or sometimes eight, so generally the ship wasn't very busy for those days as a lot of the passengers were in their cabins wishing they were somewhere else. We had been on the ship for about five months and had our sea legs, and we were pretty used to the changing seas and weather conditions. On the eve of one cruise however, we sensed an atmospheric change and thought the weather was worsening. Even while docked at Woolloomooloo, near the Sydney Harbour Bridge, it just didn't feel normal. On the main deck, the crew were closing the heavy metal doors across the viewing windows, something they hadn't done before. I was wandering around the deck when I ran into Craig, one of the officers, a New Zealander with whom I played very competitive deck tennis every day. He was looking worried.

- What's going on mate?

- Between you and me, Col, the weather is pretty shit out there. We're not at all sure we should be going anywhere tonight but we're getting pressure from head office to set sail. We have a new contingent of 1,200 passengers, and the company is probably worried about compensation payments if the cruise is delayed.

(Today, with satellites and modern weather forecasting technology, I'm sure that the cruise would have been delayed.) An hour before the scheduled departure time an announcement came over the tannoy: "Ladies and gentlemen, on our departure this evening, we are expecting some slightly inclement weather. For your safety, please be advised to place any moveable, valuable or breakable items on the floor of your cabin. We will keep you updated if there are any further developments throughout the course of the night. Thank you".

That announcement turned out to be something of an understatement. We set sail. As you leave Sydney Harbour there are two dramatic rock structures on either side of the passageway known as the Sydney Heads. Once through the heads you are out at sea and there is always a noticeable change in the ship's movement as the swells take over. But on this occasion we were no sooner through the Heads when .... Craaaaaaaaash, the Monarch keeled over to port and Craaaaaaaaaash she keeled over to starboard. Up went the stern, down went the bow. We were pitching, rolling, corkscrewing, every which way that a ship could be tossed. "Slightly inclement weather"? You're having a laugh! This was serious shit, and it got worse. I was in the bar area when hundreds of bottles and glasses smashed over the rails that were meant to be holding them in place, heavy tables and chairs were thrown like matchsticks across the room and the people followed, crashing and rolling into each other, over the furniture and anything else that got in their way. Absolute chaos! As the stern of the ship lifted out of the sea the huge propellers, now out of the water, began to spin faster and faster, emitting a terrifying, screaming, high-pitched death whine. That noise still haunts me to this day. Then the stern would crash back down and, as the propellers were again submerged, the ship, all 26,000 tons of her, jolted forwards, throwing anyone who was still standing, to the ground. It felt as if it went on interminably. The worst part was when she was rolling from side to side. She would keel so far over, you could stand on the bulkhead (wall). She would hang there for ages, and you would be convinced that she was about to capsize, but she would eventually right herself, only to keel over to the other side three minutes later and again hang there. It was torture - a kind of suspended animation.

We, and all of the passengers, had been sleeping on the enclosed promenade deck for two days as the pitching and rolling seemed slightly less severe higher up in the ship. The first officer sought us out to ask if we could do something to distract the passengers and raise morale. We suggested that we could do a singalong, preferably using the piano, which would have to be secured in some way, so he asked the crew to tie it to the bulkhead with thick ropes. We had been wearing the same clothes for two days - not that our seasick audience would have cared or noticed - but, ever the professionals, even when the ship was possibly about to go down (the orchestra on the Titanic came grimly to mind), we couldn't bring ourselves to perform without the proper frocks. So, Norm and I embarked on the perilous two-hour journey (I am not exaggerating) down to our cabins to retrieve the frocks. Properly attired, we then sang a selection of songs from musicals to a grim, green-faced audience. Not quite as heroic as those extraordinary musicians on the Titanic .... but almost!

At some point during the night, the captain decided that the situation was out of control and made a crucial decision. He hove the Monarch to. When a ship heaves to, the bow is pointed into the waves, which causes the ship to pitch rather than roll. It is much safer, helps to reduce the risk of capsizing, and is (very slightly) more bearable. We endured that force ten storm, at one point force eleven rising (force twelve is hurricane force), for three long, long, long days.

This next bit is as sad as this story gets, then we'll finish with this chapter because the whole episode still gives me nightmares to this day. At one point in the middle of that very dark terrifying second night, when we honestly thought the Monarch was going to roll over, Lesley and I decided to split up and go to different parts of the ship because we didn't want to watch each other die. One last kiss, one last hug, one last look, one last "I love you", and one last thought: would we ever see each other again? Then we both turned away. At this moment dear Reader, you're either sobbing at the thought of us leaving each other, or you're thinking "I would have stayed with my loved one till the end". Well, that's what *we* decided to do.

The ship was meant to be heading for Brisbane but limped into Townsville instead, with half our lifeboats ripped from their davits and lost at sea. Many, many passengers were injured, some seriously. A large contingent of passengers refused to continue with the rest of the cruise, and were flown back to Sydney. Who could blame them? If I hadn't been under contract, I might well have joined them. We continued the cruise with the two hundred or so remaining passengers; it was like a ghost ship.

There are many more stories to tell from our year on the Monarch and I have a thousand wonderful memories that I will cherish until I take that final curtain call in the sky. We disembarked in Los Angeles and the Monarch sailed off to be scrapped. God bless you, old girl. Many of my fellow entertainers on that year-long gig went on to have successful careers: Carl Doy, our brilliant musical director, became one of New Zealand's most outstanding musicians, best known for his multi-platinum-selling 'Piano By Candlelight albums and is now the musical director of Dancing With The Stars. Norm Walters, a cracking hoofer, became a West End Wendy (a camp name bestowed on London performers) and danced in many London shows. He also worked with Cameron Mackintosh on the show Oliver in Russia. In fact the whole team remained at the top of their game for many years to come. Well done shipmates!e After ten days in LA we flew home to Gatwick airport and into the next part of our lives and the next part of this book.

Just a little postscript to this story and a thank you to Lesley who one day said to me.

- Col, it doesn't matter to me, I love you anyway but, if you really want to take on acting roles that aren't just broad Cockney characters, you need to lose your accent. Don't lose your London accent but learn to control your Cockney one.

As well as being an actress Lesley had also trained as a voice coach. And so we started on the long, long, LONG road:

- The rain in Spain falls mainly on the plain. The tip of the tongue to the top of the teeth. He was not the pheasant plucker but the pheasant plucker's mate who was only plucking pheasants because the pheasant plucker was late. (*Try that one after three gin and tonics*) My old man's a dustman, he wears a dustman's 'at. (The last one wasn't a diction exercise at all. I just thought I would include it, in case I started to forget my roots.) My accent was so strong that, when I was speaking, even I couldn't understand what I was saying. It would go something like this:

- Wot ya tawkin' bout? Ya dunno wot I'm sayin, wot ar ya def or sumfink. Fuckinel open yerears en lizzen. duneed nun ef them bleedin' stoopid electrocution lessins.

Translation:

- What are you talking about? You don't understand what I'm saying? Is your hearing impaired? I would suggest that you pay attention. I don't need any of those tiresome elocution lessons.

You can perhaps see where Lesley was coming from, and how brave she was to try to unravel my tortured diction and grammar. Her work load was gargantuan and she almost gave up in despair. However, thanks to her, I can now speak 'proper' and am more than accomplished in a considerable range of accents, including Cockney, Royalty, Swiss, Bulgarian, outer Mongolian, Yiddish, Finnish, Scottish in fact all the 'ishes', and many, many more.

So.... "Fanks Lez, yor a dhalin".

Lesley Duff went on to have a very successful acting career and is now one of London's top theatrical agents with Diamond Management.

Scene Sixteen: Phil Silvers' Slow Death Experience in Billingham

Many years ago there was a famous American comedian called Phil Silvers. He had a massive television show in America called 'Sergeant Bilko,' in which he played a wisecracking army officer. His character was a wheeler dealer, always setting people up and getting deals on the black market. The whole series was shown in England and he became a big star here.

Phil had come over from the US to play the lead in a musical called 'A Funny Thing Happened on the Way to the Forum', written by Stephen Sondheim. It was going on tour around England before moving to the West End. Lesley was playing the female lead opposite Phil Silvers. It was a long tour, taking in some pretty grotty places around England. They were up north, and it was Christmas.

In the new year I was starting a television job for ATV in Birmingham called 'Let's Celebrate'. The programme was to replace 'Stars on Sunday' in the 5.00 Sunday afternoon slot.[11] There were four boys and four girls singing and dancing. We performed 'meaningful' semi-religious songs, and David Kossoff narrated the show.

Lesley suggested I come up for Christmas and Boxing Day and then "bugger off to Birmingham" in time to start my TV series. They were in a place called Billingham. I think it was near Teesside or Hartlepool. Anyway (sorry Billingham), not the ideal place to spend Yuletide. I was the only person who was a partner of one of the cast. The only place they could book for their Christmas meal was a sleazy pub in the back streets of Billingham. Phil Silvers was in his late sixties or early seventies by then. He had a heavy cold and was clearly feeling pretty fed up. We sat down to eat in that dingy hostelry, all trying to make the best of a bad job. I think we were the only people there,

---

11 'Stars on Sunday' was a very popular, long-running TV show. The presenter was Jess Yates who played the organ, sang hymns and religious songs, and read out saccharine-soaked dedications to sick children in hospital. He had big guest stars on the show like Roy Orbison, and the viewing figures were huge. However, Jess, who was married to an actress called Heller Toren, had been caught having an affair with a young actress called Anita Kay. There was uproar from his millions of fans. Apparently, Jess had to be smuggled out of the Yorkshire TV studios in the boot of a car and consequently lost his massive gig with YTV.

which made it even bleaker. Phil happened to be sitting opposite me. We had never met, and Lesley hadn't got round to introducing us, but he looked over at me a couple of times. After an hour, when everyone was chatting away and I felt a bit like a spare part, he looked at me and said:

- What's your name?
- It's Colin, Phil.
- Colin, I don't wanna die in Billingham.

Then he carried on talking to the other cast members and said not another word to me all evening. Or, in fact ever again.

I'd like to think Phil felt he could pour his heart out to this bloke across the table whom he didn't know, and who wouldn't judge him for being a 'bah humbug' miserable Christmas git. But maybe, just those three little words *"It's Colin, Phil."* helped him in some small way towards his return to health and fitness.

I was, and still am, a massive Phil Silvers fan. What a talent! If Phil was before your time, give him a Google. You won't regret it. They don't make them like that anymore.

Fortunately, he didn't die in Billingham.

A postscript to the Jess Yates footnote. It was widely believed that Jess was the father of Paula Yates, one of the presenters of the music TV show, 'The Tube,' but it later emerged that in fact Paula's father was Hughie Green, the presenter of one of the first big talent shows called 'Opportunity Knocks'

Scene Seventeen: The Busker of Love

As you now know, before Wall Street Crash, I was working as a jobbing singer, dancer and actor, doing whatever work I could get my hands and feet on. I had a tiny flat in Islington and sometimes, when the rent was due and I was broke, I used to go out busking with my guitar on the London underground. I was lucky because, in two days, often a Thursday and Friday, I was able to earn enough money to pay my monthly rent. I used to do the 7.30 to 10.30 morning slot at the Oxford Circus or Tottenham Court Road stations, prime spots, then go home, and start again at 4.30 and stay until 7.30. Today you have to have a licence to busk on the underground, but at that time you could busk anywhere you wanted. I was young, 17 or 18, had very long hair and, it being the 1970s, I wore stack-heeled boots that brought me up to at least a shaggable height. Some short-sighted people said I looked a tad like David Cassidy (in my dreams. Hopalong Cassidy[12] more like). I bet David would have loved a busk on the underground; he'd have had a great time.

I used to put some coins in my open guitar case so it looked as if I had already had some contributions. I would be busking away and, if a nice-looking girl came along and threw in a coin, I used to smile and thank her, and I'd carry on playing ...

- And your telephone number? *hoping she would return.*

More often than not the girls would think, "Cheeky little sod", smile and keep on walking. In the course of a session maybe two or three would come back and leave their numbers. Of course I never knew who was who. At the end of the day, I used to call the numbers,

- Hello, my name's Colin. I was busking on the underground today and you very kindly put some money in my guitar case (thanks very much) and also your telephone number. Just wondered (*hoping that she lived somewhere in London*), do you fancy meeting for a drink some time?

---

12 Hopalong Cassidy or Hop-along Cassidy is a fictional cowboy hero created in 1904 by the author Clarence E. Mulford. He was given his nickname because he was shot in the leg. "Hoppy" and his white horse, Topper, usually traveled through the West with two companions—one young and trouble-prone with a weakness for damsels in distress, the other older, comically awkward and outspoken. 66 Hopalong Cassidy films were made.

If she agreed, I would arrange to meet her in a pub, hoping that I would recognise her. They all obviously thought that I was penniless and sleeping in a box under Waterloo Bridge because, when I met them, they would always offer to buy *me* a drink.

> - No it's alright, I'm not destitute.[13] I'm an actor and haven't worked
>   for a while, so I go out busking when it's time to pay the rent.

(Some of the girls no doubt recognised me from the 'Tunes' commercial, for which I got *repeat* fees).[14] They all found the whole thing hugely entertaining and I ended up with some really lovely girlfriends who probably would never have looked twice at me in a nightclub. Sometimes, I would be out busking and they would pass by as normal on their way to work. They would give me a knowing laugh and would chuck some money in my case when, seeing them coming, I switched to their favourite song. Being a good boy, I was never tempted to play "All Night Long" or "Wake me up Before you Go-go". Sweet!

It would be ungentlemanly and totally inappropriate for me to enlarge on the bloody good luck that came my way.

---

13 Or *'prostitute'* as my mum used to say: "That woman living up the road, she's prostitute, she's got no money".

14 Have I mentioned this before?

Scene Eighteen: Gone with the Wind

I had always wanted to be in 'Jesus Christ Superstar' and, when I had finished my stint at sea, I was lucky enough to be offered a part in the West End show at the Palace Theatre. At the end of the performance there was a reprise. Throughout the show we wore dowdy brown costumes, apart from Jesus who was in white, and Mary in red. At the end, Judas flashed back to life for the finale wearing a glittery costume. For this the rest of us wore red and white angel costumes with billowing floor length sleeves to represent the angels' wings. Only our heads were uncovered. We started upstage and walked downstage (towards the audience, for those wot don't know theatre speak) in two lines, singing,

- Jesus Christ, Superstar ♪♪
  Do you think you're what they say you are?

The girls were in the front row, and we walked slowly in a line behind them, one step for each word of the lyrics. For the last line of the song, the boys would kneel behind the girls, lift their voluminous costumes, put our heads between the girls' legs, and lift them onto our shoulders. On the last long note the boys would stand up slowly; the girls' costumes would fall, and cover us completely creating the effect of a line of eight-foot angels, with only the girls' heads uncovered. It was very impressive.

We had a ballet master, more accurately a ballet *mistress*, Christopher. Because the show had been on for such a long time there was invariably someone who was off work because of illness (or because there was something good on the telly), so the ballet mistress would allocate our roles for this lift every night. It was a fluid arrangement. On this particular night, I was given Debbie to lift. I groaned. Now, Debbie had a fabulous voice but was no lightweight. (Chris said she'd had liposuction and they'd left the machine on 'blow'.)

- Chris, please don't make me do this. I'm the smallest guy in the show.
- Well, dear! There's no alternative. John's got a bad back, Brian's got a bad knee, Ronnie's got a bad neck, Tony's got a migraine and Tom's got a wobbly tummy. So you have to do it darling; put your jock strap on, engage your core, and pray to high heaven you can

get her up. You have to take one for the team, darling. Now, stop whingeing and do some squats to warm up, dear.

So, on the night, I uttered a few prayers to the Almighty,

- Dear God, I am appearing in a West End musical about your son, Jesus. I know I have been a bit lax lately, not saying my prayers or attending church. But if I promise to mend my ways, stop swearing, stop wanking, cut the joints down to sixteen a day and come off the vodka....any chance you could see your way clear to giving me a bit of a leg-up when I lift Debbie tonight?

I waited patiently for an answer, but heard nothing. He was probably off helping out David Essex, down the road in Godspell, teleporting him through the stage door, out of the crotch-grabbing clutches of his adoring fans. By comparison, my predicament would seem minor. Well sod it, I'll just have to rely on professionalism, and the expert balance I learned from my extensive judo training (yeah right!). It didn't help that, all through the show, my fellow apostles were muttering such phrases as,

- 'ang on to your wedding tackle dear, she's a big-un.

and

- Place for you in the weightlifting Olympics luv, if you pull this one off.

Amused as I was by this persiflage (a word I shall look up later!), this was of no help to me at all. I was a goner. The moment had come. We slowly walked, one step at a time to the front of the stage, as choreographed by the great Rufus Collins. The orchestra was playing the score of 'Jesus Christ Superstar', but all I could hear was Chopin's 'Funeral March'. I whipped Debbie's angel canopy over my head and stuck my head between her legs ready to lift her up.

- Do you think you're what they say you are? ♪♪

I took the strain in my legs and back and began to lift her up and, at that very moment, she let out the loudest fart I have ever heard. But it wasn't the decibel rating of the emission that bothered me, it was the storm force factor. The fart rippled around my neck like a tornado during the painfully-prolonged final chord. I thought,

- I have trained. I am better than this. A professional. And here I am, under this fucking canopy and I'm being asphyxiated.

It was horrendous. I could see the funny side of it, but only just! All I wanted was for the conductor, Anthony Bowles, to lower his baton so that the song would end and I could get the fuck out from under her flowing, fart-trapping, robes. After what seemed like fourteen years, the end of the last chord faded. I dropped her down, there was a blackout and off we went into the wings. It was always a bit of a scrum in the wings as we all fought to get to the pub before last orders.

- Oh my God!

I said to Debbie.

She burst into tears, bless her.

- Don't worry, it was funny!

She fled out of the wings. Everyone asked what was the matter.

- You won't believe it!

I said, sniggering like a child.

- Debbie farted on my neck during the lift and I was trapped under the angel canopy for what seemed like an eternity. That rustled up the laughs I had been aiming for.

Nevertheless, I had a slight twinge of conscience and thought I had better check on her, so I went to the girls' dressing room on the second floor.

- Knock, knock. Is Debbie there?
- No. What happened? She was in floods of tears. She came in, took off her costume and ran out of the theatre.
- Well, I'll tell you what happened. She farted while she was on my neck in the angel costume!

The girls thought it was hilarious, and I felt smugly pleased. Of course I shouldn't have breathed a word to anyone but, being an obnoxious little shit, after what I'd been through, I would have been happy to share the story with any casual passerby in the street, or the entire checkout queue in Sainsbury's for that matter.

On the next night, Chris was there with her list again.

- Who's on and who's off?
- Debbie's off tonight darling and nobody knows why.
- Well, let me tell you why!

I gleefully announced.

- Last night she farted under the angel costume when she was on my shoulders.
- Oh, my dear! How awful. She just said she was sick.
- I'll tell you who was nearly sick...ME!

She didn't return to work for three nights and by that time everyone knew what had happened, 'cos I had told them. The first night she was back, Chris said,

- You're lifting Debbie tonight!
- Oh no I'm fucking not!
- Only joking darling, keep ya tights on.

Before the show that night I saw her by the side of the stage.

- How are you darling? (*hypocritical little fucker that I was*)
- Don't talk to me, Col. I'm too embarrassed.
- It was just one of those things Debs. It was quite funny.
- You haven't told anybody have you?
- Told anyone? No! Of course not! How could you think that? I would never do that.
- Thank you, Col.

On stage that night as we progressed downstage towards the dreaded lift (me lifting Lucy who was as light as a feather and Dan, who was built like a brick shit-house, lifting Debbie), all of the cast were making farting noises. Even the orchestra joined in, with farty sound-effects on the electric keyboard and the trombone. Yes, I had even told the members of the orchestra. What a bitch!

We came offstage. Debbie said,

- Col, thanks for not telling anyone.
- No problem darling. I would never do anything as horrible as that.
- See you tomorrow.

Who says show biz isn't glamorous?

Mum and Dad, before he left for war

Uncle John & Uncle Bill with banjos

Dave, Mum & Col

First Band: The Scruff

Col centre

These trousers elevated my falsetto singing to Bee Gees level

Come to the cabaret my dears
Come to the cabaret

Before Strictly Come Dancing, there was Strictly Come Prancing. Camp or wot?

Ocean Monarch Yana's Bona Omies
(Robbie, Yana, Col & John)

The Northern Star

Fronting a band

London Shows

Jesus Christ Superstar
Front Row, 3rd Left

Let the good Stones roll!
Keith (Col pimping Mick)
Louis Selwyn

Thanks to Arlene Phillips.
Front row, 2nd left.

The Pinball Wizard
in Tommy 1979

Leave him to heaven.
Giving it some wellie
with Brian Protheroe

Anita Dobson

Col

Star Encounters or May
The Farce Be With You

Two for the Show!

Discography

MAGD 5045

MAG 33201

MAGL 5056

836 279-1

CD 258.624

CD 836 279-2

MAG 208

MAG 226

M 7203

M 7213

6.13915 AC

DE 3273

870 668-7

872 384-7

874.244-7

876 304-7

Wall Street Crash

Ricky Mary
Paul
Sharron Jim
Col Shaun
Jean

Wall Street Crash - The Orginals
1980

Polly Pete
Siobhan
Cori
Mary
Jim Col

Wall Street Crash - Version 2

Thank You for coming over

With Bros. TV show Belgium

Michael Parkinson Show
with Adelaide Hall.

Dean Martin's support act. London

The lads at Checkpoint Charlie

The Morecambe and Wise Christmas party.
Spot the celebrity...Col behind Des.

Astride the Berlin Wall.
Machine gun trained on my arse.

Rotterdam Harbour
Walk of Fame

WSC Acting?? Gormless twit front right

Recording studio.
Pretending to know what I'm doing!

Wall Street Crash

Karen

Polly

Colboy

Marge

Pete

Polly

Mandy

Perty

Marge

Colboy

Germany: Baden-Baden
Dougie Squires supporting
Col on skates for TV special.
Gerry, our lovely manager (L)

With some of Cols Dolls Fitness Lovelies

Teaching a step class. Note my gorgeous legs!!

Scene Nineteen: Asleep on the job

At the same time that I was appearing in 'Jesus Christ Superstar' at the Palace Theatre I was filming with Tommy Steele in a show called 'Tommy Steele and a Staircase'. I was also doing a show at a cabaret club in Piccadilly Circus. So I was pretty shattered.

In 'Jesus Christ Superstar', just before the interval, Jesus is in the Garden of Gethsemane before Judas betrays him and he sings a song called 'Gethsemane'. I was playing Peter, one of the Apostles. It was directed that three of us apostles: Peter (me), John and James, slept in the garden while Jesus sang his song, which went on for about eight minutes. The stage was warm and I was drowsy. I sank down onto the stage and Jesus started his song:

- I only want to say, if there is a way,
    take this cup away from me for I don't want to taste its poison,
    feel it burn me.

The song went on and on. I was very comfortable; the stage felt like my favourite duvet and, ever the professional, I fell fast asleep. There was a blackout at the end of the song and everyone ran offstage. Except me. The iron safety curtain was about to come down for the interval; it would have hit me, and could well have killed me. One of the crew realised that I was still onstage, and still sleeping peacefully. All the lights had come up and the audience could see everything. Everyone was calling in stage whispers from the wings, Colin! Colin! In the end a stage hand had to come on to wake me up and get me off the stage. The safety curtain was lowered.

The scene after the interval began with a blackout. We all resumed our sleeping positions and Jesus took up his place. This was the intense and poignant scene where Judas betrays Jesus. The lights slowly came up and ..... the whole audience stood up and applauded and cheered the sleeping man. Yay! I think Jesus must have had a word with the man upstairs, 'cos I didn't get the sack.

Also while in 'Superstar', I had been offered work on the TV commercial for Cadburys Dairy Milk Chocolate, starring Cilla Black, mentioned earlier. It was to be filmed in Brighton with a very early morning start. I tentatively went to ask the company manager if I could possibly leave the show slightly earlier so as to catch the last train to Brighton.

Peter was a lovely, camp guy who called everyone Tresh, as in treasure, but he wasn't best pleased about my request.

- Please Peter. It's a really good commercial and I'm going to be on repeat fees.

He took in my look of desperation for a second then said,

- Oh fuck it, Tresh, go on then, you can skip the crucifixion.

I hoped Jesus wouldn't be too CROSS, boom boom.

Scene Twenty: Leap of Faith

Another 'Jesus Christ Superstar' story. I was playing the part of Simon Zealotes. He was a rabble rouser for Jesus, whipping up the crowds. The stage at the Palace Theatre had two long ramps running up either side. It was choreographed that I would sing the first verse at the top of the ramp, which was about fifteen feet high, while Jesus, Mary and the chorus were on the stage. The chorus would sing:

♪♩♪♩♪

- Christ you know I love you.
  Did you see I waved?
  I believe in you and God
  So tell me that I'm saved.
  Christ you know I love you.
  Did you see I waved?
  I believe in you and God
  So tell me that I'm saved.
  Jesus I am with you.
  Touch me, touch me, Jesus.
  Jesus I am on your side.
  Kiss me, kiss me, Jesus.

And I would come in with:

- Christ, what more do you need to convince you
  That you've made it, and you're easily as strong
  As the filth from Rome who rape our country,
  And who've terrorized our people for so long.

And the chorus:

    Jesus I am with you.
    Touch me, touch me, Jesus.
    Jesus I am on your side.
    Kiss me, kiss me, Jesus.
    Christ you know I love you.
    Did you see I waved?
    I believe in you and God,
    So tell me that I'm saved.

At this point I would jump off the ramp, fly through the air, land on the stage next to Jesus and Mary and continue with the next verse. It was all going marvellously.

However, I'd become cockier and cockier as the show progressed and every night I was venturing higher and higher up the ramp. On this particular night I was right at the top. It was a full house; the adrenalin was high (and possibly, so was I).

The stage was constructed of three-foot Perspex squares, each of which was about two inches thick. There were three-foot voids under the squares, filled with banks of coloured lights. The lighting under each square could be electronically controlled, an advanced technology for its time. As it happened, over the years, the Perspex square that the actor playing Simon Zealotes would land on had become rather weak. Yes, you've guessed! On this night, super confident and caught up in the mood of the audience (and maybe far too many herbal cigarettes), I leapt off the top of the ramp and went straight through the Perspex square, through the lights - all of which shorted out, sparking everywhere - into the void below. The only thing that saved my life was the fact that our boots had thick rubber soles so that we could grip onto the ramps, but my legs were badly lacerated. Jesus and Mary were onstage, the chorus were in a freeze. I still had one verse to sing so, ever the professional, I leapt up out of the smoking hole I had created:

- ♫	There must be over fifty thousand
	Screaming love and more for you.
	And everyone of fifty thousand
	Would do whatever you asked them to.

Jesus and Mary were horrified, as were the chorus, as I carried on singing, lights flashing, smoke billowing and blood pouring from my leg. Luckily, this was just before the interval. The blackout was extended while the stagehands swept up the Perspex. The first aid crew came and bandaged up my leg and Peter Gardner said to me, compassion to the fore,

- Just ignore it, dear. Get on with the show. We'll sort it out in the interval.

It was a bit difficult to "Just ignore it, dear" and avoid the gaping smoking hole in the middle of the stage, but we walked around it or jumped over it for the rest of the first half. However, it took the technicians three days to get the lights working again and re-programme the computer.

For years after that, I would bump into people in and around London and they would say,

- Do you remember the night you jumped through the fucking stage at the Palace Theatre and then leapt out, pouring with blood, to sing your final verse?

Er, yes, of course I remembered!

The thing that has always puzzled me is that I never received a bonus from Tim Rice and Andrew Lloyd Webber for unstinting bravery in the face of electrocution. But I suppose I should have been grateful that they didn't send me the bill for blacking out the Palace Theatre either. So probably a result.

Scene Twenty-one: Boogying with John Hurt

The show 'Leave Him to Heaven' was enjoying a packed-out run at the New London Theatre. It was a lively rock'n'roll show starring Brian Protheroe who had a hit record at the time with that great single, 'Pinball'.

'Heaven' was a selection of all the great 1950s songs, very upbeat with really rocking energetic choreography and a quirkily funny script written by Ken Lee. It was a fictional story of a slightly washed up rock star, Conway Terle, who was trying to revive his flagging career with the help of his boy cronies who included me as Louis, his 'thinker of new career strategy ideas, but who actually had no ideas at all', and Polly as Johnnie wearing Marlon Brando leathers and a James Dean moody look. Basically we were Conway's hangers on, still trying to eke a living out of his fading career. He also had a group of adoring girls who would love him until the end no matter what, and would swoon every time he glanced in their direction.

For most performances there was a large contingent of old (and young) rockers in the audience who, when we finished the show with a long medley of up-tempo tunes, would dance in the aisles and get the rest of the audience really motoring. It was a great show and would have had a much longer run had the New London Theatre not already been booked to house 'Cats' which followed us and ran for many years.

'Heaven' was directed by Philip Headley who was having another successful run at the time with the musical, 'Happy as a Sandbag' at the Ambassadors Theatre, again written by Ken Lee. It had much the same format as 'Heaven' but was set during World War Two and included all of the great 1940s songs, with speeches from the politicians of the day: Winston Churchill's 'We will fight them on the beaches' and Adolf Hitler's famous speech at the Olympic Games in 1936. 'Sandbag' was a nostalgic show with amusing dialogue and, again, tons of great dance numbers.

The two shows complemented each other well. The 'Heaven' and 'Sandbag' companies also had a positive bond with each other because many of us had previously worked with Philip whose method involved a lot of improvisation. In fact it could be quite disconcerting because, when we started to rehearse a show, we would spend many days improvising and having loads of fun with role-playing games, but never actually opening our scripts. This proved to be a great way of getting to know the other actors inside out with the result that, when we did finally open our scripts, we were comfortable with the strengths and weaknesses of our respective characters and our fellow actors. This ultimately made the rehearsal period steam along much faster.

During the dual run of the shows Philip thought it would be a nice idea for the two companies to have a fun night out together. Quaglinos was the chosen venue - a funky restaurant/nightclub in Bury Street. It had a small dance floor and was frequented by many West End Wendys. The place was pumping. Improvisational dancing, led by Philip, dominated the evening. In magisterial tones he would command:

- Everyone dance like Anita! (Anita Dobson was in the 'Heaven' company. For both of us it was our West End debut).

So we would all have to 'dance like Anita'. Then, from Phillip (*he who must be obeyed!*), still wearing his director's hat,

- Do an impression of Paul chatting up a Bulgarian fan dancer.

And of course we did exactly that, with the impressions becoming more outrageous as the evening wore on, lubricated by considerable quantities of 'falling down water'. At one point we were all giving it max on the dance floor and I had clearly gone off into a deep cosmic dance trance, 'feeling the love' with eyes closed. I opened my psychedelic-induced terpsichorean eyes and became aware that everyone had buggered off from the dance floor, and that I was boogying on my own, well on my own apart from....John Hurt. Yes! John ('Elephant Man' and a million other fantastic films, theatre and TV) Hurt. Fucking hell! Me and John. John and *me* throwing down the shapes together. John looked as off his trolley as I felt, and must have been thinking either, who is this incredible boogie merchant getting down and dirty next to me or, who is this short-arsed twat invading my dance space? I prefer the former but it was probably the latter.

This was a slightly tricky situation because, although I have the highest respect for John as an actor, he is not someone I would have chosen to 'cut the rug' with. Yes, OK he had some good moves, I'll give him that. I was particularly impressed with his triple pirouette followed by the four-metre knee slide during 'Long Tall Sally' not to mention the standing leap straight down into the splits during 'I'm the King of the Swingers'. But, what if the next song was a ballad and John and I ended up in a smoochy dance clinch, with our hands on each others' arses gazing into each others' eyes both thinking, "How the fuck did this happen". Ermm.... what to do?

Continuing my 'getting down to my bad self' attitude and trying to reconnect my few remaining functional brain cells, I was doing my best to assess the situation and all of its possible scenarios. Would John be offended if I surreptitiously eased my way off the dance floor leaving him to his solo groove, or should I try something much more dramatic like shouting "Fire" and pointing across the room into the darkness, and hope that John would take flight in one direction so that I could take flight in the other? Decisions! I needn't have worried. Suddenly the band came to a final crescendo at the end of 'Boogie Nights' and the singer announced,

- Ladies and gentlemen, we are going to take a short break but we'll be back in fifteen minutes for more grooves that you can strut your stuff to. In the meantime, hang loose and drink the juice. Catch ya later.

John weaved off the floor without so much as a glance in my direction. He neither sent a red rose to my table, nor did he ask for my telephone number. I felt used!

Some years later the Wallies were booked to perform the interval act at the Berlin Film Festival. We arrived in the early afternoon and checked into the hotel opposite the venue. Polly suggested we have a look around before the rehearsal so we spent an hour wandering in the city before heading back to the hotel. Passing through reception Polly, with an uncanny sixth sense, spied the bar and said,

- Let's have a quick look and see who's about.

'Who was about' was... John Hurt, sitting up at the bar on his own amidst a throng of loudly chatting awards people. Polly, never one to miss out on the chance of a bit of hobnobbing with the stars, said,

- It's John Hurt. Let's go and say hello, ignoring my protestations that we didn't know the guy.

Polly was off, double time, with me lap dogging behind him. Never one to be a shrinking violet, he opened with his usual 'total strangers' gambit,

- Hi John, how's it going?

John gave him that look of "I'm sure I must know you 'cos you're being so friendly and, as this hotel has been booked solely for Festival people, you can't be a deranged fan. But for the life of me I can't place you".

- Very well, thanks. Could I get you a drink? Forgive me, I'm so sorry, but your name's totally slipped my memory.
- No! We've never met before, John. I'm Paul and this is Col. We're Wall Street Crash and we're doing the interval performance for the awards show tonight. I'll have a gin and tonic, John. Sorry mate, excuse me for a mo, I'm bursting for a piss. (*Charm school? Not!*)

And off Polly went in search of relief, leaving me with my ex-dancing partner who seemed bemused by my bandmate's turn of phrase.

- Paul doesn't stand on ceremony, does he?
- He certainly doesn't, John. Which category are you in tonight? I know you have a few films out at the moment.

And we launched into an enthusiastic conversation about the film industry. He was delightfully unpretentious company and, by the time Polly returned, John was my new best friend. He soon became Polly's best friend too and, when the rest of the Wallies appeared in the bar, John had five new best friends. We all loved him instantly and when we had to drag ourselves away to do our rehearsal, he insisted on coming along, sitting in the empty auditorium clapping and being our newest best ever fan. After the rehearsal we went back to the hotel for another couple of drinks and, after dinner, we spent the entire evening laughing and having the most brilliant time while John regaled us with thespy stories about the actors and directors he had worked with. Then, as if life wasn't good enough, an American girlfriend of John's turned up and was even more outrageous than the rest of us put together. God only knows what time we finally called it a night but I awoke with a huge smile on my face, still laughing about some of John's career exploits.

The show was televised the next evening and was followed by a lavish party at the venue for all involved. Champagne flowed from a fountain, accompanied by bucketloads of caviar (I was gagging for a cheese roll). Then the band kicked off and we were all on the floor giving it max. It was déja vu all over again: strutting the floor with John Hurt à la Quaglinos. I felt less inhibited this time seeing as he was my new bezzy friend, and we and the other two hundred guests boogied the Berlin night away. A bona night was had by all, dear.

Scene Twenty-two: Cheers Wolfie

My birthday fell during that same run of 'Leave Him to Heaven'. After the show the gang suggested we all go to Macreadys to celebrate. Macreadys, the members-only actors' club, was spread over three floors. On the middle floor there was a cosy little restaurant, not too flashy, with good wholesome after-show nosh. Every evening, we were entertained by a pianist who knew every song that had ever been written for any musical and also all the old Cole Porter and Irving Berlin standards. If guests were in the mood they would sing a few songs while they were waiting for their table. During the course of any evening an impressive selection of performers would casually do a turn, occasionally duets, and sometimes, in the early hours when quite a few drinks had been imbibed, a crowd would sing whole shows from start to finish. Some memorable nights were had around that piano, with some great singers.

On the top floor there was a much posher restaurant. This was where you would take your agent, manager or casting directors who had been to see your show. A lot of business was done on the top floor of Macreadys. The basement bar was dark, seedy but very atmospheric. This is where you went if you fancied making a lot of noise and having a good laugh and it is where we ended up for my birthday celebration. You would always meet people from other shows whom you hadn't seen for a while so a lot of catching up and memory lane stories would be the order of the night. Sometimes Macreadys was jam packed with performers from the Royal Shakespeare Company, the National Theatre, the Royal Ballet and every West End theatre and club. I sometimes mused that if someone dropped a bomb on Macreadys it would be the end of showbiz for a very long time.

My birthday was going great and in the early hours the usual "Happy Birthday to You" burst into life and a grand theatrically-themed birthday cake appeared from the kitchen. Toasts were drunk and a few riotous speeches were delivered. Great stuff.

Everything was settling back to normal when one of the waiters appeared with a bottle of champagne in a bucket.

- Happy birthday, Col. Birthday wishes from Robert on the top floor.
- Many thanks Chris, but Robert who?

131

- Lindsay. He's having dinner upstairs and he asked me to give you a birthday bottle of bubbles from him. Shall I give him a message?

Robert Lindsay was, and still is, a massively successful actor. He has had a brilliant and well-deserved career in theatre, musicals, TV and film. At the time he was riding high in a TV series called 'Citizen Smith', created by John Sullivan. The character he played was Wolfie Smith, an anarchic, power-to-the-people urban guerrilla from Tooting who was hell bent on causing trouble for the authorities. In reality, he is an unemployed wastrel and small -time criminal. It was a hilarious series and Robert excelled as Wolfie.

- No thank you Chris, I'll pop upstairs and thank him myself.

I fought my way through the usual melee of the West End crème de la crème and searched for Robert's table. He was dining with three friends so I thought I would just say a quick thanks.

- Hi guys, sorry to interrupt your meal. I'm Colin and I just wanted to thank Robert for the lovely bottle of birthday bubbly. It was such a surprise. I know we've never met or worked together so you've caught me completely off guard, but thank you very, very much.

Robert stood up shook my hand,

- I heard the birthday singing and asked Chris whose birthday it was. He said yours and that you were in 'Leave Him to Heaven' which I saw last week and really enjoyed. So, although we've never met, I just thought I'd send you a little something and hope you have a lovely evening.

I've never bumped into Robert since, but will never forget his kind and thoughtful impromptu gesture from one thesp to another. Many thanks Robert.

Scene Twenty-three: Through the Roof in Monte Carlo

The first gig we did at the Sporting Club in Monte Carlo was a whole new experience for the Wallies. This beautiful club overlooking the Côte d'Azur has hosted some of the world's finest performers: Frank Sinatra, Sammy Davis, Tony Bennett, Whitney Houston, Bette Midler, the Eagles, Kylie and hundreds more. To stand on that stage is a great honour. On the flight over we were both excited and nervous. This was our first big gig abroad and it was daunting for it to take place at such a prestigious venue. We were desperate to get everything right and we kept going over the order of the numbers and the links (who says what between the songs). Should we chat a little bit in French? (When I say 'we' I mean Polly, as the rest of us were still struggling with English, especially me.) We had recently put together a medley of swing numbers, the catch being that I kept getting the songs wrong. We had performed the medley at our live gigs and on a number of TV shows in the UK and it had always gone down a storm. 'Swing Swing Swing', as the medley was known, became our finale for many years to come.

The transport took us from Nice airport to the Sporting Club. We stood on the stage, awestruck as the stage manager pressed the magic button that opened up the entire width of the domed roof, exposing the sky. It was breathtaking. We were introduced to the brilliant resident orchestra who had, over the years, backed so many famous performers. We gave the musical director our charts (arrangements) which he handed out to the musicians, raised his baton, and counted them in. 1 2 3 4. Note perfect, they played our arrangements the first time around as though they had been *our band* for years. Such was the quality of those musicians.

We were to perform for seventy minutes, finishing with our swing medley. The head honcho of the Sporting was Bernard Lyon, a very experienced long-serving veteran of the club. He was known to everyone as Monsieur Lyon (including his wife and kids in all probability). There was none of that "Hey Bernie, how's it hanging? Give me a high five, dude" shit with this guy. Total respect was required at all times. (Of course we called him a wanker behind his back because he was a bit up his own arse but, even then, I think we called him Monsieur Wanker.)

M. Lyon had watched the rehearsal from the centre (royalty) table and was pretty subdued throughout so we had no way of knowing how he felt about the performance. However, when we finished the swing medley, he rose to his feet and, almost in tears, exclaimed,

- Formidable, formidable, fantastique, très très bon. Parfait!

He was applauding like a man possessed. I think he liked it!

- This is the perfect act for Le Sporting Club: sophisticated, elegant, sexy (*me*), such talent! Le Sporting welcomes you. Formidable, formidable! Clearly Bernie didn't know how to say " you are the dog's bollocks" in French. Hang on a mo, I'll look it up now.. Ah! here we go: "Vous êtes les testicules du chien." Sounds OK to moi.

He leapt onto the stage '*formidabling*' like mad, embracing us all and kissing us with just a slight hint of garlic breath (don't react guys, he's *the* man).

- You must perform your act exactly like this, you are the most exciting, energetic, warm-hearted performers to appear here for a long, long time. Formidable! Formidable! Now tell me, this swing medley is the very last piece you perform, oui? It is very important that I know this is the final musical piece.
- Oui, Mr Lyon, 'Swing Swing Swing' is our closing medley. Then we take our bows, fuck off, and all get outrageously pissed. (Of course we didn't *really* say the get pissed or fuck off bits because he may not have thought that was terribly formidable.)
- So 'Swing' is definitely your *last* song?
- Oui.
- Formidable!

We had a couple of hours before getting ready so we had a wander around Monte, the Palace and the casino. Then back to the hotel to prepare. As I was soaking in my French-perfumed bubble bath the size of a small ocean liner, I mused, Is this the life for a backstreet boy? Oui! Oui! And oui! again.

Show time was upon us. Mr Lyon took centre stage and announced,

- Tonight, from London we have the most exciting, exhilarating, sophisticated act I have seen for many years. I know you will love this group as I already have come to love them. Your Royal Highness, Ladies and gentlemen......Wall Street Crash.

Bang! Off we went into our first number 'Gone At last', a kick-arse, rocking, soul, foot-stamping, up-tempo winner of an opener. We leapt around the stage, never missing a beat; our dazzling finely-tuned choreography was faultless. Our singing and harmonies were right on the money. We looked fab! The girls in their Anthony Price (very expensive) dresses, us lads in our sharper-than-razors Savile Row suits. We were the real Monte Carlo deal. We were motoring, we were hotter than a monkey's arse on a Bunsen burner. We were *the* biz.

The number finished, we held our final pose and waited breathlessly for the rapturous applause............Nothing! What? Had we all gone deaf? Nothing! apart from a mild smattering of half-hearted feeble clapping somewhere at the back. Nothing!

We shared a quick puzzled glance with each other. Keith, our mentor and musical director, was 'on the stick' (conducting the orchestra) and counted the orchestra into the next song, at the end of which.....nothing! Nothing continued throughout the whole show. Sixty minutes of Nothing! Even when Polly chatted to them in French....Nothing! We were coming up to the final swing medley. There was just one more number, 'Saved', to be followed by 'Swing'. As Polly was bravely introducing the penultimate number, Mary caught my eye and mouthed.

   - Tell Keith to cut 'Swing'.
   - Really?
   - Yup, we're dying up here. Let's do 'Saved' and get off.

While Polly was still nattering to them in French I caught Keith's eye, gave him the cut-throat finger sign, and mouthed,

   - Shall we cut the Swing medley? Let's finish on 'Saved'.
   - I agree. We're outa here.
   - Cool!

We finished 'Saved', took our bows to a very polite applause, and got off the stage. Fast.

We were standing in the wings shell-shocked and baffled when, through the stage entrance, appeared a furious, ranting, raving, swearing Bernard Lyon.

   - Merde! Crétins. Imbéciles. Vous avez fucked up the whole finale.

What happened to the last number? You promised me the 'Swing' thing for your finale. Why did you not do the Swing thing? Ce n'était pas professionnel. You tell me one thing then do another. Why, why, WHY did you not do the Swing thing?

Mary spoke:

- Monsieur Lyon. We were dying out there. They hated us. They hardly applauded anything. They just wanted us to go!

The boss, starting to calm down a little:

- Are you crazy, êtes-vou fous? This is a Monte Carlo audience. They don't applaud anyone. They have seen every great performer there is and, even if they are over-the-moon impressed, as they were this evening, they never applaud.
- Hold on, did you say, they were impressed this evening?
- Mais oui! That was the best response I have heard in Le Sporting for years. Three weeks ago Frank Sinatra walked off. The silence so comme la mort that, if anybody had dropped a pin, you would have heard it. This is Monte Carlo. They are the most discerning audience in the world; the response you got tonight was equal to a standing ovation.

When we later discussed this debacle with the French musicians, they confirmed that Sinatra had received such a lukewarm reception that he vowed never to return. The boss went on to explain why he was so pissed off that we had cut the swing medley. Apparently there was a long-standing tradition at the Sporting Club. At the end of every show as the last number finishes and the performers take their applause, the roof is slowly opened and thousands of fireworks are launched, lighting up the night sky above the audience. These fireworks are prepared all day in sites along the beach, manned by an army of launchers holding lit tapers, all of whom are waiting for the cue on their headphones. To be sure there are no misunderstandings Mr. Boss Lyon gives the final word "GO!" and, with military precision, the blue touch papers are lit and the fireworks go off in unison. What follows is a spectacular pyrotechnic display which lasts for thirty minutes. Oh dear! We didn't do the last number so nobody lit the fireworks. Whoooooops. You would have thought that he-who-must-be-obeyed would have given us the heads up on the modus operandi.

The following day we received the most amazing write up in huge print on the front page of the Nice Matin, the paper that is circulated all over the south of France. Guess what? They said Wall Street Crash were "FORMIDABLE!". Bernie forgave us and Monte Carlo became almost our second home for many years. And a fabulous almost second home it was too. Oui, oui, oui. And there were fireworks aplenty from then on.

Scene Twenty-four: The Death of the Monte Carlo Digger

At the Sporting Club our glitzy act and the way we worked meant that we were used to interacting with classy audiences which, on a number of occasions, included Prince Rainier and his influential friends. So how did it come about that Polly and I were in our hotel room at 2.30a.m., blacking our faces with burnt cork, and donning the sort of dark clothing used in undercover warfare?

Our reckless charade had started two days earlier, when we checked into the Mirabeau Hotel at the beginning of our week-long engagement at the Sporting. We went to our swanky rooms to unpack and organise our frocks for the first show, which was scheduled for 9p.m. that night. We had a regular habit of checking out each other's rooms, just in case one or another of us had an extra two inches on their balcony, or better-designed plastic tape across the loo. This juvenile exercise was entirely pointless because, by the time we returned to our rooms, we were always three-parts pissed and would cheerfully have slept in a cowshed. But, there's nowt so queer as folk.

As always, the afternoon rehearsal with the Sporting Club's resident orchestra went well. We had a stroll along the prom, a quick bite to eat (nothing too heavy as we would later have to run around the stage like blue-arsed flies), then back to the hotel for a shower or bath, a vocal warm up and a team-tactics talk about the gig. We usually said the same things, like:

- Don't fuck up the dance steps.
- Stick to your own fucking harmony lines.
- And check your flies before you go on!

All this was a complete waste of time as we rarely fucked up the dance steps and had enough trouble remembering our own harmony lines, let alone nick someone else's; but it was our pre-show ritual and it seemed to bond us and vibe us up for the gig.

The show went surprisingly well considering that Polly fucked up the dance steps, Perty sang my harmony lines and I went on with my flies undone. Of course, being the consummate professional, I had applied enough makeup to cover all possible contingencies.

As always, when we were in Monte, we would pop over to the Tip Top restaurant after the gig, five minutes' walk from the club, where our lovely waiter friend,

Salvatori, would have our usual bowls of spaghetti bolognaise, warm bread, and gallons of wine waiting for us. Heaven! We would finish most nights by singing endless acapella songs for the punters who would, in return, buy us copious amounts of booze. One night the 'Tip' was full of American sailors, all wearing their whites. The fleet was in port on one of those goodwill visits for which all of the local dignitaries would don their best frocks and pitch up at the captain's cocktail party for idle chit chat, bubbly and vol au vents. These American matelots must have been really starved of entertainment because they thought we were the best thing since momma's apple pie. Wow! Those guys and gals really knew how to party. They were dancing on the tables and in the street. They bought us so many bottles of wine that we had to get Salvatori to stash them in the boot of his car for later consumption; we were well set up for the whole week. Yo! for the Yanks. Those GIs were right up our strasse. At chucking-out time, 5am, we would assist each other down the hill to the hotel where we would *eventually* find our keys and rooms and fall, generally fully clothed, into bed, and sleep like babies.

On this particular night, I was woken at six in the morning by an earth-shattering banging and vibrating that all but threw me out of bed. What the fuck! World War III must have just been declared. Jesus H Christ what on earth was going on? I threw open the curtains and there before my eyes was something I couldn't believe I had missed the previous day. Immediately next to our hotel there was a one-hundred-foot hole filled with cranes, a monster digger the size of ten double decker buses, trucks and two hundred workmen scurrying around like ants. I rang reception.

- Yes sir. They are building another lovely hotel that will be the pride of Monte Carlo in about three years' time.
- What?! But surely all your guests must be complaining?
- No sir. All of our guests, apart from your group, are on the other side of the hotel and can hear very little. We hope to move you there today, tomorrow or maybe the next day. It was our mistake; we are overbooked and these are the only rooms available for you at the moment. So very sorry. Merci.
- Mer-fucking-ci! You're avin' a giraffe. I'm a sensitive artiste, I can't perform on two and a half hours' sleep, I have to cosset my vast vocal range of three and a third notes, I'm not some fly-by-night 'sort of' bloody pop star. I'm the real 'sort of' fucking deal, don't ya know?

She said something in French that sounded vaguely like piss off you stupid short-arsed talentless English twit and the line went dead. I pondered, 'How could a person I have never met know me so well?' Bitch!

With that, there was a knock at my door and Polly appeared, followed by Marge, Perty and Mandy. We were all furious and rang Gerry in England. He was also angry and promised to have us moved to another hotel, post haste. He called back a bit later with bad news. Every hotel in Monaco was booked because the Monte Carlo Rally was on. We would have to cope until the hotel management could move us to the other side.

The same thing happened the following night. We carried on with the shows of course but felt despondent. Because we usually slept until mid-afternoon, we were tired, and it affected our singing. Salvatori kept filling our glasses and was as pissed off as we were. He joked,

> - It's a pity the digger doesn't blow up.

We looked at each other, and Polly said.

> - That's it! We'll kill the digger.

We all (half pissed) agreed,

> - Yeah!!

Silence. Then,

> - How?

Polly:

> - Col, we can do it together. We'll put on dark clothing, black our faces and get a weapon of some sort. You will somehow get to the bottom of the hole and.....kill the digger.
> - Me? Why me?
> - Because you're a nippy little short-arse and you will get down there and back quicker than anyone else.
> - Not bloody likely. Do it yourself.
> - Don't be such a wuss. You're the right man (*gullible prat*) for the job. Now come on, we've got to prepare. *(I noted the "we")*

So, we blacked our faces with burnt cork from the Tip Top, we donned our darkest clothes and...and.... what about our weapon? We should have borrowed a big kitchen knife from the restaurant. By then it was too late as it had closed. We scanned the room and discovered a fruit knife lying seductively in the fruit bowl. It was about three inches long and very blunt but it seemed to be all we had. What would the SAS do in our situation? Well, it was quite clear what the SAS would do. They would throw the fruit knife in the bin, strap on their Heckler and Koch machine guns, and shoot the shit out of the fucking digger. Job done, feet up. Polly reached for the fruit knife and we left the room. The mission was on.

After scaling the security fence, we peered over the edge of the vertical drop into the blackness, and Polly pointed to what he thought might be a good route down.

- I'll stay here and keep watch. If anyone comes, I'll sneeze loudly and you'll have to take cover wherever you can (ever the hero to the last).

We hugged in that really camp way that blokes do when they think that one of them (me) is going to die.

- 'ere mate, what am I going to do when I get down there?
- Improvise.
- Improvise?
- Yeah! Break a leg, mate.
- Break a leg? Break a leg?[15] Don't give me any of that theatrical shit when I am about to launch myself into a black abyss and almost certain death. How did I get tricked into this?
- Who dares wins.
- Fuck off! Give me the bloody fruit knife.

It was 3.30a.m.by then and as dark as pitch. And I was scared. Really scared. I eased myself over the edge of the gaping hole and gingerly rested my weight on a piece of jutting rock. The rock gave way with a horrible crack, and I felt myself falling through space, tumbling, rolling, sliding for what seemed

---

15 This term has a theatrical origin. When a performance has been well received the cast will return to the front of the stage to receive the applause and will show their gratitude to the audience by bowing to them. In Elizabethan times this would take the form of a genuflection, a bent knee curtsy, or 'breaking of the leg'. This can happen any number of times with the curtain rising and falling. The more times they repeat this action the more chance they have of tripping and actually breaking their leg.

like an eternity. In reality it was much longer than that. I came to a painful halt, smashing into the wheel of the giant digger, winded, bleeding, crying, swearing, angry.

- Right, you fucker, I'm goin' to 'ave you.

Night vision restored, I searched for a suitable location to wield my pathetic little weapon (and my fruit knife). I found a big metal door, heaved it open and discovered an array of rubber pipes and wires. I chose the thickest one, and started to saw through it - with my fruit knife. There was a loud hissing noise, which encouraged me to think that I must be doing something suitably destructive. Suddenly, all hell broke loose. Search lights flashed across the site, loud French voices were shouting and sirens were wailing. I was doomed. Would death be instant? Would guard dogs rip me to pieces? Would a bullet pierce, and silence, my fast-beating heart? I dived under the digger and covered myself with loose earth (I saw some idiot do that in a film once), and I lay there as still as I could. After about twenty minutes, the uproar began to die down and the voices faded into the distance. I slowly started to climb my way out, and up, one step at a time. It took me an hour to reach the top. I was exhausted. Polly, my loyal partner in crime, was nowhere to be seen.

Back at the hotel I knocked on his door. He greeted me with:

- Hello mate, did you hear all that kerfuffle? I think they had an attempted robbery at the casino. Gendarmes all over the shop. I legged it back here as fast as I could. Sorry, I forgot to do that sneeze thing. Anyway, where've you been? I thought you must have come back and gone to bed.

Had I still had the fruit knife I would have plunged it into whatever bit of him was within reach. I was so tired I merely turned around and went to my room, emptied the entire contents of the mini bar down my throat, and passed out. I was awakened at 9.30a.m. by the heavenly sound of birds singing on my balcony and *no digger noise*. I peered down to the scene of my nocturnal mission to see several men standing around the evil machine scratching their heads and looking puzzled. THE DIGGER WAS DEAD. We had a celebratory bottle of bubbly at lunch, did a cracking show that night, got pissed with Salvatori and, when we returned to the hotel, they told us they had moved us to quiet rooms on the other side of the hotel. Heaven.

My entire body ached like hell and I was very sore for the next few days. Fortunately I suffered nothing worse than cuts and bruises, and a lifelong fear of three hundred foot deep black holes in the middle of Monte Carlo.

Did my effort with the fruit knife kill the digger, *or* did the Great God of Showbiz take pity on the Wallies and knobble it for us? I guess we'll never know.

Scene Twenty-five: You Never Know Who's Out There

Wall Street Crash had a three-week gig at the Sporting Club. As it was the end of the season, the management decided to put us into the Cabaret Club, a nightclub underneath Lowes Casino. It was a smaller venue and better suited for the last couple of nights. When we went onstage to do the show we found that there were only four people in the audience. We boys were singing an acapella song while the girls were doing a quick change for their next number. It was ludicrous because there were three of us onstage and four in the audience. We started to get the giggles and, once begun, we couldn't stop laughing. We were helpless and the more we tried to pull ourselves together, the worse we got. We came offstage to change and the girls passed us as they went on. They were not happy. Quite right too.

- You're so unprofessional. You're in serious trouble.

We expected to get a further ear-bashing from the girls later, and boy did we.

After the show, as we three 'unprofessionals' sat in subdued silence (scared of the girls? YEAH!), the maître-d' came backstage and gave us a business card that had been left for our attention. It was from Canale Cinque, Channel Five television in Italy.

When we got back to London Polly rang the number. The Italian guy said he had seen the ('giggling bastards') show and, unbelievably, he thought that Wall Street Crash would be perfect for a big, new television show, 'Attenti a Noi Due Due', that was due to be filmed in Milan. It would be screened all over Italy at prime time on Saturday nights. They wanted us to perform one of our own songs every week for eight or ten weeks, and also to record a signature tune that would open every show. They wanted a ballad, because Italians like ballads, to be sung half in Italian and half in English. We came up with the idea of doing 'You Don't Have to Say You Love Me', Dusty Springfield's big hit. It was originally written in Italian, and English lyrics had been added. So, we got hold of it. None of us could speak Italian so we hired a translator. We sang the verses in English and the chorus ("You don't have to say you love me just be close at hand") we sang in Italian: "Io che non vivo, Più di un'ora senza te, Come posso stare una vita, Senza te Sei mia, Sei mia".

We sent it to the head of Channel Five in Milan. The answer came back,

- Perfect. Come out and start filming next week.

So we recorded the song and it was played at the beginning of every show. It turned out to be a massive hit, our most successful record. In 1982 we won the 'Song of the Summer' and, in Verona, we were awarded the Silver Cat, the Oscar of the television network. Peter Gabriel won best male solo vocalist and we won best group. We continued to work in Italy for over two years, most of which we spent in Milan doing all of their pop programmes and the original show as well. We had the most fantastic time, and WSC became famous all over Italy. It pays to remember "You never know who's out there".

Every week there was a guest artist on the show. One week it was to be the Bluebell Girls from the Lido in Paris. About twenty girls arrived: Danish, Swedish, English, German, American, French, all six foot three with their shoes off. They were such a laugh. They did one show and were then asked to stay on for another four or five shows because they were such a success.

We had been accommodated in apartments in a place called Milano Due, a whole town attached to Milan and owned by Silvio Berlusconi. Next to the flats was the hotel where the girls (or the Blubes as we called them) were living. There was constant partying. We'd fly back to London or Amsterdam to do a gig, and the girls would give us a farewell party. Then they would throw a welcome back party two days later when we returned. They were the best fun.

It was one of those serendipitous things that the hit record and our long career in Italy were the direct result of singing/giggling to an audience of just four people in a cabaret club under Lowes Casino in Monte Carlo. It was probably the most unlikely gig to have brought us such huge success. We also recorded an album to follow up the success of the single, again mixing English with Italian; the formula was a hit and the album sold really well. Most of the time we had no idea what we were singing about; we just sang the Italian words parrot fashion in the studio in London.

On one occasion the record company suggested an Italian song which we all thought sounded a bit dull. Keith Strachan said,

- This is a bit dreary, let's jazz it up.

Our Italian translator wasn't around that day so we thought sod it! The lyrics are probably nothing special anyway, so why don't we record it as a fun, "Let's all have a party" calypso, which we did. A few days later we rocked up to C5 in Milan with our latest masterpiece. Davide the Italian TV director gave us our instructions,

> - OK Wall Street, perform the song for the production team and then we'll work on the camera shots.

So, hugely excited and proud of ourselves, we launched into our fab, flamboyant calypso number, embellished with big dance moves which involved lifting the girls in the air and swishing them around, all of us yelping and having great fun. Party time! We got to the end of the number and there was an unusually heavy silence in the studio. The camera crew and most of the production team slowly walked away. Davide, with an expression of total disbelief asked,

> - Do you know what the lyrics to this song are about?

We had to fess up that we didn't, explaining that our translator was away when we recorded it.

> - What's the problem Davide?

Davide, now almost in tears, answered,

> - This song is about the children of Italy dying in poverty on the streets. They have no shoes, they have no food, they have no homes or shelter, they have no one to care for them, they are ... DYING!

(*Oh fuck!....So you don't think it works with the calypso feel then?*)

> - Please return to London and re-record this song, and please give it the respect it deserves.

Erm, we made a bit of a bollocks with that one......

The moral of the story is.....if a song in a strange language sounds sombre, it has probably been recorded that way for a very good reason. So, don't think you know better, you Cockney twats.

Scene Twenty-six: You Only Live (or Die) Twice

This was another of our frequent gigs at the Sporting Club. Before the end of our week-long commitment Gerry rang up and said he had booked us for a job in Berlin on a big television show for ZDF, one of the main TV companies.

- They want you to do three songs. The show will be networked all over Germany and other countries at prime time. It's a great gig but I'm having trouble getting you back to Monte Carlo to do the show. I'm trying to get you a direct flight.

Half an hour later he told us that he had spoken to ZDF and they had offered a private plane. On the next day we went along to Nice airport to board a tiny eight-seater jet. At that time the Berlin Wall was still standing. Flying restrictions meant that you were only allowed to fly within a vertical one-mile air corridor and there was only one American aviation company who could do this. If you strayed outside the corridor you could be shot down. The pilot appeared: a very jolly, very tall 6 ft 10" Texan called Chuck.

So we climbed into the plane: the pilot, co-pilot and the five of us. It was a lovely summer's day. We took off and headed towards Berlin. Quite some time into the flight, Chuck turned round and said,

- Hey guys, it's going to be a bit bumpy up here. You'd better tighten your seatbelts.

A bit bumpy? You're 'avin' a laugh! We were suddenly in the biggest storm you can imagine. One minute the plane was on its nose, then on its tail, on one wing, on the other wing, and then dropping five hundred feet. You could see that Chuck was struggling to control it.

He shouted back to us,

- There's nothing I can do to get out of this. I can't climb higher because they'll shoot us down and I can't go below the storm because they'll shoot us down. We just have to ride it out.

For about an hour we were thrown all over the sky like a cork in a storm.

Our little jet might have been small but it was perfectly equipped. Each seat had a personal fridge beneath it. Mary, feeling fatalistic, said,

- We're all going to die, so let's just get pissed.

Not that we *ever* needed an excuse, but it seemed like a good way to go. So we opened our fridges and drank our bottles of champagne, getting totally legless, and blessedly anaesthetised, while the plane was being randomly tossed around.

Finally, we began the descent to Berlin airport. I will never know how Chuck landed that plane. As we came in to land we were practically on one wing. When we got to the end of the runway he gave a shout of triumph and raised his hands above his head in a victory gesture,

- I wanna tell you guys, I flew 180 missions as a helicopter gunship pilot in Vietnam but that was the most scared shitless I have ever been.

We did our three songs for ZDF; heaven knows how in the state we were in.

Chuck was waiting at the airport for our return flight,

- Great news, it's all going to be fine, the weather's going to be good all the way back to Nice.

So off we went, relaxed and playing scrabble. On our approach to Nice we were told to buckle our seatbelts ready to land. We were almost on the runway when the plane accelerated rapidly and shot straight up into the air. When it had levelled out and we could gather our breath we asked Chuck what had happened. He said that another plane had come onto our runway just as we were about to land and we had almost collided. He had missed him by little more than three feet. He said it had been the worst flying day of his life.

So we nearly died twice in one day. It took every last ounce of Wallies camaraderie to pull off the show that night.

Scene Twenty-seven: Ben Wa Bleeper

We had done a gig in Frankfurt and were held up at the airport because of a long flight delay. We were bored out of our brains and wandering around aimlessly. Then we remembered that there was a Dr. Müller's Sex Shop in the airport. Dr. Müller's is probably one of the biggest sex shops in the world. After debating whether to go there or to the lecture on the uses of tree bark in Finland, we had a cup of tea and a sticky bun, and opted for Dr. Müller's (this may surprise many of you).

One of the girls, who will remain nameless to protect the innocent, noticed an intriguing item on display and asked what it was. It was a pack of Ben Wa balls (Ben Wa balls for the uninitiated, which included us, are two round silver metal balls which, when inserted into a private female orifice - excluding the nose I presume - give a pleasurable sensation with the movement of the body). Anyone interested to know exactly what function they perform should do a Google search - I just did and discovered that they have more uses than a Swiss army knife.

This girl, who must remain nameless in case her mother is reading this book, said,

- What are these for?
- Well, presumably they do what it says on the tin. You insert the balls, you rock around, walk around, stand on your head, or swing from the chandeliers and a good time is guaranteed (or, you can go back to the lecture on Finnish tree bark).
- Ooh! That sounds like a great idea. How much are they?

They were, in sterling, about £30.

- Thirty quid! Well, I'm not paying that much for them. What if they don't work? I could buy a bottle of Bolly for that.

One of the guys in the band, who shall also remain nameless to protect the (slightly less) innocent, said,

- Look, I'll buy them for you if you insert them and wear them on the way home so that, when the plane takes off, and with luck there is

149

a bit (or a lot) of turbulence, we can see what happens. It will be a laugh, and good research for future trips.
  - Alright then (sez the girl with no name) if you pay for them, I'll do it.

So off she went to the loo, clutching her balls. Of course being certifiably The Thickest Band in the World, given that these were metal balls, it never occurred to any of us that we would have to go through the metal detectors. We didn't give it a second thought. We were walking through security, eagerly anticipating what would happen when the plane took off when, suddenly, beep, beep, beep! Oh fuck! A security girl came over and asked our novice Ben Wa user if she had any metal on her.

  - No, no. Just these rings and my watch.
  - No, zer is somesink else and ve need to investigate. Iz zer some metal in your leg or anyzink like that?
  - No, nothing like that.
  - Vell, you vill follow me to the strip search area. (*I think maybe she was a cousin of Klaus, the coach driver to whom you will be introduced in a later story and who was a star graduate of the Berlin School of Charm.*)[16] Ve vill have to find vot iz making viz the bleeping noise.

By this time, being a sympathetic lot, we were hysterical with laughter. She-who-travels-incognito, was taken off for an intimate body search, and the Ben Wa balls were revealed. The security girl (who probably had to 'de-Ben Wa' about fifty people every week), bless her, put them into a brown paper bag and they went through security separately. We picked them up at the other end and off we went.

The anonymous one then decided to reinsert the balls.

  - I'm not going to waste these. You've paid all that money. We're through the detector now. I'm putting them back in.

So off she went, reinserted them and we all got on the plane.

---

16 See Scene 32

Well, the plane gathered speed: 50 mph...80 mph...400 mph, Mach one...Mach two, depress clutch, engage first gear, floor the accelerator.... the Lufthansa beast leapt into the air, and so did our girl. YES! YES! YES! came the orgasmic screams from seat 48b (the lady in seat 48d said, "I'll have what she's having", a line which was later used in a film). The turbulence didn't let us down, the plane soared to ever increasing heights and so did she. The high pitched screams were even louder than the previous night's audience for our final encore. Everyone joined in the chorus and...and ....and....

Of course *everything* from 'the plane gathered speed' is completely fabricated *cobblers,* designed to titillate you, dear reader. The truth is, we were so knackered after our late night gig that we all fell asleep as soon as we collapsed into our seats on the plane. I have no memory of any orgasmic screaming, metal balls rolling down the aisle, or the plane being diverted due to a Ben Wa terrorist alert. Or, maybe they just don't work? Maybe Ben Wa balls are a complete fake and Dr. Müller is a charlatan? What a bastard!

Scene Twenty-eight: A Pipe Down the Trousers

When I was about seventeen I was in a pop group. I answered an ad in the 'Melody Maker' for the lead singer in a band that had been together for some time but hadn't found the right vocalist. I went along and got the gig. It was a heavy metal band who, after I left them, went on to be incredibly famous all over the world. I rehearsed with them and really enjoyed the music even if it was a bit heavier than stuff I'd done before, but they were all a bit druggy, which was a problem for me. Contrary to what you might have assumed, I was a fairly clean-living bloke and they were on pretty well everything apart from roller skates, but they were a really great bunch of very talented guys. The first gig I did with them was at a club somewhere out in Surrey.

We were in the dressing room just before we went on, and their manager came and put a hose pipe attached to a belt onto my dressing table. I thought it was a bit of a wind-up.

- What's this for then John?
- What do you mean? It's obvious. You wear the belt and stick this down your trousers. The girls love it.

This was when flared trousers were in fashion.

- You're 'avin' a giraffe, ain't ya. It'll just look like a piece of hose pipe down my trousers.
- No, no, the girls love it. They really do. Just put it on.

So I decided to go along with it. *They'll all piss themselves laughing, and then I can take it out and we'll get on with the gig.* I did as requested.......and the other guys put *their* hose pipes down their trousers. What?!

- This is a wind up, right?
- No, no, man, we always put the pipes down our strides. The girls go mad for it.
- But it just looks like five blokes with great big pieces of hose pipe down their trousers.
- No, honestly, Col, the girls go gagging mad for it.

We went on stage. The guitarist was a brilliant musician. He performed with one foot up on the speaker, like all rockers do. When he went into his first solo,

I could see that the belt had come undone and the hose pipe was slipping down his leg. You might think that I am making this up, but I'm not. The girls were going raving mad, "Ooooo!!!" I watched as it slithered out undulated onto the front of the stage. He was so off his trolley he hadn't noticed. The club was packed with girls but none of them laughed; they just got more and more excited.

I did a few gigs with the band before they went off to America and fame and fortune, each one with a long piece of hose pipe down his trousers. The group were always off their heads, spending much of the day smoking 'Camden Cornets', but they still played brilliantly. (However, one night, Terry the bass player wasn't well and so had laid off the gear before the gig. He went on stage but couldn't remember how to play a note; he stared at his guitar as if he'd never seen it before, clearly not knowing whether to strum it or blow it, and the other guys had to cover for him.)

As for the lead guitarist, I would always know when he was going to go into a solo by the I'm gonna rock this fucking place demonic look in his eyes, but I would have no idea how long he would play for because he was always higher than Trump Tower. From experience I knew it could last for five or ten minutes, or it could go on forever (one night I had a bath, read 'War and Peace', serviced my car, ran the Boston marathon, and he was still playing). I didn't like to stand there looking a complete prat - there's only so much clicking your fingers, playing a poncy tambourine and looking moody you can do, so I used to go offstage and wait until he had finished showing off. Sometimes, if I thought we were in for a long one, I would head to the bar at the back of the auditorium and watch the band like a spectator rather than the lead singer. Eventually I would see him look round to see where I was and I would run like crazy, jump onto the stage, grab the microphone, and start singing again.

I did a few gigs with them around the country. I hadn't even passed my driving test at the time but, because they were all permanently stoned, I used to drive the van, perhaps from Manchester back to London or wherever. It was an old transit with lipstick messages written on the side: 'I love Geoff...Tony's got a big knob.....Col's a wanker' - that sort of thing.

On one occasion, I was doing about 70 miles an hour down the M1 when there was a frantic banging on the metal partition which separated the driver from the back of the van.

- Col, *Col*! Stop the van! Stop the fucking van! Mick's fallen out.

(Mick was the drummer.)

- You're joking.
- No, seriously man, pull over!

He had actually fallen out of the van. He was so stoned that he'd opened the back doors, and had ended up rolling down the motorway after the van like a runaway wheel. He probably didn't feel a thing. I screeched to a halt, leapt out and hot-footed it down the hard shoulder. When I finally reached him (the others were still so stoned they were finding it hard to negotiate their way out of the van through, you know, that tricky device called the doors), I thought he was a goner,

- Mick, Mick can you hear me ? Mick, can you hear me?

I was desperately trying to remember how to do CPR (Dr. ABC: Danger, Response, Airways, Breathing, Circulation). Thank fuck for that St John's course. Gradually he opened his eyes and said, in a voice right out of Spinal Tap,

- Wow, man, what a blast.

He'd broken both arms (always a good move for a drummer) and his ankle, and was admitted to hospital. I decided there and then that maybe this wasn't the gig for me.

As I said, they went on to become incredibly famous. (I'm not revealing the band's name or the guys' names because, after telling you what a bunch of heads they were/are, they might just sue the shit out of me for libel. I don't think for a minute they would find reading this story anything other than very funny because, after years of 'doing it in' with enough high octane substances to re-launch the Apollo Space Programme, it's doubtful they would remember it ever happened. But hey! Better to be on the safe side, eh?)

A really great band, and a really great bunch of guys. Incidentally, the singer who replaced me remains their singer forty odd years down the line. Definitely made of sterner stuff than me.

Scene Twenty-nine: Champagne Through the Curtain

The worst job I ever had was at the Stork Club, a hostess club in London's Piccadilly Circus run by a Greek guy called Nick. There were two shows a night, at midnight and two o'clock in the morning, seven nights a week. The Monday night show was often poorly attended. When I mentioned to Nick that the club was often empty for the midnight show and that I couldn't see the point in performing without an audience, his meticulously considered reply was,

> - Tough shit! You still have to do the show because someone might walk in. It's advertised outside.

So, every Monday night, if the club was empty, we would do the twelve o'clock show and just muck around. I would make up funny, lewd words to the songs and the dancers would do outrageous camp routines. We did it for our own entertainment and for the hostesses' amusement as they had to be at their tables, ready for action if the billies[17] came in.

For the 'proper' show, I would sing and dance, while the six girls wearing feathers and very little else, danced around me. The clientele was usually a mixture of very wealthy businessmen, actors, showbiz celebs, and a large contingent of East and South London gangsters. One evening the dressing room curtain was swept aside. A very broad-shouldered man with a cauliflower ear the size of a football, and a nose that had clearly seen some action and was positioned more to the left of his face than the centre, bulldozed in.

> - 'ere son, my missus's favourite song is 'My Way'. Do it for 'er will ya? 'ere's a ton. (£100) ow!, so I did it for 'er, and it will come as no surprise that...

I've never sung 'My Way' better than I did that night.

A Polish guy, Tardik, was the other new act on the bill. He played the guitar and sang when I wasn't on stage with the girls, singing and flitting around. There were two tiny dressing rooms on either side of the stage, each about 5-foot square with no doors, just curtains. The girls were on one side, and Tardik and I were on the other. We were sitting there playing chess on the first

---

17 The punters were known as "billies", the 'Billy Bunters'.

night when suddenly a hand came through the curtain holding three quarters of a bottle of champagne. I thought I should take it - just to be polite, of course. I called through the curtain,

- Thanks very much.

I poured a glass for each of us and we carried on playing chess. Tardik was a brilliant player. Fifteen minutes later another bottle came through the curtain, also three quarters full.

I said to Tardik,

- What do you think this is? Maybe one of the billies is rewarding us for our outstanding work.

He had no idea.

This kept happening throughout the night until we had nine bottles of champagne on our dressing room table. It all became clear when one of the girls came in.

- I hope you don't mind us doing this. We get commission on every bottle of champagne we can persuade the billies to buy. We don't want to keep drinking it, but we want them to keep buying it. Do you mind if we pass them through to you? You can do what you like with them. Pour them down the sink if you wish.

For three months we did that gig, seven nights a week. And every night at least ten part-bottles of champagne were delivered through our dressing room curtain. I thought I was making the best ever, most brilliant chess moves in the history of the game, but Tardik trounced me every night. By comparison I was a mere amateur at both chess and alcohol.

I was having a bit of trouble with one of my front teeth at the time. When I was a kid I belonged to a boxing club and we did a lot of sparring. I couldn't afford one of those posh, made-to-measure gum shields and, as I wasn't much good at boxing and only a littlun, I used to get bashed about quite a bit. Years later, one of my front teeth started to turn black because the root had died from the constant walloping (not a good look for a 'sort of' pop star of the future). I don't think my trainer ever got around to teaching me the very important skill of ducking. My dentist said he would have to remove the tooth and the root, and fit a tooth on a bridge which would be attached to the teeth on either side. So that's what he did. It seemed to work OK until, one night at the Stork, I noticed that the tooth was a bit loose and wobbly when I was singing. I decided to go to the dentist on the following day. However, when I was singing my big number, 'Bridge Over Troubled Water', the tooth seemed to be vibrating more. Like all good cabaret performers, I hopped off the stage onto the small dance floor to get more intimate with the audience. Quite frankly, being preoccupied with the hostesses and the champagne, the billies really couldn't have given a shit if I was alive or dead. I was nearing the big finale to the song and giving it some right welly in an effort to get at least one person to look in my direction, apart from the hostesses who always applauded as they were passing yet another bottle through the curtain to Tardik. (In the meantime, *he* was taking the opportunity to slyly move his chess pieces into a better position to whoop my arse.)

I went for the big note.......'LIKE A BRIDGE.........♪♪...' when.... ziiiiiiiiiiing, *my* bridge came flying out of my mouth, arced into the air and landed on the dirty, smelly, champagne-soaked dance floor......ugh!

What were my options?

(a) I could pretend nothing had happened, keep singing, and pick my tooth up during the thunderous lack of applause at the end of my act....I only had one more song, but even so, not a good look.....nice tuxedo, expensive bow tie, and a great big hole in the front of my moosh where my tooth used to be (or not to be) or

(b) I could pick up the gunk, slime, stale booze-covered tooth and shove it back in my otherwise pristine mouth, try to hold it in place with my tongue, and sing at the same time (talented or wot?).

So that's what I did. My final song that night was 'The Party's Over', and it was for me too. The next night was my last night. Bye-bye Stork Club.....I was freeeeeeeeeeeee..

Scene Thirty: Pork Pie Punchup

I was at the Queens Theatre in Shaftesbury Avenue, London, playing the Pinball Wizard in the rock opera 'Tommy', written by Pete Townsend of 'The Who'. I had that signature song:

- *Ever since I was a young boy*
  I've played the silver ball
  From Soho down to Brighton
  I must have played them all

I was dressed in skin-hugging silver leather and wore a helmet with flashing lights. It was a great part. I also played the part of Tommy's father at the beginning of the show. Tommy's father was an RAF Spitfire pilot who had been horribly burnt when his plane crashed and was thought to have been lost in action. Tommy's mother was played by Anna Nicholas.

To backtrack. Before the show opened a film had been made of Tommy's parents' wedding with me in my RAF uniform, extras throwing confetti and all the works. When we got married on stage at the Queens Theatre they ran this film behind on a big screen. It was a device they used throughout the show. I went off to war, was shot down, got horribly burnt and everyone thought I was dead. They made me a grotesque mask, like a Phantom mask, to show the burns. When I was missing in action my wife took a lover. I turned up out of the blue and my wife was there in bed with her lover, played by an actor called Steve Devereaux, with whom I shared a dressing room. When he saw me approach, he would get out of bed, and we would fight. The fight was like a dance, choreographed to the music by a fight director, and had also been pre-filmed. It was shown behind us as we fought on stage. Our movements on stage had to correspond precisely to the action on the film.

One night we were in the dressing room putting on our makeup before the show.

- What's the matter Steve? You look a bit fed up.
- Well, Col, I *am* fed up actually. Today, I went to the supermarket with my wife and I put a pork pie into the trolley. We got to the checkout, loaded everything onto the counter, and my wife said, "What's this?" "It's a pork pie." "A pork pie? You're going to eat a

pork pie? This revolting unhealthy thing?" Everyone in the line was looking at her. We ended up having an awful, very public, argument and we drove home in silence. I haven't spoken to her since.

At that moment a voice came over the tannoy,

- Ladies and gentlemen, this is your ten-minute call, ten minutes everyone.
- Oh blimey mate, what a bummer! Anyway, see you on the green.

About ten minutes into the show, Steve was in bed with my wife and I came onto the stage as the wounded RAF pilot. The music was playing. We were about to go into our fight sequence in which he would grab me by my hair and kick me in the face, all supposedly perfectly in sync with what was happening on the screen behind us. I walked towards him, the music pounding. He had a demonic look in his eye, and I couldn't help myself. I said, under my breath,

- Fancy a pork pie?

That was it! We both collapsed in uncontrollable laughter and, instead of the fight that was on screen behind us, we looked more like two girls with handbags, slapping each other around the face and rolling around on the stage. All the audience could see were these two grown men behaving like idiots, while this perfectly choreographed violent fight scene, clearly with the same two characters, was screened behind them. It was a disaster. By the time it ended we hadn't managed even one of the choreographed moves. The blackout came and we went into the next scene.

We got into terrible trouble and were up before the beak, the company manager, the next day.

- I have never heard of anything so unprofessional in my life. What caused the laughter?

I thought, "I'm going to have to 'fess up' about the pork pie comment."

Steve intervened gallantly,

- Oh, we just got the giggles. We were both to blame and it was really unprofessional. Sorry John, it won't happen again.
- Yeah,

I added eloquently, trying to be helpful.

John replied, barely able to put two words together,

- In all my years of theatre, I've never...ever...... I didn't see it, but I heard about it. We had complaints from the audience. These two idiots giggling and rolling about on the stage.

We were suitably abashed.

Anyway, it turned out that Pete Townsend had been in to see the show that night. There was a knock at our dressing room and a voice through the door said,

- It's Pete, I've got something I need to say to you two.
- Oh, shit!!

Steve and I thought were in for another bollocking,

- Oh, hi Pete, what is it? (waiting for the onslaught)

Pete said through the door,

- Anybody fancy a pork pie?

He could have gone raving mad but he thought it was as funny as we did. It turned out that the stage manager had seen the whole sorry episode from the wings and had 'dobbed us in'. He thought Pete would skin us alive but no luck buddy! Good man, Pete.

Scene Thirty-one: The Berlin Wall is Falling Down

In 1989 I was in Berlin with Wall Street Crash. We came off stage after the show at about 11p.m. Our driver was waiting for us and said that there had been some sort of an incident; he didn't know what it was, but thought we would have trouble getting back to the hotel because the place was log-jammed with cars. There might have been a crash or a fire. He suggested that we stay in our dressing room at the theatre while he tried to find out what was going on.

He came back about twenty minutes later and told us that there were hoards of people at the Berlin Wall; it was being demolished by the crowd, and that was the reason for the crush of traffic. We asked if he could get us to the wall but he said no, there was too much traffic and he thought it could be dangerous. He told us that we would have to walk back to the hotel. So, with our costumes, and the band with their instruments, we walked back to the hotel, about half an hour away, through streets thronged with people. We spent the rest of the night watching the unfolding events on TV and the crowds surging through the streets.

We were flying back to London the next day. In the morning, we asked our driver if we could possibly get to the wall before our flight. He agreed to give it a go. He picked us up and we got there to see hundreds of people hammering at it with whatever they could lay their hands on. There was a guy standing on a ladder and I asked if I could climb up. I climbed to the top and sat astride the wall. On the east side there were soldiers on motor bikes with machine guns, one of them trained on me. The guard had a look on his face that said 'Mach weiter punk, mach meinen tag'.[18] The east side was otherwise deserted, an extraordinary contrast to the scene on the west, where thousands of people were tearing at the masonry, giving vent to years of anger and frustration. There was nothing that the East Berlin guards could do about it except keep their machine guns trained on the wall in case things got out of hand. I put a big chunk of the graffitied wall into my suitcase and, when I got home, I broke it up and gave bits to my friends. Unfortunately, I forgot to leave a small piece for myself.

So, it was a memorable moment for me when I sat astride the Berlin Wall as it was coming down, and even more gratifying that I didn't get shot up the arse by a grumpy East German guard, which was a bit of a result.

---

18 Go ahead punk, make my day

Scene Thirty-two: Pit-stop on the Autobahn

We were heading from city to city on a big tour bus in Germany after a Wall Street Crash gig. Before we left, the driver declared in a staccato voice,

- You must be very avare before ve go that ze toilets on ze bus are not vorking. They are *kaput*. We could not get another bus in time for ze trip. Zerfore you *vill* all go to the toilet before we leave. On the autobahn we cannot stop. Ya Vol.

We had a few drinks, had a bit of a sing song ('White Cliffs of Dover', 'Who Do You Think You're Kidding Mr Hitler', 'Goebbels Was a Prick', and other patriotic ditties), and settled down to a self-satisfied doze. Suddenly one of the group, Mary, who was fond of a drink or nine, woke up and slurred,

- Golla have a pee.

I tried to explain,

- Marge, we are doing 140 miles an hour on the autobahn and we can't stop.
- I golla have a pee. I'm desperate.
- Hang on a minute. I'll go and have a word with the Fuhrer.
- I'm sorry (to the driver), but one of the girls is desperate for a pee.
- (shrilly) We can NOT stop ze bus once we have started on ze autobahn. I am doing very fast miles per hour.
- I'm very sorry Klaus, but she is really desperate.
- Ve can *not* stop.
- (to Marge) I'm sorry luv, but Himmler said, "We are going faster than shit off a shiny Sherman tank, so you're just going to have to hold it." It's about another thirty minutes.
- I can't hold it. If he won't stop I'm going to pee all over his bus.

I explained this to the Gestapo, and he very reluctantly pulled over to the side. By this time everyone had woken up: the band, all the musicians, the crew, chef and so on. It was about 4a.m., pitch black with no ambient light, in the middle of the German countryside.

- Be very, very quickly, othervise there vill be a problem. (I don't think he said, "And you vill all be shot at dawn", but he definitely wanted to.)

So about twenty-five of us lined up at the side of the motorway, not realising that we were at the top of a steep embankment. Anyway, Marge, bless her heart, dropped her knickers, lost her balance, fell arse over non-bollocks and rolled down the embankment, disappearing into the black of the night.

Everyone was laughing, but I thought I had better run after her. (She was rather essential to the act after all, being the choreographer and the only one who could remember all of the harmonies.) Therefore, in the interest of the survival of the band, I selflessly braved the thickets, brambles and thorns, and rushed down the embankment,

- Where are you?

All I could hear was her screaming,

- I'm over here!

By sheer luck I found her, knickers around her ankles, a hair's breadth from certain drowning in a dark, torrential river. I dragged her back up the embankment, with no help from any of the others, who were now not only still pissing (they drank a lot, those guys), but pissing themselves laughing. I heaved her back onto the bus, knickers reinstated. I apologised to Kraut-head, who closed the doors with a loud hiss, and all but a heil Hitler salute, when Mary said,

- I still haven't had a pee! I golla have a pee.
- I can NOT open ze doors again, you fucking stupid Englanders. Ve vill all be arrested.

I reminded him that we fucking stupid Englanders had won the stupid fucking war but he seemed unimpressed. The engine roared into life, and off we went.

I can't remember how Marge dealt with her predicament and it's perhaps best not to know. An empty chianti bottle? (This was not unknown.)

Is there an award for being *The Classiest Group Ever'*?

Scene Thirty-three: Getting Steamed up with Larry Grayson

Larry Grayson presented the successful TV show 'The Generation Game' for a few years. He was outrageously camp and had a repertoire of suggestive catch phrases which he delivered to camera, such as, "Well, my friend Everard". The game involved two teams who would be given certain tasks like cooking, juggling, trick-cycling and so on. The teams had about four minutes to learn their task and the winner was then judged by the person who had taught them.

Wall Street Crash were invited onto the show to sing 'Steam Heat', a swing number, and to teach it to each team. Larry asked which two of us wanted to judge. Cori, a Canadian girl in the group, and Peter, volunteered to be the judges. The remaining four of us did the choreographed number with the two groups. Team A had an enthusiastic applause from the studio audience.

- Lovely, lovely, lovely, darlings, said Larry. Team B, come on. Line up with them.

And off they went,

- ♪ I got (clang) (clang) s-s-s-steam heat,
  I got (clang) (clang) s-s-s-steam heat,
  I got (clang) (clang) s-s-s-steam heat,
  But I need your love to keep away the cold

Team B had a much more energetic applause.

- Lovely, lovely, darlings. Now Cori, Peter, who do you think were the best team?
- Team A, Larry.

There was a deathly hush from the studio audience and then suddenly, an uproar. It was clear to us that team B had been better by a million miles. The audience went bonkers. "A load of rubbish! It's a fix!!!" etc., etc.

Larry said,

- Oh fucking hell darlings! I don't think my friend Everard will agree with your decision at all, dears.

The studio was in chaos. Fortunately the programme wasn't going out live.

The director came onto the floor and said,

- You can't say that team A was better, because they weren't.

Cori and Peter (*Getting a bit arsey*)

- Well, in our opinion, they were. Larry said,
- No, no. Don't be stupid dears. I can't put one foot in front of the other or sing a bloody note in tune, but clearly team B was better by far.

The director decided that the whole segment had to be recorded again and, this time, Cori and Peter must declare team B to be the winners, whether they liked it or not. Cori and Peter were not happy with this. We told them to shut up and simply go along with the director.

So off they went again. This time both teams were much the same.

Larry:

- A lovely performance by both teams, dears. Cori and Peter, who is the winner?
- Well, Larry, *team B* were better by far, by far!

The audience were falling about. And that is the show that went out. The TV viewers, who of course didn't know the whole story, must have been puzzled as to why the studio audience was laughing so much.

After the show and a few bevvies in the green room Larry was typically entertaining,

- What the bloody hell were you two thinking about? You must have had your heads up your arses, dears. I mean, darlings, clearly team B were miles better. Anyway I fancied the husband so, even if they were shit, I wanted them to win.

The drinking went on for quite some time and Larry had us crying with laughter. He just got camper and camper (if you can imagine such a thing) and funnier and funnier, with his showbiz stories about the people he had worked with.

A lovely, lovely guy, Larry Grayson. Rest in peace, Larry.

The Interval

It is the custom with full length theatre productions to have an interval approximately half way through the show. So, as this book is in reality a theatrical memoir, and we are approximately half way through, let's keep with tradition and have an interval now. This may be a fitting place to throw some reflective light on how 'The Business' worked in the 70s, 80s and 90s. Light entertainment was still thriving then, with fantastic TV shows and great cabaret venues like The Talk of the Town in Leicester square, Blazers in Windsor and the Lakeside Country Club in Frimley, where WSC were awarded the 'Club Act of the Year' trophy in 1983. Others outside London like the Circus Tavern in Purfleet, the Night Out in Birmingham and many, many more were still packing in the crowds in their droves, all coming to see the top headliners of the day: Neil Sedaka,Tom Jones, Englebert Humperdink, the Four Tops, Gilbert O'Sullivan and Shirley Bassey, along with some great comedians: Tommy Cooper, Freddie Star (I could write another whole book about his antics both on stage and off but I'm pretty sure in wouldn't get past the censor), Morecambe and Wise[19], Bob Monkhouse, Little and Large, Cannon and Ball, Jimmy Tarbuck and Bruce Forsyth amongst others. The evening would consist of a chirpy compère who would warm up the audience before introducing the first act of the evening, usually an up-and-coming band or comic. For WSC's first gig at Blazers we supported Joe Brown and the Bruvvers. When the act had performed, food would be served, usually chicken in a basket (or chicken in a bastard as it was known), or steak, chips and petit pois. With a big build-up, the compère would then introduce the main event of the evening. The performance would usually last for about an hour or, in the case of Ken Dodd, four hours and fifty minutes. Many's the time the management had to physically drag Ken off the stage, not because he was boring the punters, he was brilliant, but because the staff and musicians wanted to go home to their beds. WSC played all of these clubs and many more all over the country. It was a great way to learn your trade. You could try out new material, songs and patter and, if it flopped, you would try something different on the next evening until your act was as razor sharp as it could possibly be. It was a luxury that

---

19 WSC appeared in the Morecambe and Wise TV show where Eric and Ernie did one of our routines with us. It was to the song, Alexander's Ragtime Band. We rehearsed with them for three days and although Ernie had been a song and dance man before they got together Eric was actually the better dancer and the quickest at picking up the steps. It was recorded at Teddington TV studios and Ernie had us in fits of laughter for the whole three days.

today's performers don't enjoy. Because there were so many clubs, sometimes two or three in each town, you would often get together after your show with the acts appearing at a club nearby. A message would arrive at the stage door from say Bucks Fizz or Brotherhood of Man with the meet-up point, and a good time was had by all. I've lost count of the number of times WSC stayed up all night getting sloshed with the Nolan Sisters who, for the record, could drink us all under the table - and we were no slouches in that area.

Going back to the TV shows: 'Britain's Got Talent' and 'The X Factor' have a massive following for sure but, being a bit peevish and an 'oldish' git now, I can't stand all the shouting and screaming. These shows have nothing on the old greats. The Michael Parkinson show of course was incredible and, in my opinion, the very best. Michael launched many new performers on the road to stardom. Jamie Cullum never looked back after Parkinson, and neither did WSC. And then there was Terry Wogan, Russell Harty, and the music programmes like Top of the Pops (with Pan's People, choreographed by the brilliant Flick Colby, doing their dance routines in between the band numbers). These shows gave new groups a huge leg-up. If your group was on TOTP not only did your record shoot even further up the charts, selling tons more singles, but your performance money in the clubs increased tenfold. Not forgetting, of course, the ground-breaking Kenny Everett Show featuring Arleen Phillips' Hot Gossip dance group wearing very raunchy, and very minimal costumes.

Of the more serious TV shows there were the satirical programmes like That Was the Week That Was hosted by David Frost, with Ned Sherrin and Millicent Martin sending up the latest news and scandals of the week. Great entertainment.

Being an actor, dancer and singer in those decades was, looking back from a modern-day perspective, like going back to the dark ages. These days everything is done through social media and by computer. Back then, every actor had to have 10x8 photos which you would send off to prospective employers, accompanied by a resumé (much of which was fictional) in an effort to secure an audition or interview. My resumé stated that I was 5ft10 (I didn't mention the Cuban heels and elevated inserts in my shoes), that I could ski, ride horses, drive heavy goods vehicles, skydive and perform a vast array of other talents which were way above my pay grade! Like every other actor, I figured that if I got through the audition door I would just bluff my arse off.

At that time you also had to be a member of Equity, the actors' union. This was a masterpiece of confusion because you couldn't get a job in London unless you were an Equity member and you couldn't get an Equity card unless you had a job. EXACTLY! How you got around this dilemma was by getting a job in a remote rep company or by doing a summer season, which entitled you to a provisional membership. You then had to work for fifty-two weeks out of London before you were awarded the magic full membership.

The 80s was also the time when the hideous AIDs virus was at its most destructive. Along with many outside the theatre profession, HIV and AIDs took a huge toll on the performing family. I personally lost many friends both gay and straight, dancers, singers and actors in quick succession, sometimes attending two or more funerals in a week, often listening to the delivery of the oh so poignant W H Auden poem, Funeral Blues ("Stop all the clocks, cut off the telephone"), which perfectly expressed our feelings throughout this horrendous period. My very dear friend, Ian Calvin, was one of those who succumbed, in 1986. Ian had the most amazing tenor singing voice; he was a real talent who would have gone on to do wonderful work. He was appearing in the West End production of Les Misérables when he lost his battle. I was working abroad and couldn't get to his funeral but I'm told that the cast sang the barricade song from the show at the service.

The recording industry was also a vastly different animal back then. Before streaming, downloading and all of the other malarkey of today, a band or solo performer would record a single, followed, if successful, by an album. It could be purchased from one of the good old record shops; the sales would be totted up and your royalties would appear in your bank account. Easy peasy. Also sadly missed must be the album record sleeve with all of the lyrics, so that you could sing along, as well as some classy photos of the artist. And of course the sleeve also served as the perfect platform for the rolling of a Camden Cornet if you were that way inclined.

Well! I hope this little interval has given you a short respite and a brief insight into the glory days of way back when. So fasten your seatbelts and let's get on with the show.

Scene Thirty-four: Thank you for Coming Over

In 1980/81 Wall Street Crash did their first Royal Command Performance. It was at the London Palladium and we were the new act on the show that night. The performance was watched by the Queen Mother and Prince Charles. The usual form is that, at the end of the show, after the curtains fall, all of the acts remain on stage and form a receiving line in the shape of a horseshoe. The newest acts are always at the beginning of the horseshoe, and that year it was Wall Street Crash. The last person in the line-up is the star of the show.

The star of the show that year was Jimmy Cagney a brilliant all round performer and, along with Sammy Davis Junior, one of my all-time heroes. "Here's looking at you kid." "I'm up top of the world, ma!" He could sing, act and he was a brilliant tap dancer. He didn't do anything in the show that night but he was given a standing ovation when he walked on stage. He just stood there and the audience applauded for about eight minutes, acknowledging his extraordinary career.

When we lined up in the receiving line, Jimmy Cagney, at the other end of the horseshoe, was only about eight feet away from me. We were waiting for the royal party to arrive. I must have been staring at him and he looked over at me and said,

- You OK kid?

Wow! Jimmy Cagney just spoke to me.

- Yeah, all good Jimmy, thank you.

I didn't know what to say to him. He just gave me a wink, but that wink will last me a lifetime.

If one of the royal party speaks to you, protocol dictates that you answer them but you must never speak first. You address the Queen Mother as "Your Majesty" initially, and then "Ma'am" if she speaks to you again. The guy who was briefing us said,

- You must say ma'am as in spam not 'marm' as in 'farm'.

So, the royal party came out. Prince Charles chatted away. He said he had really enjoyed the show and had seen us on Michael Parkinson and on Morecambe and Wise. He moved on and the Queen Mother was suddenly opposite me. She looked me in the eye, stoically feigning an interest,

- Thank you so much for coming over.

She thought we were American. I didn't know how to respond. I felt like saying,

- No problem, Your Majesty, it only took me twenty minutes from Islington on the bus.

Thank God, I didn't say that. Many a man has suffered cruel punishments for lesser crimes in the annals of history. I would probably have been hung, drawn and quartered - and possibly electrocuted as well - which may well have increased my vocal range, if not the length of my career.

We discovered in a rather strange way that WSC had been chosen to appear at the Royal Command Performance. One evening after rehearsals Polly and I were driving along the less than salubrious Holloway Road in North London when he stopped the car for me to pop into a newsagent. It was a horrible wet, cold night. We were both knackered and a bit fed up as the heating had packed up in the rehearsal room. It was mid-January and we had been freezing all day. I was waiting for the man to put my purchases into a bag when I glanced down at the newspaper on the counter. On the front page was a huge photo of WSC with the headline 'Star night as hopefuls join the royal set'.

- Bloody hell! That's me, I declared to the man behind the counter.

Focussing on the complicated transaction, he clearly couldn't give a toss,

- That's six pounds eighty please.

I bought every copy that he had and legged it back to the car.

- Polly, Polly look! We're going to do the Royal Command!
- Great mate! Did you get the crisps?

When he realised that I wasn't pulling his plonker we each let out a loud girly scream and suddenly that shitty January night in London turned into April in Paris.

A few months later we were asked to do a performance for the Prince's Trust, Prince Charles' charity, at the Grand Theatre in Blackpool. Prince Charles was watching the show from the royal box. The last time we had met the prince was at the London Palladium when he was with his grandma. After the show we were getting changed when a knock came on the dressing room door. It was His Royal Highness.

At the time Siobhan (Shiv) was a member of the band. Born in Dublin, she had a small part in the original 'Evita', joined Wall Street Crash, was with us for eight years and then returned to the theatre to play the lead in 'Evita' in the West End. From then on her career flourished, with a principal role in 'Les Misérables' and the original mum in 'Mama Mia'.

Shiv answered the door and welcomed HRH like an old friend in her finest Dublin accent.

  - Charles, bless ya for coming round. Would ya ever come in and have
    a beer with us?

Before he had a chance to decline the offer, Shiv had taken him by the sleeve and whipped him into our microscopic dressing room. His bodyguard (or so we assume) came in with him, which left us all standing in intimate proximity to each other. The heir to the throne said,

  - I had to pop by and thank you so much for your contribution to the
    show. So nice to see you all again. After meeting you at Mum's show
    a couple of months ago, and thoroughly enjoying your performance,
    I must say your act has improved enormously (he obviously thought
    we were shit the first time round). With that, Shiv thrust a warm can
    of lager into his hand and asked,
  - Now tell me Charles, how would the plans for the wedding be going
    then?

(Charles was due to marry Diana in two months' time.)

  - Yes, yes. It's all going tickety-boo, thank you. I am so sorry but I
    can't remember all of your names.

Without a moment's hesitation Shiv said,

  - It's Siobhan, Charles, but you can call me Shiv.

At that time all three of the girls had very brightly-coloured hair. This had been clocked by HRH.

- I must say *Shiv*, I *love* the colour of your hair.
- Well I havta tell ya Charles, it's not a *dye*.

With an embarrassingly theatrical flourish, she slapped our future king on the shoulder and, in an Irish falsetto lilt,

- Oh jaysus Charles. Did I ever say dye then? 'Cos when I said dye, Charles, I didn't mean Di, as in your intended. I meant dye as in our hair colour. Does that make any sense to you at all, at all, Charles?

HRH looked at Shiv as if she was a raving lunatic and was surreptitiously eyeing the door and tipping the wink at his (alleged) bodyguard. But Shiv was having none of that and continued in her attempt to extract further prenuptial revelations. Throughout this performance, the rest of us were little more than mute bystanders, watching in apprehension as Shiv was busy consolidating her relationship with her new best friend. To his credit HRH remained with us in our shoebox dressing room for a further twenty minutes, and was great company and thoroughly charming.

Over the next few weeks we waited for the arrival of our wedding invitations. They must have been lost in the post. Had Shiv been secretly invited by her new besty? We scanned the TV footage. Was that Shiv in that veiled millinery creation in the front row? If it was, she never fessed up.

Scene Thirty-five: The Roller-Skate Stunt Man

I was offered a TV commercial for a Spanish company called Kelme Sportswear. The commercial would only be shown in Spain but would be broadcast right across the country. My agent asked,

- Can you roller skate?
- I used to skate as a kid but haven't done it for about 25 years.
- Mmm. They're looking for someone who can do trick skating.
- When are they shooting the commercial?
- Not for about three weeks.
- I can buy some skates and practise.
- I sent your photo and resumé and they think you seem right for the part.
- Well, I'll 'get my skates on' and get moving.

So my agent called them and I was given the gig. I kept practising and my skating improved but still wasn't great. On the day we were filming (at a school near Goldhawk Road in London's Shepherd's Bush) I met Julie, the girl who was to play my girlfriend in the advert. She was a dancer and a very good skater. She asked if I had done a lot of skating. I told her that I had only come back to it over the last three weeks and wasn't very good. She looked alarmed as she'd just seen the script and there were some tricky, not to mention dangerous, moves. I asked if she could help me out, and get me up to a decent level.

- Have you got five years to spare?

This didn't boost my already flagging confidence.

The first shots were easy. The director gave his directions in Spanish and they were translated for us by an English director. Wearing the brand sportswear, we had to skate out of a classroom, along the corridor, into another classroom, and then skate around the playground. I was doing OK and holding my own, confidence improving by the second.

The plan for the next day was to go to the Kings Road and leap onto a moving bus with our skates on. We were to skate along the pavement, jump onto the road and catch up with the bus. I would hang onto the pole and hoist myself on, and then help Julie onto the bus. (It was an old double decker without doors, so you could just hop on and off). Fair enough, again, not too difficult. With a bit of luck maybe I could pull this off without too many broken bones.

We were all lined up on the Kings Road: the camera crew, make-up, hairdressers, Kelme sportswear stylists etc. A bus came along, moving quite fast.

- Action! shouted the English assistant director.

Off we went, skating like mad to catch up with the bus. I grabbed hold of the pole, grabbed Julie by the hand, and she leapt on. With that, the conductor came flying down from the upper deck,

- What the fuckin' 'ell do you think you are doing?! What the fuckin' 'ell's going on?
- It's OK! I think we got the shot. I think we've done it alright.
- What fuckin' shot?
- You know, the camera shot. You must have been told. We're doing a TV commercial.
- No one's told us about no fucking commercial.

He rang the bell furiously. The bus stopped and the driver came back.

- This bloke 'ere and his sidekick, these two comics 'ere, they got on the bus with their roller skates. And there's cameras over there.

They both went raving mad and went off to a public phone to call back to their depot, and probably the fuzz.

I said to Julie,

- We'd better leg it, Jules. Get off the bus sharpish. Let's get the hell out of here.

So we skated back to the director and told him that the bus driver and conductor knew nothing about the filming. Apparently, the Spanish director had said that it had been cleared with London Transport.

- Well, they're going raving bloody mad! I think we'd better clear off, pronto...

So we packed up as fast as we could, and the whole crew scarpered down the Kings Road with the irate driver and conductor yelling,

- You should be locked up, you bloody hooligans.

We took cover in the Land's End pub and regaled ourselves with several large bevvies.

That night, we were told that the big shot would happen on the next day.

I asked the director, trying to hide the trepidation in my voice,

- What will that involve?
- You just have to come out of the classroom, skate along the corridor at top speed and jump over five chairs.

Fuck me! I couldn't even jump over a stool, never mind five chairs.

- Right! No problem, I said, in a slightly higher pitched voice than normal.

The director said,

- It's going to be a bit hairy but we should get it in a couple of takes.

Julie whispered,

- You won't be able to jump over five chairs. You'll break your neck. I'm a professional skater and I couldn't jump over five chairs. You'll have to come clean. You've got to fess up.
- I can't do that! My agent blagged this job for me. (*It was the 70s and we were getting about £500 a day, the going rate for 'proper' skaters.*)
- What are you going to do then?
- I'm just going to go for it.
- Are you fucking mad?
- Yup.

The next day, after a sleepless night, and a lot of praying to the God of all skaters, I came into work. Julie looked bleary-eyed,

- I haven't slept all night. You can't do this. I'm going to tell them.
- Julie, I'm just going to do it. It'll be ok. (*yeah right*)
- Well, I'm not going to watch.

The director said we were ready to go. I asked him to make sure that all of the cameras were properly lined up to catch every angle because we may be able to get it in one take. (As if there was ever going to be a second take.)

175

- Bloody hell, mate, that's a helluva task.

He spoke to the Spanish director and the camera crew.

- Colin's going to try to do this in one take so make sure everyone's clear to roll. All clear? Sound? Cameras? Colin, you're sure you want to do this in one take? You don't want a couple of goes first?
- (*No I fucking don't, was what I was thinking!*) Are you sure *all* the cameras are lined up?
- Yes, let's go for it.

The next sequence of events seemed to happen in slow motion. I skated out of the classroom, building up speed along the corridor. I could see the five chairs about thirty feet in front of me, sneering, as if to say "*Jump over us lot? In your deluded brain mate!*" Vroom Vroom! Shoom Shoom! I took off like a bat leaving hell. I felt as if I was in the air for about an hour and a half. Everything slowed down around me. As I came down I slightly clipped the last chair with the wheel of my skate. All I could think was,

- Keep your balance, keep your balance, don't screw up now, you're almost home and dry.

I slowed down and swerved to a halt at the end of the corridor. There was a massive cheer from the whole crew. (They were undoubtedly thinking, "Who is this finely-tuned daredevil hunk, and why isn't he famous?")

The English director said he would check that everything was OK with the Spanish director.

- Colin can do a second safety take if you want it.

I said to myself,

- No, Colin absolutely can't.

The director,

- Are you sure Miguel?
- Yes! Certain!
- OK, it's a wrap. Well done everybody. Drinks in the headmaster's study.

My legs still shaking uncontrollably, I went into the playground where I found Julie sitting on a bench, her head in her hands.

> - I can't believe it. I thought I would be visiting you in Northwick Park Hospital. I was waiting for the sound of the ambulance sirens.

So, I did it! I BLOODY DID IT! The god of skaters and all wheeled chancers had waved his wand and saved my neck. I never saw the commercial as it was only screened in Spain. It's amazing what 500 quid a day can do for your courage, or your mental equilibrium (aka insanity).

A few years later, when I was playing the Pinball Wizard in Tommy, the director, deep in thought, kept glancing at me in a strange way. He came over and said,

> - Colin, I've just been thinking...maybe it would be good if you played the Wizard on roller skates. The cast could whizz you around the stage and you could bounce off the buffers as they light up on the pinball table, as if you're a human pinball. What do you think darling?
> - Balls to you,

is what I thought.

> - Can you roller skate?
> - (*Can I roller skate? I'm the Kelme sportswear stunt skater, don't ya know*).

So for the next three weeks we rehearsed the show with me, once again, on skates. It was bloody difficult, especially as I had to sing at the same time. This was years before 'Starlight Express' and their excellent skating tutors, so I was winging it as I went along. Then, the god of all skaters skated to my rescue once again. When we moved into the Queens Theatre in Shaftesbury Avenue, we discovered that the rake (the incline of the stage) was very steep, in fact the steepest rake in any London theatre. With the best will in the world, I would probably have been propelled into the front row of the audience. As funny as it would have been, that wasn't quite what the part was about. The director saw sense and the skates were ditched. Phew!

Scene Thirty-six: Snake Bite

When I was working in the clubs my agent called and said that he'd arranged a gig for me at the Twilight Rooms, a hostess club on the Charing Cross Road. As usual I went along for a rehearsal with the resident band in the afternoon. The guy who was looking after the acts said that I would have to share a dressing room with the other performer because they had only two rooms, and one was being decorated. The other act was a stripper. Fine by me. I had worked with loads of strippers and found them great fun. The dressing room was tiny, about four-foot square.

- There's only one chair in there, mate. You'll just have to muck in.

When I came back to do the show in the evening my co-performer said,

- 'Allo luv, are you Colin the singer?
- Yeah.
- I'm Lily the stripper. It's a bit cramped in 'ere but what can we do love, ya know? I'm using this chair. You'll have to sit on that basket.

So, following directions, I sat on the wicker basket, and we chatted away.

She said,

- I do a bit of stripping. I work as an accountant as well but I don't make much money as I'm still training. I'm trying to get enough together for a mortgage.

We had been nattering away for an hour or so when the MC came in,

- You're on in ten, Lily. Break a leg.
- Oh, I'd better get myself together, love.

As she was doing her makeup, she turned to me,

- Can I have Sid, love?
- Sid?
- Oh, sorry darling, Sid's my snake.
- (falteringly) Your snake, Lily?
- Yeah, in that basket you're sitting on there's a snake, his name's Sid, he's part of my act. Some say he's the *best* part, but everyone's a critic, ain't they?

I leapt up, with considerable velocity, and she opened the basket to reveal a terrifyingly huge and unquestionably deadly snake (an anaconda the size of a small bedsit), which she casually removed and wound round her neck. I backed into the corner of the room, but was still within spitting distance of Sid.

- I'll see you later, love, have a good show...

was her fond farewell as she disappeared, adorned with her co-performer, Sid. The music burst into life. So did Lily and so did Sid. They were a tough act to follow.

Scene Thirty-seven: Let's Dance

I had never forgotten the thrill of seeing, at the ripe old age of six, the rock'n'roll jive dancers in the carnival at Southend, and I had long wanted to get into dancing. I was in awe of the Young Generation on TV, a group of ten boys and ten girls who were choreographed by Dougie Squires. At the time they were on the 'Rolf Harris Show' every week. I told my mum that I wanted to dance like that, but thought nothing more about it. Anyway, she made some enquiries and found some modern jazz dance classes at the Dance Centre in Covent Garden. The teacher was Mollie Malloy and her assistant was Arlene Phillips, who later went on to be a judge on 'Strictly Come Dancing'. She had done loads of other things; she was a well-known choreographer and choreographed 'Cats' and other musicals.

So, I went along to the Dance Centre. I was wearing jeans and a pair of old plimsolls. There were only three guys in a class of about thirty. They were wearing tight leggings and snazzy dance gear, and there I was in my tatty old clothes. I felt like a fish out of water and decided that it wasn't the place for me. I was creeping surreptitiously towards the door when I heard a clarion voice,

> - Hi, there! Where are you going?

It was Arlene Phillips.

> - I don't think this is for me. I've got all the wrong clothes on. I think I should leave.
> - No, no. Please stay. Do the class. It doesn't matter what you're wearing. I'll talk to you afterwards and tell you where you can buy dance clothes. Just do the class.

Well, I stayed and I absolutely loved it. Arlene told me to go to a dance shop in Baker Street called Gandolfi. I got the kit and went to the class four times a week.

Not long after, an audition notice appeared in *The Stage* magazine for girl and boy dancers for the Young Generation dance group, the same group I had seen on TV. I decided to have a go and try the audition. Although I hadn't done much dancing, I had done judo and gymnastics all through my younger years so my balance was good and I could move quite well. There weren't many guys at the audition (*Yes! Surely this would work in my favour?*). Jamie Phillips, who managed Trends Entertainment for Dougie Squires, was running the audition.

He commented,

- Clearly you're not a trained dancer but you're a good dancer and you have the right look. When there's another opening would you be interested?
- Absolutely!

About a month after that, I had my first Young Generation gig on the Les Dawson Christmas Show.

There's another part to this story. When I went along to the first day's rehearsal in Richmond, I was really nervous. There were all of the girl and boy dancers I had seen on telly so many times, and I felt very intimidated. Dougie Squires, the choreographer, bless him, suggested we do a warm up class. That got me chatting to people and it broke the ice.

I found out later that they had flown in from Canada only that morning and had hardly slept on the plane all night. The last thing they needed to do was a warm up. They wanted to get on and learn the dance routines (and probably go home to bed), but they generously gave it their all rather than throw me in at the deep end.

So, only four months after I told my mum that I would really like to do what the Young Generation were doing, I was part of that very group and on the telly with them. Many years later, when I was with Wall Street Crash, I bumped into Arlene Phillips. I told her that I couldn't thank her enough, and that she was the person who got me into dancing. I recounted the story about how she had called me back into the dance studio, persuaded me to stay, and how that led to a dancing career.

Scene Thirty-eight: The Wizard Without a Voice

We were doing the previews for 'Tommy' in which, as you know by now, I was playing the Pinball Wizard. That afternoon at the rehearsal my voice was clear and in good nick. The half-hour call came over the tannoy. I was sharing a dressing room with my mate, Steve Devereux, and chatting about the afternoon rehearsal.

- You were in great voice this afternoon, Col. I'm looking forward to the show. Are you?

I tried to say "Yeah", but nothing came out of my mouth. *Nothing!* The fifteen-minute call came over the tannoy.

I mouthed to Steve,

- I've lost my voice.

He said,

- Stop fucking about, you tosser!

I wrote on a piece of paper, "*Steve I'm not messing about. My voice has gone.*"

- Oh, shit. What are we going to do?

I mouthed,

- I don't know.

In a panic we rushed to the company manager's office. Pete Townshend was there to see the show before it opened. By that stage Pete was almost deaf from playing loud rock music for so many years.

- Oh shit! What happened?

I wrote:

- I don't know, Pete. My voice has completely gone.

So, the understudy, a guy called Berwick Kaler, was called. (Berwick went on to be a very good Shakespearean actor.) He looked panic-stricken.

- I don't know it well enough and I am not sure of the choreography.

The show was still at the preview stage. At that time, under equity rules the understudy was not obliged to be thoroughly familiar with a part until the opening night. There was a big build-up to the part and timing was important.

> - Ladies and gentlemen, your five-minute call. *Five minutes*! Thank you.

Pete said,

> - I've got an idea. I'll get a mike at the side of the stage. You go on, mime the song, and I'll stand in the wings and sing the part, in the dark. Give me the script.

He needed a script because the song in the musical was different to The Who's original single record that had been a number one hit. The version in the show was much longer.

The show has already started. I tried to explain the order of the verses to Pete. But he couldn't hear and I couldn't talk, so it was a less than ideal situation. The introductory music started, I went on stage, paraded up the stairs ready for my entrance, wearing my skin-tight silver calf leather costume topped by my helmet of spiked flashing lights. I made my grand entrance down a gantry covered with billowing laser-coloured dry ice. The stage was set up as a pinball machine and I was the pinball, thrown by members of the cast from bumper to bumper causing them to light up.

Boom! The first big chord exploded. Boom! The second great big chord. Right, fingers and eyes crossed, I'm in! Please, God of Showbiz, help me now..

> - Ever since I was a young boy ♩♪
>   I've played the silver ball
>   From Soho down to Brighton
>   I must have played them all....

I could hear Pete's voice as clear as a bell. It was all going marvellously. We got to the second verse and I began,

> - Even at my favourite table

And Pete sang,

> - He stands like a statue.

BOLLOCKS !!!! Pete was singing the wrong lyrics! And continued to do so for the rest of the song. We never once managed to get back on track. God only knows what the audience made of it.

By law, critics can't write full reviews until the opening night. But, in the Evening News the next day, there was a report: *Last night I was at a preview of the rock opera 'Tommy', written by Pete Townshend. It was a most amusing evening. For the big song of the evening, 'The Pinball Wizard', a very hoarse Pinball Wizard mimed onstage while Pete Townshend, trying to help the struggling voiceless thespian, was clearly singing the **wrong** words in the wings.*

Marvellous stuff!

An ENT voice specialist was brought in. He diagnosed a vocal cord virus, prescribed the necessary medication and advised me not to use my voice until the opening night, two days later. The opening night came. I had a cautious practice in the afternoon, just to make sure that something was going to come out of my mouth when I opened it, hoping that nothing would go wrong. The music started up. I descended the magic staircase again, lights flashing, heart racing. I grabbed the mike. The two massive chords exploded again. Here we go.

- Ever since I was a young boy ♪♪
    I've played the silver ball

Bollocks! I couldn't believe it. This time my *voice* was working, but the *microphone* wasn't. Not a sound. Shit! The rest of the cast were on the stage around me. Thank God, one of them found another mike and handed it to me. I had only missed a few words, but I felt doomed.

The show was a huge success and ran for seven months. My voice stayed in good nick, and Pete never had to come to my rescue again...bless his cottons.

Scene thirty-nine: Drake's Downfall

In the late 50s, early 60s, Charlie Drake was a massively successful comedian. I was doing a pantomime in Liverpool. During a run we would always get together with other theatres and have an inter-show party because you always knew somebody who was in the show down the road. I was at a party in one of the theatres and I was talking to one of the girls I had worked with in a different show. She was a great looking girl, a dancer. Charlie Drake came over. He was a tiny, not very attractive man. His catchphrase was "Hello, my darling." So he sidled over to me and this girl. He looked at her and said,

- Hello, my darling, what would you say to a little fuck?

She looked him over and said,

- Hello little fuck.

And with that, the little fuck fucked off.

Scene Forty. I Never Forget a Face

I was in Hampstead Garden Suburb, queuing up in a sandwich shop to get a cup of coffee. It was a long queue. This guy kept staring at me. I kept looking away. Eventually he said to me,

- I know you, don't I?
- I don't think so.
- No, I never forget a face. I've seen you around. Where would I have seen you?
- I don't know. I work around here quite a lot. I'm a personal trainer.
- Nah, I don't recognise you from around here. I'm sure it's somewhere else.

He went on and on. Finally, thinking it was my moment of fame, I said, in a smug-ish way.

- Well, I used to sing with Wall Street Crash, a vocal harmony group, and we were on the telly a lot.
- No, no. Didn't you used to drive a bus in Watford?

WHAT? Of course, what I wanted to say was, *"No I fucking didn't ,you dickhead. I was a 'sort of' pop star you know, and I did a Tunes TV commercial for which I got repeat fees. And I sat astride the Berlin wall as they were knocking it down, with some pissed off East German border guard training his machine gun on my nuts."*

- No, I can't drive a bus.

To the girl behind the counter:

- Can I have a tuna and cucumber sandwich please? And, a cup of boiling water to pour over this tosser's head?

Dear Reader...you may feel that you detect a slight hint of bitterness that my glittering showbiz career had been reduced to being (supposedly) an ex-Watford bus driver. If you do....... YOU'RE BLOODY RIGHT.

Scene Forty-one: In Chicago with Ben Cross

I'm proud to say that I was one of the original cast members in the UK production of 'Chicago', the brilliant Kander and Ebb musical that is still in production and remains a huge international success.

We rehearsed for three weeks in London under the musical direction of the talented David Firman, and then transferred to the Crucible Theatre, Sheffield, for our final ten days of rehearsals before the opening night. I was playing the role of Sergeant Fogarty, a hard-bitten Chicago cop investigating a murder scene and I had the opening lines in the show.

- And your wife, Roxy Hart.......

After I'd delivered my lines I was then pretty much in the background for the rest of the scene. Most actors will testify that it is much more difficult to have little to do on stage; you either start inventing activities, fiddling with props and generally faffing about to avoid looking like a spare part, or you do *so* little that you actually *do* look like a spare part. I will never forget the sage advice a director passed down to me when I was playing a very minor role in a fringe repertory play. I had virtually nothing to do in a particular scene and, in rehearsal, due to my lack of acting experience, I was busy building up my non-part with all sorts of pointless nonsense, fiddling with a flower vase, fluffing up my hair in a mirror, flipping noisily through a magazine. The director who was doing much more useful things like directing the actors in a crucial scene, and who had clearly had enough of me farting around in the background and being bloody annoying, stopped the rehearsal and bellowed in a voice that would have put Brian Blessed to shame.

- Colin! for fuck sake! Don't just *do* something.....*stand* there!

Note taken.

Back to Sergeant Fogarty's three lines in Chicago. I hadn't realised that Ben Cross, who was playing the role of Billy Flynn, the handsome, flamboyant whizz kid lawyer, was sitting in the dark at the back of the empty theatre watching the rehearsal. When we stopped for a coffee break in the backstage artists' bar I was pondering how to embellish my big opening scene moment to give it some impact. Ben wandered over to me and very sympathetically said,

- Col, I was watching the rehearsal and it's pretty clear Peter (Peter James) is giving all of his attention to the other actors because they have much more to do, but don't allow yourself to be overshadowed. You may only have three lines *but* they are the first three lines and they need to be acknowledged by the audience.
- Thanks Ben. I'm not sure how to play it. It's difficult as I'm stuck up-stage while all the action is going on down-stage.
- Exactly! So, when the lights come up you should walk straight down to the centre front of the stage. You will then be in a commanding position and all eyes will be on you.
- Thanks Ben, but do you think that will piss Peter off?
- Do it and if he's not happy, then so be it, but it's worth a try.

After the break Peter said,

- OK, let's run it from the top.

The lights came up and, as Ben suggested, I walked purposefully to centre front stage,

- And your wife Roxy Hart.....

A booming directorial voice announced,

- Good Colin! Good! Do exactly what you did then. It's much stronger and gives much more focus to your character's authority. Good, good. Much better. OK, continue everyone.

Ben had been out front watching and in the next break we high-fived. After I'd thanked him, he said,

- You might be able to help *me*. I'm struggling a bit with the high notes in 'Razzle Dazzle'. Any suggestions?

Ben has a great voice and certainly didn't need singing lessons from me, but I had noticed that the top notes fell in the break of his vocal range when he moved from chest voice to full voice. I suggested it might work better if he used his head voice for the tricky crossover notes and then he could slip into full voice and he would be OK. At the next rehearsal he did exactly that and it worked perfectly. We high-fived again. We were even.

Apart from the 'huge' role of Sergeant Fogarty, I was also one of the dancers, which was great fun. There are so many fantastic songs in 'Chicago' and Gillian Gregory's choreography was outstanding. Towards the end of the run in Sheffield we heard that we would be transferring to town, opening at the Cambridge Theatre. Great! One night just before the show my agent, the ever camp Kitty Whittle, rang saying he had an audition for me at ten the following morning in London for the role of the Pinball Wizard in 'Tommy' which, after rehearsals, would go straight into the Queen's Theatre in Shaftesbury Avenue. So after the show I would have to get the overnight train down to the metrop. Unfortunately, because of a football match in London, the train was crammed with Sheffield Wednesday supporters, singing and drinking all through the long, long night. I couldn't find a seat and so I sat on the floor and propped myself up against a wall in the corridor. Throughout the seemingly endless journey I was trodden on and tripped over by a constant stream of pissed supporters who, 'probably unintentionally', dripped warm lager over my head. Not the best way to travel to an audition. I arrived feeling tired and reeking of stale beer. I gave it my all and rushed to catch the last train possible to get me back to Sheffield in time for the show. Kitty rang the stage door phone just as I arrived to say that I had the part in 'Tommy'. Yippee! As much as I loved 'Chicago', and was honoured to be part of the original UK production, 'Tommy' was a much better option for me. I told the management that I would not be transferring with the Chicago company, wishing them all the luck 'that they definitely wouldn't need' as we all knew the show was going to be a smash hit from the first day of rehearsals. Whilst doing my round of goodbyes, Ben told me that he was only going to do a limited run with the show as he felt that he had done enough musicals for a while, and wanted to return to some straight acting. We wished each other luck and agreed to meet in town for a catch-up drink when both shows were up and running.

Both shows opened and both were smash hits. One afternoon in between shows, I was wandering along Shaftesbury Avenue when I heard a familiar voice call from across the road.

- Col! Col. Hang on, I'll come over.

Ben crossed the road and we were chatting away like mad when we realised we both had to get back for our next performances. Ben said his time in 'Chicago' was nearly up and I asked if he had anything in the pipeline.

- Not really. I did go along to meet David Puttnam for a possible role in a low budget film that he's producing. It's a great part, but I know they're having trouble raising funding for the film so I don't think it's going to come to anything.
- Oh OK! Well, all the best Ben. See you soon. By the way, what's the film and the part?
- The part is Harold Abrahams and the film's called 'Chariots of Fire'.

'Chariots of Fire' scooped four Oscars and Ben became an international star. It couldn't have happened to a nicer bloke.

Sadly Ben passed away on the 18th August 2020. Ben, I know that you'll be Razzle Dazzling your audiences up there as much as you Razzle Dazzled them down here. Nice one mate!

Scene Forty-two: Mandy Versus the Speaker

Mandy (also affectionately known as Brand and Brandy Balls) Franklin has one of the loveliest natures you could ever come across. Nothing was ever a problem for Mand. When the rest of us were grumpy after a late night gig and an early morning flight Mand simply 'got on with it'. And when we decided we needed new 'whites' - our posh costumes with the tails which, even back in the 1980s, would set us back a few grand, Mand said,

- I can make them.
- Really?
- Yeah! It'll take a while but let me measure you all and... I'll just get on with it.
- Great, Brand! How much do you need?
- £50 a pop.
- £50 for a set of tailed whites with proper lining and everything?
- Yeah, that should be enough.

We gave Brandy Balls fifty crisp ones each and...well...she just got on with it. If you ventured into Mand's hotel room/tailor's workshop, it would be festooned with white fabric in all shapes and sizes, lengths and widths hanging off doors and light fittings. These she would bundle into a massive suitcase and transfer to the next gig every time we moved on. Mand was like a lunatic sewing professor with steam coming out of her ears and a demonic look in her eyes.

Over the next two months on tour while still wearing our old whites/off-yellows, embossed with sweat stains, makeup and the random scars of life on the road, Mand would beaver away on her sewing machine every moment she had free, day and night. After a concert, when the rest of us were high as kites on adrenalin and no small amount of lubrication, Brand would be in her room sewing away for hours on end. Sometimes she would have the audacity to appear in the hotel bar (usually around 3a.m.) and sometimes even (how dare she?) seek us out in a bar nearby, and ask very politely if we would call by her room for a fitting so she could 'get on with it'.

- Sorry to be a pain guys but would one of you pop up to my room for a fitting? I won't keep you long.
- *Hic!* Flitting? Waya talkin' 'bout? *Hic.* Carn ya see, *hic,* we'ze in *hic*

the muddle of 'avin fun 'ere, *hic*. Stop bein' boring an' com'n 'ave a drinky with us.

- No, don't worry. We can do it tomorrow (*I always sew better on twenty-eight minutes sleep*).
- Yeah! Gool idea, *hic*. Lez do it *hic*, toomozza *hic*.

In no time at all Mandy had made five sets of fantastic whites which fitted like gloves and had fabulous linings, and would have put a Savile Row tailor to shame. These whites lasted through the hell and high water of gigs for the next ten years and never lost their shape, even if some of *us* did. Actually that's not quite true. There is nothing like a life on the road to keep you slim and trim. Anyway that's a little example of what a lovely, easy-going person Mand is.

We were doing a concert tour of Holland, performing one or two nights in each town or city. We arrived at the theatre for this particular gig to discover that the shape of the stage was rather strange. It was half in the round with unsettling sight lines, as a result of which the audience seemed slightly off centre. It wasn't a serious problem but it put us a little off balance.

Mand had a big emotional ballad which she sang alone on the stage in a single spotlight. It was called 'Locking my Heart Away' or, as it became known, 'Stuffing my Face all Day' 'cos Mand liked the odd KitKat or two. (By the way, she had a gorgeous figure - she was one of those people who really pissed you off because she could eat everything she could get her hands on, and never put on an ounce. Bitch!) The song had been written by one of Mand's friends especially for her. With our usual sensitivity, we often used to change the lyrics, just for a laugh. You know, something really grown-up like this:

The first line was.

- How many hearts have you broken? I tell you I've learned my lessons well.

But, at the sound check, the rest of us might sing,

- I've got a McDonald's token, a big mac and fries would do me well.

This would completely bugger up Brand for the evening performance because she couldn't get our version out of her head and would get the giggles. We would be listening off-stage and would feel very smug and amateurishly self-satisfied.

On this particular afternoon, Mand was rehearsing her song on the weird asymmetric stage. She had to walk on from the wings in the dark and 'find her light', which was an overhead spotlight, not easy to do at the best of times. She said,

- This is really strange! I feel as though I'm walking diagonally to the audience and my overhead spotlight isn't where I think it's going to be.
- Yes! We know what you mean Mand! We'll all just have to be aware of the oddness and concentrate on our entrances and exits.

Facing us across the front of the stage, about six feet apart, were four monitor speakers, each approximately four-foot square. From these speakers our stage-left sound engineer was able to give us some of what the audience was hearing but, crucially for us, they made our voices more prominent than the band, enabling us to clearly hear what each of us was singing and blend our voices together to get the right vocal balance. This was before the days of headset microphones. We used lead microphones which, choreographically, became part of our act. Show time arrived and everything was going brilliantly. The audience was enthusiastic and energetic, the band were playing out of their skins and the sound was perfect. What could possibly go wrong? We finished 'Call a Reporter' which was a Marge and boys' number. There was a blackout at the end, and the four of us exited stage left to change into our next frocks. Neil counted the band into 'Locking my Heart Away'. We could hear Neil and the band playing the gentle, melodic intro. It was one of those songs that, when you heard the first few chords, it made life feel infinitely better and generated a warm glow inside. Even though we were rushing to change because we would be back on as soon as Brand had finished, we felt pleasantly calm. Calm, that is, until we heard an almighty CRASH, followed by a sharp intake of breath from the audience. Still frantically changing we were asking each other,

- What's happened? What's happened?

We heard Mandy begin to sing, although she sounded a little shaky.

- ♪♪ How many hearts have you broken?

CRASH!

Bloody Nora what's going on?

What was going on was this…..

Mand had walked on stage but there was no spotlight for her to head towards. (Lighting boards can differ from one theatre to the next so it can be very confusing for technicians on tour). It was pitch black onstage and she could only see the green exit lights at the back of the theatre, but they were in a strange position because of the odd angle of the stage. Being a pro she walked to where she thought the overhead light should be, hoping that it would be turned on to illuminate her. However, disorientated by the unusual configuration of the stage, she walked too far forward and fell over the monitor speaker which was close to the edge of the stage. She would have fallen off the stage and into the audience if she hadn't been ignominiously pushed back onstage by some helping hands. Being a real trouper, Mand picked herself up and tried to get into position. Finally the overhead light came on but she was nowhere near it. Still in darkness, she started the next line,

- ♫ I tell you I've learned my lessons well,

CRASH! She fell over the next speaker.

The audience, as one, went,

- Ohhhhhh.

And Mand (with her accustomed eloquence) said,

- Fucking hell!

Followed sharply by,

- For fuck's sake!

Then adding,

- Where the fuck am I?

At last our lighting guy found the switch for the main bar of overhead lights. Only he didn't! What he found was the switch that turned on the house lights. So now there was only one overhead light on stage but full illumination of the auditorium and a very confused audience. Our lighting guy was now panicking and flicking every switch he could find, creating a kaleidoscope of lighting madness. The audience must have wondered if this was a failed attempt to replicate the 'son et lumière' at the Acropolis in Greece. Mand continued singing but she was so confused that she couldn't remember the lyrics and started singing our bastardised version from the afternoon rehearsal.

- ♫♫ I've got a McDonald's token,
  I think I'll have fillet'o'fish and fries.

By this stage we had finished changing and we leapt onto the stage to help the battered and bruised, shocked and confused Brandy Balls. We grabbed our mikes and started singing like one of those choirs run by that bloke in the glasses on the telly. Even the audience were trying to sing along, despite the fact that *they* didn't know the words because they had never heard the song before, bless them. I could hear vague references to food items you can purchase in Mickey D's: cheeseburger, shake, side salad, egg McMuffin, none of which scanned with the metre of the song, but at least they had a go. Hallelujah! As we sang the final lyrics, now reduced to using Wimpy for inspiration, the lighting returned to something resembling the norm.

After the show, our lighting guy was distraught and almost in tears. We told him not to worry and that it could happen to anyone. We then found his van in the car park and rigged his brakes so that they would fail on the first steep hill he drove down. (Admittedly not too much of a danger in Holland.) Mand, after we had smothered her bruised legs and bum with Arnica cream, was able to see the funny side of it. She said,

- When something like that happens, you just have to 'get on with it'.

Good on ya, Brand.

Scene Forty-three: The Boys in the (WSC) Band (You Can Count on Freddie)

Over the years we had many fantastic musicians playing with us and some huge personalities. The quality of the musicians (never to be called musos because they hate that term) can make or break an act, and we were lucky and honoured to work with the elite. The Wallies started off with eight singers but, for the last twelve years or so, we worked really well as a five-piece. We would sometimes travel with ten musicians and one or two sound crew. Because of the cost of transporting a large music ensemble, a financially expedient alternative was to use 'pick-up bands'. Our management would find the best musicians wherever we were booked to perform. It was great if we were able to fit in a rehearsal with them on the day before the gig but sometimes we would meet up with them for only a few hours on the day, so it was all rather hit or miss. Generally, however, we were fortunate and the musicians, apart from very few occasions, came up trumps for us. We had musical arrangements for nearly every configuration of band, from five musicians up to orchestras of fifty or more.

Gerry called one day to arrange for the 'big band' parts (arrangements) to be sent to America. We were booked to do a one night stand in a huge venue in Berlin and we were to be backed by an American big band who would play their own set, after which we would join them for a ninety-minute gig. As they were busy working all over the world we would only be able to rehearse with them on the afternoon of the gig, so they wanted the parts in advance to familiarise themselves with our music whenever they had a chance. It was a little worrying but we were assured that they were the top guys and that there wouldn't be any problems. We arrived in Berlin and were taken to the venue. As we came through the front entrance we could hear the band rehearsing a swing song I had written called 'Susie's Bar'. Wow! They sounded fantastic. It was a massive sound and they were really swinging the arrangement. We came through the auditorium doors to the incredible sight of the Count Basie Orchestra: the whole outfit with all the famous faces *and* they were playing *my song* which I had written in my tiny basement flat in Islington one wet Sunday afternoon. I was walking on air. We waited for them to finish, applauded their fantastic playing and introduced ourselves. Freddie Green was their guitarist, a music legend and one of the all-time greats. He must have been close to eighty years old and the coolest dude imaginable. He was scrutinising the music on the stand in front of him. He looked up and you could see the eyes of a man who had lived life to the full and loved every second of it. Very slowly with the coolest American accent he said,

- Hey......who wrote this song?

My mouth was so dry with nerves and admiration that when I opened my mouth to fess up nothing came out. Was he going to say "I've never played such a heap of shit in my life!"? Mary came to the rescue.

- Col wrote it, Freddie.
- Hey Col, good to meet you, man. Say this is a cool piece bro. Just got one little issue if you don't mind me stickin' my ten cents in.

Oh fuck, here we go, he's going to pull the thing to bits and tell me to shove it up my arse.

- See this chord here, man, this B flat seven?
- Yes Freddie (c'mon let's get it over with).
- It would sound much cooler if it was a B ♭ 7, ♭ 9, aug 5.
- Of course Freddie. (*If only I knew what B ♭ 7, ♭ 9, aug 5 was.*) Oh OK, thank you very much, much appreciated, Freddie. (*Grovel, grovel*)
- Want me to change it for you man?
- If you would, Freddie, that would be great. Thanks so much. (*More grovelling*)
- Well let me show you what I mean first man and if you don't like it we'll just leave it as it is. Your song, man, your call.

This is *the* Freddie Green, the same Freddie Green who had played with Sinatra, Sammy, Tony Bennett, all the greats, and he was asking *my* permission to change one little chord. Holy shit! Of course I could have let him play it, then said, "Erm it's OK Fred but I like my chord better and mind your own fucking business. In future, when I want your opinion I'll give it to you."

- Thanks Freddie I really do appreciate it. Thank you. (*Far too much grovelling*)

197

He played the chord. I heard angels singing; it was the best chord I'd ever heard in my life, and I've heard a few chords I can tell you.

- That's brilliant Freddie thank you. Would you mind changing it for me?
- It would be my pleasure, man.

He changed the chord and shook my hand.

- Great song, man!

I could have happily died and gone to heaven.

Scene Forty-four: The One and Only (thank God) Neil Drinkwater

As for the musicians in the Wallies band, I have to start with *this* man: Neil Drinkwater. He was a fantastic keyboard player, musical director and arranger, and one of the funniest guys I've ever met in a piss-taking-I've-got-no-time-for-this-crap sort of way. We were doing a long tour of the Netherlands. It may not be the biggest country in the world (not much more than 150 feet long) but we somehow seemed to play hundreds of venues from one end to the other and we had brilliant audiences.

We were opening with a great number called 'Be There'. It really motored and got the crowd with us from the get go. When the band played the opening chords we would come on up-stage in a line as though we were going to go straight across the stage and exit on the other side. When we got to centre stage we would all turn sharply and come down quickly to the line of microphones that were in position for the five of us. We would launch straight into the song,

- ♪♫   Gonna be there, Gonna be there,

getting the audience clapping with us straight away and lifting the already great atmosphere, then bosh!

I had the first few lines to sing:

- ♪♫   Early in the morning,
  in the dead of the night,
  You know babe
  I'm gonna be there.

The endorphins were always on overdrive! One night, and I still don't know why, I opened my mouth to sing, and not a sound came out. Before the show we had been vocally warming up as usual and my voice was absolutely fine but now: nothing! In such times of stress and panic your brain goes into overdrive and speeds up. In that split second I knew what would be going on all around me. Dicky, our sound guy, would think the microphone wasn't working and would be pushing all the faders on his desk trying to get some volume out. One of the Wallies would be rushing to get a spare mic from Arjan, our side-of-stage sound guy. But, just as Perty was handing me the spare mic and singing my lines for me, my voice suddenly came back and, bizarrely, was completely normal. It was fine throughout the concert. This has never happened since. It remains a mystery.

In the interval our Dutch tour promoter came backstage and asked me what had happened. I said,

> - I've no idea Robin. Everything was completely fine until I opened my mouth, and nothing came out.

Neil, who was sitting close by, reading a girly magazine, without even looking up, intoned in his very slow nasal drawl,

> - I thought it was an act of God!

Isn't it encouraging to have the admiration, support and respect of your contemporaries?

Scene Forty-five. The Applause not the Clap

Here's another Drinkwater classic. In the second half of the concert we would always sing an acapella song. It made a nice change from the band giving it max and we had a chance to show off some of our tricky vocal arrangements. During the preceding number I would introduce the musicians one by one and they would each play a funky solo which the audience always appreciated, and duly applauded. It would go something like this:

- Ladies and gentlemen, many people call this man a virtuoso but quite frankly what he chooses to do behind closed doors is his business. Please give a huge round of applause for the finest saxophone player this side of the Mississippi delta, Mr. Philip Kolb.

Philip would then go into a kickarse solo which always guaranteed a massive response from the crowd. He would take his bow and I would move on to the next musician.

- This man owns the largest collection of guitars in Europe. Unfortunately he doesn't know how to play any of them, so tonight on drums Mr. Steve Sanger.

Steve would whack out a massive drum solo that would rock the foundations and lift the roof off the venue, followed by huge applause.

- For your further delight this evening - a hunk (of whom it has often been said.....but never proven, has the fastest fingers ever to grace the bass) - give it up for Andy Herbert!
- Philip Kolb has the finest wingmen in the Netherlands and, if you're feeling horny, these are the only horns you'll ever need. Go mad for Stylus Horns!

And that's how I carried on until they had all had their moment in the spotlight. The musicians, apart from Neil, would then leave the stage to get as much booze down their necks as possible in the space of the next eight minutes when they were due back on. When they had all gone I would turn upstage to Neil who was sitting at the keyboard, and I would say.

- Good evening Neil how are you?

To which he would reply,

- I'm very well indeed Colin and all the better for seeing your smiling face.
- How kind. Neil, would you be so kind as to give us an arpeggio in E Major please?

Neil would play the arpeggio; we would hum our individual harmony notes...

- Mmmmmmmmm 𝄢

Then we would launch into our unaccompanied song. When this ended and the applause kicked in we would bow and Neil would count the band (who had now returned looking much happier for a couple of stiff drinks and a few tokes on a Camden Cornet) into the next number.

- 1.2.3.4

and off we would go again. It was a nice little interlude in the show.

Well! One fine evening Neil was in one of those moods in which anything could happen. As usual I turned upstage to him and said,

- Good evening Neil how are you?

In a particularly testy, adenoidal tone,

- Well I'm not feeling too well actually, Colin!

Fuck! He's going off-script. What's he up to? Improvising, I said,

- I'm very sorry to hear that Neil, and what is ailing you?

(Now bear in mind the concert hall is packed to the rafters with people of all ages, ranging from fifteen to seventy-five.)

- Well Colboy, I think I've caught a dose of syphilis.

Help! This was totally out of left field. Half the audience laughed, half the audience gasped and one or two headed for the exit. Still frantically improvising, I said,

- I'm so sorry to hear that Neil and only yesterday I was thinking how well you looked. I suggest a couple of litres of penicillin and ten hours' rest in a darkened room. Would you be so kind as to give us an arpeggio in E Major please?

Which he did. Unfortunately, by this stage we, and the audience, including the ones who had been gasping, had started to giggle, at first in embarrassment and then uncontrollably, with the result that the next four minutes of acapella singing were a total farce, with not one note or lyric in time or in tune. By the time we had shambled our way to the finish line, the audience were in hysterics, the band (who had now returned) were pissing themselves, and so were we. Neil's face was as deadpan as usual. He counted the next number in...

- 1.2.3.4

and our very 'high-class' concert (with the exception of the previous eight minutes) continued.

What a rascal, eh?

Scene Forty-six: Neil and his Gang go Undercover

On this occasion, Neil was aided and abetted by his scurrilous cohorts Steve-let's-get-one-over-on-the-Wallies Sanger, and Andy-let's-stitch-up-the-turn Herbert, our fab bass guitarist.

Perty had written a song called 'She's Undercover'. It was set during the Cold War and I was playing the part of an English agent, helping to secure other agents' safe passage across the border from the east into neutral territory in the west. Perty would be positioned under an overhead light corner-stage, singing the narration surrounded by swirling fog (dry ice). I was dressed in the usual agent garb of a mac and a trilby hat and would be pacing back and forth across the stage, also in dense fog, waiting nervously for my agent to appear to give her the false identity papers, map and the route necessary for her to negotiate the enemy lines to safety.

Agent Mandy would appear out of the fog carrying her suitcase, very apprehensive because of the dangerous situation she was in. I would rush to her and shine my torch (this was in the dead of night) onto the counterfeit papers and the map and quickly point out the route she was to take through the forests and the countryside to meet with other agents who would guide her further along the escape lines. At this point, we were rumbled. As searchlights were trained on us, we scattered in different directions. I was shot dead and Mandy was caught and taken away to be interrogated. Off-stage you heard the final shot as she was executed. It was the sort of light-hearted piece that would make the audience feel cosy and relaxed whilst having a fun evening out at a Wallies concert!

Well, one evening, Drinkwater and his cronies thought they would liven up the proceedings a little. They found house bricks and put them into Mandy's suitcase, they purloined the false papers from the pocket of my mac and glued pornographic photographs inside, and they persuaded the theatre electrician to rig my torch so that, once I had turned it on, it wouldn't switch off. (As you will no doubt conclude, Wall Street Crash and our associates were an exemplary, professional outfit).

The show was rocking along when we came to 'She's Undercover'. Perty was in his fog being all dramatic and emotional and I was pacing up and down doing my very best "Where's my secret agent?", "It's bloody cold out here" acting. Suddenly off stage in the dark I hear Mandy's muffled expletive,

- Fucking hell! What's happened here? Jesus Christ, I can't lift the fucking thing.

Scraping noises ensued and Mand appeared out of the fog dragging her suitcase across the stage with both hands, her hat on sideways, huffing and puffing and looking very pissed off.

I rushed to help her and we both managed to pull the case into the pool of light. I reached for my torch, switched it on, and shone it on a photo of two people copulating in the thirty-ninth position of the Kama Sutra. I looked at Mand, she looked at me, and we both burst into laughter. We tried to conceal this from the audience by turning upstage. When I went to turn off my torch the switch was locked, so I stashed it in the pocket of my mac, with the result that the beam was dramatically illuminating my groin.

As in the script, we parted and went our separate ways. In the billowing fog, Mand crashed into the immoveable suitcase, fell arse over tit and ended up sprawled, legs akimbo, in the middle of the stage. The East German border guards (Polly and Marge) entered and I, with my illuminated crotch, was shot in the back. I was lying dead on the stage, the audience no doubt wondering what was so significant about my wedding tackle that it needed a special lighting effect. Mercifully Mand was dragged off, still laughing uncontrollably, and shot. The stage went into blackout, a blackout that would have been complete if it had not been for my glowing willy lighting my path as I stumbled offstage. End of number. God only knows what the audience thought, but Fagin Drinkwater and his gang dined out on that shambolic scenario for months.

Scene Forty-seven: Sanger Loses his Timing

Steve Sanger, drummer extraordinaire and all round lovely guy, was having a spot of trouble with his love life or, to be more accurate, the lack of it. Steve hailed from Dorset. He spoke with a lovely West Country accent which had been only slightly mellowed by his time in London and sounded (sorry Steve) a bit country yokel-ish. One day on tour in Holland we were having a chat on the 'magic bus' and he said to me,

- 'Ere Colboy can I bend yer ear about something ?
- Anything! Shoot Steve.
- Well I've not 'ad much luck with moy love life of late, ya see, as I'm not much cop at the old Charlie chat like wot yous is and I waz wondering if you could give me a few pointers. See, I fancy Marja and I don't know how to go about chattin' 'er up like, and oy don't want to look like a plonker.

Marja was our new Dutch percussionist, a fantastic musician and a cracking looker. This was her first tour with us. In the past we had used a great guy named Eddie Conard who was American, sharp, black, hip, uber good looking, ultra cool and a genius on percussion. Eddie was a big time player with the ladies and had this great expression which he would trot out whenever you bumped into him.

- Y'know Mother Nature's been *very* kind to me!

A quick glance at his wedding package and you knew he wasn't talking about his wins on the lottery. But Eddie wasn't on this tour. He was probably off somewhere showing some gorgeous girl how kind Mother Nature had been to him. So Marja had joined us, and Sanger had the hots for her.

I said,

- Look mate tomorrow, when we board the bus, I'll sit next to her on the pretext of chatting to her about the percussion fills in one of the numbers. If you saunter by, I'll get you involved in the conversation because you're the drummer and a kindred spirit. Then, when the timing's right, I'll say, "You sit here Steve. I've just got to talk to Andy about something". You take my place next to her. Just be yourself and get chatting about how she came to start playing percussion, who she's worked with, where she lives, has she ever been to London - you know, all the usual 'getting to know someone stuff'. Then, when it's all nicely relaxed, say you've never really seen much of Amsterdam and, on our next day off, would she fancy meeting for a coffee and showing you around, with maybe a bit of tip-toeing through the tulips?

- That's great, Colboy. Thanks for yer help.
- Cool!

The following day our plan rolled into action. I engineered my way into the seat next to Marja and was waffling on.

- Great having you on tour with us Marja. I was saying to *Steve* how much I love the way you're using the toms on 'Call a Reporter'. That fill you're playing in the middle eight is awesome, it cuts brilliantly across the back beat that *Steve's* playing. I don't know how you're managing to play six things at the same time. Brilliant! Oh, hi Steve. I was just saying to Marja how much I love her playing on 'Reporter'. It really complements what *you're* playing; you blend *really* well together. Listen, I've just got to ask Andy something. You sit here Steve and I'll be back in a mo.

I swanned off and left them to it. Occasionally I would glance down the bus, peering through the mild marijuana mist (those Dutch boys liked to fire up the boilers early, usually at around 6.30a.m.) to check up on the progress of love's young dream. Marja seemed to be talking animatedly while Sanger listened intently, gazing at her with his puppy-dog, slightly lustful eyes. It seemed to be going OK so I settled down with my Sony Walkman. There was a long drive to the next gig which was somewhere near the German border and I wasn't sure whether Vivaldi's 'Four Seasons' or Meat Loaf screeching his bollocks off in 'Bat out of Hell' would be the best way of passing the time. Meat Loaf won. I must have dozed off, even though Meat was doing his nodule-ravaged vocal cords some serious damage in 'Paradise by the Dashboard Light' at seven thousand decibels. I awoke to Steve tugging my arm, looking slightly worried.

- Hi Steve, how did it go mate? Marja seemed to be chatting away nicely. Do you think you've made any headway?

- Well oy don't roightly know. Ya see, once she started talkin she didn't come up for air. She was goin' on big style about all (and these were her words Colboy) the men who have fucked her over all through her life, been unfaithful, into drugs and gambling and, worst of all, most of them were musicians and raving alcoholics who fucked with her head and screwed up her fucking life. She said she'd never, ever have a relationship with another fucking drunken musician for as long as she lived, and that she'd like to cut off all their cocks and shove them up their arses.

- Ermm! So it's not looking great for a visit to Anne Frank's gaff and a wander through the tulip fields then?
- I think oy'd better swerve this one, Colboy. What d'ya think?

- Well! Let's not be negative about this. Look, I've known you for some time now mate and I know you like to go out on the lash and get completely bladdered every so often. I still remember that time when we were recording with the BBC orchestra at Lime Grove and you had a few too many at lunchtime. You came back to the studio early and peed into that drippy, self-satisfied musician's baritone saxophone and, next time he blew it, bubbles flew out of the top and showered the other musicians. Thank God they never got to the bottom of that little episode. Oh and then...

- Oh all roight! I know I've had a few indiscretions over the years, but oy'm not a bad bloke.

- That's exactly what I was going to say Steve. You're a lovely bloke and, as long as you behave yourself, I think you and Marja will get along great. After the gig tonight get chatting to her again and tell her you completely understand the hurt she must feel after being treated so very badly by those other insensitive, horrible drunken musician bastards, and that you would never in a trillion years treat a lady in that deplorable manner. Ask her to give you the benefit of the doubt so that you can try to restore her faith in men because they're not all the same. Suggest that she meet you tomorrow at that little bar on the corner of Dam Square for a nice quiet, no-strings-attached lunch, and a stroll around the canals. I know you can do it Steve. Break a leg mate!

All through the gig I could see Sanger giving it max, smiling at her and knocking out flirty little progressive drum riffs around her intricate percussion fills, seducing her with a foreplay of tympany. Well, all this percussive peacock strutting seemed to do the trick and on the journey home they were nattering away happily. We arrived back at the hotel at 4.15a.m., and Sanger told me he was meeting Marja for lunch at two that afternoon.

> - Great Steve, now go straight to bed so you're nice and rested. In the morning have a sauna and a swim so you're feeling relaxed, wear your nicest casual clothes. Oh! And a small bunch of flowers wouldn't go amiss either. It's Sunday tomorrow, we don't have a gig so you have all day to enjoy yourselves. Have fun, mate. Keep me posted.

I drifted off to sleep feeling like a self-satisfied male version of Anna Raeburn at her agony aunt best.

Late Sunday afternoon there was a tentative knock on my door. I called out,

> - Who is it?

I was always careful not to open the door without checking first, just in case I was faced with a horde of excited fans who would become much less excited when they realised they had the wrong room and it was me and not that good-looking hunk, Perty.

> - It's me, Sanger.

I opened the door and beheld a nightmare vision of a person who, in a hideous Zombie-like way, only vaguely resembled Steve Sanger. What was left of this poor wretch can only be described as a dead man, reeking of alcohol, unshaven, wearing a vomit-stained Iron Maiden t-shirt, with eyes that were not piss holes in the snow, but piss craters of untold magnitude on the side of Mount Everest.

I will deliver the next section of this story in the words and voice of Steve 'why-oh-why-didn't-I-listen-to-my-life-coach-Colboy' Sanger.[20]

---

20 Dear Steve, if you are a tiny bit pissed off by my portrayal of your Dorset accent, and are considering tracking me down and beating me to death with your drumsticks, please note that I have changed my name and moved to Azerbaijan.

- 'allo Colboy! I stand 'ere a man ashamed. Not worthy of the help you bestowed on me. I am a useless excuse for a human being who should be cast asunder and ....
- Steve, for fuck's sake, drop the melodrama and get on with it. I'm losing the will to live here.
- Awright then. This morning you told me to go straight to bed but as I passed Drinkwater's door I could hear raucous laughter coming from Neil, Andy and the Stylus Horns boys, so I thought I would knock and say goodnight. This, Colboy, was my idiotic downfall, for which I should be punished in hell. I should be strung up by my bol.........
- Steve. Hopefully I have another forty years left to live. I would prefer *not* to spend them in this bloody doorway. PLEASE.
- Quite roight, Colboy. So I knocked, and was lured into their den of hedonistic deloight. I 'ave to confess I weakened and partook of various concoctions but some'ow managed to crawl back to my room. The next thing I remembers is a frantic banging on moy door at a volume and intensity you can't imagine. Someone's screaming very, very loudly and yelling words like fucker, bastard and dickhead. I jumped up sharply only to feel the searin' pain of the bells of 'ell clangin' inside moy 'ead. I ran to the door, threw it open and there, standin' in the 'allway, before my slits for oyes was......... Marja, sobbin' and angry. Colboy her words are still ringin' in moy ears. "Just like every other drunken musician I have ever met. Why did I think you would be any different? You're all the same. Selfish, mean, insensitive, uncaring, unworthy. I hate you all." She turned around and walked straight ahead, and out of my life. Unfortunately straight ahead led her three steps across the 'all and into the chambermaids' cupboard which was full of buckets, brooms, toilet rolls, cleaning fluids and three 'undred of those little plastic bottles of shampoo and conditioner. There was an almighty rumpus as the whole roomful cascaded on top of her. She fought like a woman possessed, Colboy, strugglin' to free 'erself from the mountin' of domestic supplies. She stood up with all the dignity that someone with their head in a metal bucket could muster, threw it off, glared at me one last toyme, turned (the right way this toyme) and stalked off down the 'all. All I could do was stand and sway in a still

'alf-inebriated mess. And 'ere I am. What am I goin' to do, Colboy?

- Well! Suicide seems the immediate first option but, as we still have twenty-three gigs left and it might be useful to have a drummer, I think the biggest, most-grovelling apology in the world and a life of wearing sackcloth may be the way forward. Shall I come with you?

We were given Marja's address by Mark, the tour manager. After three enforced showers and when five mugs of strong black coffee had been decanted into Steve, we set off in a taxi to face, what? We knocked on her door and..... waited with baited breath for the onslaught to come. We were both bricking it and suspected that turning up out of the blue would go down like a French kiss at a family reunion. However, when Marja opened the door, she took one look at us standing there like carpeted schoolboys.....and burst out laughing. The broom cupboard had saved the day. She and Sanger never 'fell in love' but they 'fell into' a firm friendship.

Some years later I heard that Marja had married a rock keyboard player and that they had three kids who are all musicians. Steve Sanger continues to play drums brilliantly with a vast array of top bands and works non-stop as a much-in-demand session musician. You's awright you is, Steve, the toppest of top blokes.

Scene Forty-eight: The Nude Balconist (no elevator required)

The Wallies were doing a TV show in Frankfurt, Germany. It was a big variety show with a mix of different performers: dancers, musicians, comedians and the great British bandleader and brilliant jazz trumpet player, Humphrey Lyttelton.[21] Humph, as he was known to one and all, was without doubt one of the finest British jazz musicians of all time. He was born at Eton College where his father was a housemaster. Whilst he and his mother were watching a cricket match at Lords in 1936 they became a trifle bored and slipped out of the grounds, hot-footed it down to London's Charing Cross Road, and bought Humph his first trumpet. He was fifteen, and he soon became a fast rising star in the jazz clubs around London and later the world, playing with all the greats.

We met Humph briefly during the afternoon rehearsals but unfortunately didn't have a chance to hang out with him. That would have been awesome as he would have had so many fantastic stories to tell. The show went really well and there was an after-gig party at our hotel where all the performers were staying. We kept an eye out for Humph but realised that he must have bailed out early and nipped off to bed. The party wrapped up at around two thirty and everyone drifted off to their rooms. Despite the late hour and having arrived in Germany on a very early flight from a gig in Switzerland the night before, I was wide awake. It was the middle of summer and my room was very hot. I don't think the aircon was up to much, and clearly the hotel had seen better days. There was only one channel on the telly which was showing a riveting documentary about the germination and life span of the bonsai tree, some of which can apparently live for a hundred years. I made a note to order boxed sets to give as Christmas gifts to my bank manager and other people who bring joy to my life. By 3.15a.m. I was so bored that even the bonsai tree (now in its fifty-third year) was starting to look interesting. Erm, what to do? *I'll ring Polly, of course.*

- Hi Polly, are you asleep?
- If I had been I would be awake now because you just rang me. Dhuuur!
- Soz mate. I'm bored.

---

21 Louis Armstrong referred to Lyttelton as "that cat in England who swings his ass off".

- Oh, OK, and what exactly would you like to do to rectify this dilemma, at 3.25 a.m. in downtown Frankfurt? I mean the list of options must be endless. Anyway, I'm watching a programme about the germination and life span of the bonsai tree. So bugger off!
- Don't be tetchy luv. OK, I'll leave you alone. See you later.

Boring sod! So what am I gonna do now? 3.27a.m. and no one to play with. Oh the heady life of a sort-of pop star! The bonsai tree had sprouted another leaf. Yippeeeeeee. 3.28a.m. *Right, I can't take the excitement any longer. Drastic action is needed.*

(Dear Reader, before I continue with this next section I must put out a stern warning and disclaimer to you all. DO NOT UNDER ANY CIRCUMSTANCES TRY THIS AT HOME OR, FOR THAT MATTER, AWAY FROM HOME. You may think that what is to follow is pure fiction but, scout's honour, it is exactly what happened.)

As my room was unbearably hot I had de-robed and was now wandering around in the altogether whilst formulating my masterplan. Yes! I would visit Polly and cajole him into humour of some sort. Unfortunately, this would mean getting dressed, taking the lift up three floors, walking the length of the corridor and knocking on his door (which he would probably ignore, assuming that it was a deranged fan who had tracked him down wanting first, his finely-tuned body, and second, to learn the finer points of bass counterpoint harmony singing). I would then have to reverse tracks back to my room only to be faced with a clock reading 3.52a.m.

No! This was my *Cunning Plan.* I knew that Polly's room was three floors up but, crucially, was directly above mine. I approached the minibar with the determination of a man who has made a pivotal life decision; from this moment there would be no turning back. I opened the minibar and selected a quarter bottle of champagne. This exact brand of champagne varied in price dramatically, depending on the hotel and country you were in. For instance, the same bottle in Spain cost you thirty euros, in Italy forty euros, in Bulgaria three euros - and in Monte Carlo it cost two hundred and fifty euros just to open the minibar door and three hundred and fifty euros for the champagne. However, on this occasion I was in the Fatherland and the cost was a reasonable twenty-five euros. Onwards! Not wanting to be caught out underdressed, I selected one of my very snazzy ties from the wardrobe and, using a reef knot that I learned in the boy scouts, secured one end to the neck of the bottle and wound the other end around my neck. I was now ready for lift-off. Using the 'crack-climbing' skills learned in my misspent youth shinning up high rise flats, I heaved up onto the railing of my balcony, took a firm grip on the bottom rail of the balcony above me, and started my climb to Polly's room. To add to the tension of this story it may be worth pointing out that my room was on the eleventh floor. I repeat:

DO NOT IN ANY CIRCUMSTANCES TRY THIS AT HOME.

Very, very carefully, relying on my innate cat burglar dexterity, I inched my way skywards (don't forget that this ludicrous foray was being performed not only without a safety net, but also without any clothes, apart from my carefully-selected tie). Eventually I managed to hoist myself up to Polly's balcony. I couldn't have planned it better; his sliding door was slightly ajar and he was lying on the bed engrossed in the bonsai tree programme. With a flourish, I slid open the door and casually asked,

- Hello mate, fancy a drink?
- Oh! Hello Colboy how did you get here? (*dumb!*)

Polly was completely unfazed by my unorthodox entry, as I was known to do this sort of thing on a regular basis.

- Well, it was starting to get light and I thought you might be a bit thirsty so being a good friend I took a short cut up. Much quicker than the wimpy lift route.
- Great! Let's crack open the bubbles then. Oh, do you want to watch the end of this programme?
- No thanks mate. Cheers.

We downed the bubbly, had a few laughs, and (not pushing my luck) I borrowed a dressing gown and took the sensible route via the lift back to my room. Oh dear….having had no pockets in my skin-toned climbing outfit and, having overlooked the fact that I might need a key to get back in, I found a chambermaid and explained that I had been sleepwalking and had locked myself out of my room. She gave me that look that said "Yeah right, Liebling! Rick Parfitt from Status Quo did exactly the same thing". Oh well! So much for originality, then. Back in my room. 5.50a.m. The Bonsai was still growing, slowly.

The following day we were checking in at Frankfurt airport when I felt a gentle tap on my shoulder. I turned to see Humphrey Lyttelton's smiling face. He said,

- I know you, you're the Nude Balconist!
- Oh hello Humph. Sorry, what was that?
- Last night, it was so hot in my room, I couldn't sleep, and I was bored watching a programme about the gestation and lifespan of the bonsai tree, so I thought I would sit on my balcony to get some fresh air. Lo and behold, across the courtyard on the balcony of the room directly opposite mine, I beheld a bizarre vision. Some chap without a stitch on but with a bottle of something hanging around his neck clambered up the side of the hotel then disappeared into a room three floors above. At first I thought it may have been that man from the Cadbury's Milk Tray commercial, but this fellow looked a bit short in stature for that. Then, in a blinding flash, I recognised him as a Wall Street Crash person. From this day forth you will forever be known to me as the Nude Balconist.

Some months later we were doing an open air jazz festival in Rotterdam and Humph and his Big Band were on just before us so he introduced us to the audience.

This is how it went:

- Ladies and gentlemen it's great to be back in the Netherlands and performing in one of our favourite cities, Rotterdam. I know you are all fans of the next group. So please give a big round of applause for Wall Street Crash, featuring the Nude Balconist.

Humphrey Lyttelton, many thanks! It was an honour to share the stage with you.

Scene Forty-nine: Revved up in the Rain

When I was working on my own, my agent arranged a cabaret gig at a small hotel somewhere in the middle of Essex. I had an old Hillman Minx that I had bought for about 50 quid. I could always rely on my car - that is, I could always rely on it to let me down, because it was absolutely knackered. As I was not due on stage until ten o'clock, I decided to get dressed for the gig before I left. This would mean that I could get there ten minutes early, put on my makeup, do my act, and then head for home. It was tipping down with rain. I got into my tuxedo and set off. About an hour away from the venue, my good old Hillman Minx gave a shudder, and ground to a halt. I am not great with cars. As I see it, cars are there for one purpose which is to get me from one place to another, but on this occasion my old banger had failed me miserably. Wearing my tux and bow tie I peered under the bonnet. That's what guys do isn't it? It made as much sense to me as the inner workings of a space rocket. Not a single car had passed me, and I couldn't see any houses nearby. This was before the days of mobile phones and there wasn't a phone box in sight. Then, I heard an approaching throaty roaring sound. A motorbike came speeding past me, splashing muddy water over my tuxedo. It disappeared over the hill and I resigned myself to my soggy-wet sorry state. However, a moment later, I heard the throaty roar again and the bike skidded to a halt, this time spraying me with mud,

- Can I help? (the rider beamed through his visor)
- Well, my car's buggered, mate.
- (Noting the tux) Are you going to a wedding or something?
- No, I'm a singer and I'm booked to do a cabaret act at the Elm Park Hotel. It seems to be in the middle of nowhere.
- I know that hotel. Blimey mate! You're still about forty-five minutes away.
- I know, and I'm supposed to be on in forty-five minutes.
- Well, I don't have any rainproof gear you can wear, but I can take you on the back of the bike. My name's Geoff by the way.
- My name's Col. Thanks Geoff, you're a diamond. Would you mind?
- No, but you're going to get very, very wet.
- Geoff, you're a lifesaver.

So I got my music out of the car and climbed onto the back of his huge bike, a Harley Davidson or something equally butch. We roared off, with me clinging on for dear life, the monsoon tipping down, the tux getting thoroughly soaked. Forty-five minutes later we screeched to a halt outside the hotel.

- There you go! Have a good show.
- Thanks Geoff. I'll never forget you.

I walked up to the reception.

- Hi, my name's Colin. I've come to do the cabaret here this evening.

The receptionist gave me a withering look,

- *Like that?*

I explained what had happened.

- Oh, dear! You're meant to be on soon. Let's see what we can do.

She took me into what appeared to be the hotel laundry which was festooned with drying bed linen, and told me to stand in there for ten minutes..

- See if you can dry off. I'll have a word with the MC to see if he can delay your act for a bit.

The MC came in and stared aghast at the drenched wreck of a man masquerading as his next performer.

- Blimey mate, you're on in a couple of minutes. What shall I do? I could introduce you as a *steaming* cabaret act?! How about that?

As I and my tux had almost disappeared behind a cloud of water vapour, it seemed appropriate.

- Yeah, introduce me as the steaming cabaret singer if you like. They might just take pity on me.

It was time to go on.

- Now ladies and gentlemen, we have a new act for you. He had a bit of a to-do on the way, his car broke down, he arrived here on the back of a motorbike in the downpour; he is literally a steaming singer and you'll see exactly what I mean in a minute. Ladies and

217

gentlemen, you've heard of the group Wet, Wet, Wet, well this bloke's even wetter. Please welcome Colin Copperfield.

I walked onto the stage, which was hot because of the lights. And I sang.

- When they begin the beguine ♪♪
  It brings back the sound of music so tender
  It brings back a night of tropical splendour
  It brings back a memory evergreen ......

The steam was rising in front of my face and got denser as the act progressed. It turned into more of a comedy act, seen through a blanket of mist. The audience loved it, and when I started singing 'Bridge Over Troubled Water' they went crazy.

In case I get caught in a 'pissing down with rain' situation again I've now included in my repertoire 'Singing in the Rain', 'Raindrops Keep Falling on my Head', 'Crying in the Rain', 'Don't Rain on my Parade', 'Stormy Weather', and a few others. I probably should have considered making it a regular feature. My tuxedo was never quite the same again.

Scene Fifty: Change Your Act

My agent rang,

- I've got you a gig for tomorrow night.

It was at a pub in Romford, in Essex.

- It's a big, big, big pub and I want you to do two forty-minute slots.

As always, I rehearsed with the resident band in the afternoon. I was doing lots of funky jazz: 'A wonderful night for a moondance...' and so on. We got to the end of the rehearsal and the pianist asked, somewhat tentatively, if that was the sort of act I normally did in that sort of venue.

- Er, yes. It's the only act I've got!

He said,

- Well, they're a bit of a rowdy crowd. I'm not sure that's the right material. But anyway, it's your act. Go on and do it and we'll play your stuff as best we can.

I got up on the stage later that night to face a noisy and boisterous audience. My act went down like a strip act at a meeting of the church deacons, for a full forty minutes. It felt like forty hours. I came offstage and the piano player was backstage. I told him I was the wrong guy for the venue. He gracefully avoided the "I told you so" routine, but he agreed with me.

He said,

- Look, you've still got to do another forty-minute set, so let's go through some stuff. Do you know a song called 'When Your Old Wedding Ring was New'?
- No.
- Well, it goes like this ...

And he sang it for me.

- Do you know 'Danny Boy'?

Yes, I did. So he went through about ten songs that I vaguely knew.

- Well just busk them. We know these songs. We play them all the time. We'll find which key you sing them in. I'll keep cueing you as to which song we're going to do.

About half an hour later I was introduced on stage. The noise was even louder. So I started,

- When your old wedding ring was new... ♪♫

Suddenly everyone stopped talking.

- And each dream that we dreamed came true. ♪♫

Five hundred people joined in:

- I remember with pride how we stood side by side......

And on it went. "Oh, Danny boy, the pipes, the pipes are calling". "'Old it, flash, bang, wallop, what a picture".

"Yeah, more more!!" Standing ovations, huge applause. "We want more. We want more." I didn't know any more!

I was a huge success, a legend in my own lunchtime. I thanked the piano player who had saved my life, and the band, and went out to the bar to get some drinks for them, and to have the biggest drink I could get my hands on. This bloke came up to me and he said,

- Colin, can I buy you a drink?
- Lovely, thanks very much.

He said,

- I just wanna tell ya. You started out a wanker and ended up a diamond.

I want that on my gravestone when I eventually end up in that great, green room in the sky.

COLIN COPPERFIELD
He started out a wanker,
And ended up a diamond.
Rest in Peace

Scene Fifty-one: The Name Game

My agent called to say that he had arranged a great gig at Dagenham Working Men's Club in London's East End. Several thousand workers were employed to build Ford cars at the plant, so their social club was sizeable. I went along and was waiting to do my rehearsal with the resident band in the afternoon when this guy came up to me and said,

- Hello there. My name's Derek. I'm the compère. Welcome to Ford's. Looking forward to your act. What's your name, mate?
- Nice to meet you Derek. It's Colin Copperfield.
- You'll be on just after the ventriloquist and before the knife-throwing act at about quarter or half past ten. Have your rehearsal with the band and I'll show you to your dressing room later.
- That's lovely, thanks very much.
- What's your name again?
- Colin Copperfield.
- Alright Colin, have a good rehearsal.

I did my rehearsal with the band and he turned up again.

- Everything good?
- Great. A really good band. Thank you
- I 'll show you where your dressing room is. Sorry, what's your name again?
- Colin Copperfield. [*Wanker* ☺]
- Yeah, yeah, come with me mate.

So he took me to my dressing room which made a Primark changing room seem spacious, and said,

- Can I get you anything?
- No, I am absolutely fine, thanks.
- I'll pop back later to see how you are. Sorry mate?
- Colin Copperfield. [*You thick git* ☺] You know like 'David Copperfield' but Colin instead of David. [☺*Not that you would know how to spell it, you talentless fuckwit.*]
- Yeah, of course, like in that book they made a film of, 'Pride and Prejudice' wasn't it?

[*This man's a bloody genius.* ☺]
- Why don't you write it down, Derek?

He looked very indignant.

- Write it down!? **Write it down**!? I've been compèring here for nearly eleven years and I've never had to write anybody's name down.
- [*Tosser* ☺} It's Co-lin Copp-er-field.
- Alright, mate, I'll see you later on.

At about 9.45 he knocked on the dressing room door,

- Hello there. You'll be on in about twenty minutes. Can I get you anything?
- No, absolutely fine, thanks very much, Derek.
- Run it by me again mate.
- [☺ *Lord, give me strength!*] **Colin Copperfield.**
- Alright mate, I'll give you a shout when you're on.

I was standing at the side of the stage about twenty minutes later when he announced to the audience,

- Ladies and gentlemen, we've got a new act for you this evening. He sings, he dances, he'll tell you a few jokes. Please give a big round of applause for....*Clive Chipperfield!!*

So, I went on and performed as Clive Chipperfield. Luckily, Clive's act went down pretty well. I came off stage and went to the bar. People came up to me,

- Nice act Clive, can I buy you a drink? Any records out, Clive?

That was the one and only performance by Clive Chipperfield, God bless his soul.

It's possible that, a few years later when Wall Street Crash were doing really well and appearing on TV every week, some of those who had been in that audience at Ford's for the one and only performance of Clive Chipperfield, were watching TV and saying, "Doesn't that bloke look like Clive Chipperfield? I wonder what happened to him?"

Scene Fifty-two: Pies 'ave Coom

Another club story from when I was working on my own doing a cabaret act. I got a gig at a club up north, in Eccles near Manchester. I think the club was called the Talk of the North. It was a genuine working men's club. They used to have a van that came around from the bakery in the evening, usually at around 9 o'clock, bringing hundreds of steaming hot meat pies. They would be wheeled in; everyone would buy their pies, return to their tables with them, and carry on drinking. The arrival of the *pie van* was the big event of the evening.

I was due to go onstage at about ten o'clock when the MC came up to me.

- I just wanna tell you lad, the pie van hasn't been yet.
- The pie van?
- Yeah, yeah. Everything stops for the pies. Anyway you're on in five minutes.

I had no idea what he was talking about.

I had been onstage for about ten minutes and was giving it a bit of welly when suddenly the MC walked on stage. He was like the double of Bernard Manning, the fat Northern comic. He took the microphone out of my hand and explained,

- Sorry lad. That's it for you. We'll pay you anyway.

And to the audience:

- Ladies and gentlemen, the pies 'ave coom! And could we have a big hand for…... Colin Copperfield! Thanks for coming lad. Nice act. See you again.

Everyone rushed over to get their pies and that was the end of my act. I had driven to Yorkshire to sing three songs and be upstaged by a meat pie. There's no bizness like pie bizness.

♪♫♪♫♪♫

These clubs could be tough going. I was doing my band rehearsal in another venue somewhere up north when the MC said to me,

- Aye lad, there's meant to be another act on with you tonight but they haven't turned up yet, so you might have to do a bit longer if that's alright with you. We'll give you a few quid extra.

223

- No probs.

Ten minutes later the other act arrived: two very harassed boys and a girl. Having broken down on the motorway they were full of apologies but Mister Miserable Git was having none of it.

- Well just get on with it and do your rehearsal. You'll not work 'ere again after tonight. Bloody unprofessional.

Poor buggers! They had broken down and it wasn't their fault. Steam was still coming out of the bonnet of their very tired old van. They were the opening act so I decided to watch them from the wings. Grumpy Git, the MC, went on-stage to introduce them. It was one of the biggest build-ups for an act I can ever remember..

- Right then, we've got an act for you tonight who turned up an hour late for rehearsals, so they must be crap. They say they won 'Opportunity Knocks', but they all say that don't they? Anyway, they won't be working here again. Ladies and gentlemen, 'Two Hits and a Miss'.

I felt so sorry for them. They were actually a very good act, but of course didn't stand a chance with the audience 'cos, Knobhead had set them up so badly. I did alright though, and my act went down pretty well.

As I was driving home I saw smoke rising from the hard shoulder of the motorway up ahead. 'Two Hits and a Miss' had broken down again. I slowed down, considering my options, decided there was nothing I could do, gave them a double thumbs up 👍 👍 and accelerated into the night. Always ready to help fellow thesps in need.

Scene Fifty-three: Lost in Translation

I was working at a tiny hostess club on the Charing Cross Road called the Starlight Room. I had been putting more and more comedy into my act and it seemed to be going well. I decided to tell a few more jokes between the songs and the dancing. On this particular night I was introduced in this way,

- Ladies and gentlemen, direct from performing on a round-the-world cruise where he regaled audiences with his witty repartee and vocal dexterity, this performer is heading for the top and beyond. When you see this outstanding talent you will have witnessed a performer of such magnitude you may never, ever recover from the experience. So savour the moment, count your lucky stars because tonight, here to delight you and you alone is …..

I thought, *"Who?"* This guy sounds amazing. I looked behind me, rather resentfully, to see who was about to eclipse me, but I was the only one there.

…………the one and only Colin Copperfield.

Crikey, so no pressure then!

Onstage, because the spotlight is on your face, you can never see anyone in the audience. There could be four people or four hundred. I sang a few songs and then went into my comedy routine. There was no response. Nothing. Not even a titter. I had done the same routine during the previous week and it had gone down well. I persevered. Still nothing. So I decided to go straight into a song and cued the pianist. I thought, "I don't get it but, anyway, I'll leave the gags out tonight."

I was totally confused by this. I went back to my dressing room, mulling over my abject failure. There was a knock. It was one of the girls,

- Look mate, I thought I'd better tell you. You're out there doing all these jokes, and it's a funny act. All the girls are loving it. But tonight is a corporate event. There are three hundred Japanese men sitting out there and they haven't got a fucking clue what you're talking about. I would stick to the songs if I was you.

Not to be beaten by this, I moved to Tokyo for three years, now speak fluent Japanese, am worshipped all over Japan and do my comedy act all the way from Honshū to Hokkaidō where my name (Colin Copperfield in case you've forgotten) is in lights: コリン・カッパーフィールド Yeah right!

Scene Fifty-four: Two for the Show

I was doing a musical play at the Roundhouse in Camden, in London. There are two theatres at the Roundhouse, a big stage, and a smaller theatre which seats about two hundred, where they try out new productions. I was in 'Star Encounters or May the Farce be with You', a very camp send-up of 'Close Encounters' and 'Star Wars'. I was dressed as a Luke Skywalker character with the addition of big Cuban-heeled boots. The show had been running for about four days when it came to the Saturday matinee. We were only just getting into it as we hadn't had a long rehearsal period.

The equity ruling at that time stated that if there were more people on stage than in the audience, you didn't have to do the show but would still be paid for it. On this particular Saturday we were getting ready, putting on our makeup and discussing what was right and wrong with the show. Two of the guys were in drag, so they were wearing loads of makeup.

The company manager came by and said,

- Everybody, take it easy. There are only two elderly ladies out there. Yeah! I know this sounds like the old theatrical gag but there really are only two old ladies in the audience, and one of them has a dog. You have an audience of two old ladies and a dog. You don't have to do the show.

We all looked at each other.

One of the guys said,

- Look, we've put on all this makeup. Why don't we just treat this as a rehearsal? We still have some things to sort out. We'll do the show properly. Go and have a word with the two ladies, and the dog, and ask if they want us to do this. As there will be twelve of us onstage and two in the audience, get them to come down to the front and we'll do the show for them, if they're happy with that.

The manager came back,

- Yeah, they're up for it. I think they come from 'oop north'. They've brought their sandwiches and a bottle of pop and are happy to sit and watch, especially as it's pissing down with rain outside.

227

So the two ladies and the dog moved down to the front row. The show, which was a bit raunchy, lasted for an hour and fifteen minutes. They proved to be the best audience in the world, laughing and applauding, and the dog barked along as well. At one point he got up and peed on the front of the stage (so we realised we needed to work on that bit!). They made comments all the way through the show,

- Ooh, I liked that song, Hilda!
- 'ere that woman singing now looks a bit like a bloke.
- Pass us the crisps, love.
- Ay, this is better than the bloody telly. I'm glad we came down 'ere.

We got through the whole show and they, and the dog, gave us a standing ovation at the end. We shared the rest of their sarnies, had some photos taken, gave them a backstage tour and then we all went out and waved them off. A tale to tell their grandkids. Bet that's never happened to the cast of 'Phantom of the Opera'.

Scene Fifty-five. The Phantom Trouser Dropper

My mate Dave Mackay and I had written a musical called 'Paradise Lane'. He had produced the New Seekers and Bonnie Tyler, and had had a lot of success with a number of groups in the 70s and 80s. He had also written 'That's Livin' Alright', the theme tune for 'Auf Wiedersehen Pet', for which he won the Ivor Novello. He was a good writer, Dave. While we were working on 'Paradise Lane' he mentioned that some guys might get in touch with me as they were writing a book about his career, and he asked me to give them a story.

This is what I wrote:

Great that you are writing this book about such a fantastic bloke, bless your cotton socks. In 1981 I was a member of Wall Street Crash, signed to Magnet Records. We were to make our first album and Dave was to be the producer. From the get-go we all loved Dave, a down-to-earth Aussie with a great sense of humour. During the recording sessions at Dave's studio, the Factory, in Woldingham, those of us not required to warble on a particular track would lounge, pop star fashion, around the outdoor swimming pool attached to the studio, catching the summer rays.

Siobhan was in the vocal booth and, due to nerves, was having some trouble recording her lead vocal. Dave has to be the most patient, sensitive, encouraging record producer in the universe. But, after quite a few hours of poor Siobhan sodding up the takes, Dave came out to the pool (very annoying when you're topping up your 'sort of' pop star tan) and said in his finest Aussie accent,

- *Jesus, mates, will somebody go in there and make her laugh or something, or we're going to run out of time and budget on this one track.*
  (Magnet's budget of £22.75 per track was never going to go far anyway.)

- *Col, go and make her laugh. Good on ya cobber.*
  Well, being the dedicated pro wot I am, I stripped off me trunks, strode into the vocal booth buck naked, stood next to the sobbing

229

Siobhan, put the cans on and started to sing along to the track. She laughed (whether at my manhood or my gesture I will never know), but she nailed the song on the next take. And Dave was a very happy man.

Twenty years later, having lost touch with Dave, I had an idea to write the Cockney musical, 'Paradise Lane'. I knew Dave would be the perfect person to co-write it with me, so I tracked down his number and, blow me down, after twenty years, Dave's voice was on the end of the line.

- *Dave, it's Col from Wall Street Crash..*
  expecting him to say,

- *Hello mate, I still remember those great vocals and those tricky harmonies you did and the songs you brought to life with your extraordinary talent.*
  But no! The first thing Dave said to me after twenty years was,

- *Hi mate, still dropping ya trousers and making the girls laugh?*
  It's lovely to be remembered with such reverence.

In the rough and tumble and sometimes cruel world of the music biz, Dave Mackay will always stand out as one of the good guys. A brilliant record producer and a real top bloke. Anyone who knows or who has worked with Dave will be the richer for it. GOOD ON YA MATE.

Scene Fifty-six: Whose Job is it Anyway?

When I used to go for auditions for musicals, the people running the audition would hire in a pianist. You usually had three or four minutes to go through your music with them. The pianist could make or break your audition so a lot of us would take our own audition pianists along with us.

One night, when I was doing 'Jesus Christ Superstar', I got chatting to the stage manager, Alastair. He had trained in classical piano and had also worked with rock bands. He said he read music well so I asked if he would consider doing some auditions for me. He lived in town, which was an advantage. I would go to his flat, have a brief rehearsal and warm up, and then we would go along to the audition.

A big musical called 'Mardi Gras' was coming up. They were looking for a matador-looking guy to play the lead. They had already auditioned a lot of guys. You had to be able to play flamenco guitar, sing, act and dance. I had been to two or three recalls, and it was down to me and another actor called Nicky Henson. He was a good looking chap, and a good singer. I think he was living with the actress Susan Hampshire at the time. The last auditions were at the Talk of the Town in Leicester Square. I did my audition first; I sang, danced, did an acting piece and played some flamenco. It went really well but I knew that Nicky Henson was going to get the part. He was perfect for it.

He auditioned after me, and it was clear that he was the man for the job. The director, producer and choreographer had a chat and then came over to tell me that, although I had done well to get to the last two, they were giving the part to Nicky. I agreed with them, and said so. The director said that he was sure we would work together in the future. We would stay in touch and he would call if something came up. With that, he turned to my pianist Alistair and said,

- What are you doing at the moment?
- I'm stage manager at the Palace Theatre for 'Jesus Christ Superstar'.
- Right. Could you get out of that contract? Because we are looking for a good rock pianist for the show.
- I can do that.
- Great! You're hired.

So I came out of the audition without getting the part, but my rehearsal pianist got the gig, and went on to do it!

Without being cruel to anyone, there was a slight saving grace. I decided to go and see the show at the Prince of Wales Theatre. I went along on the opening night, fully expecting it to be a good show. It was absolutely dreadful. I didn't even stay for the second half. Everyone was good in it, including Nicky Henson, but it was a really shit show. The critics slated it and it lasted for a very short time in the West End. Pheeeeew! That was a narrow escape. Of course, if they had chosen MEEEEEE, the show would have been a runaway success, and still running to this day. Wankers!

Scene Fifty-seven: Out of Time

We were doing a big TV show in Sweden. In the 80s and 90s these live TV performances were very popular. Benny Andersson was performing at this particular show. At the backstage party I was standing with my great buddy Perty.

- Oh my God, there's Benny Andersson. I grew up with Abba. They're one of my favourite bands ever. I'm in the same room with Benny Andersson!

He was droning on and on.

At that moment I caught Benny Andersson's eye,

- Perty, Perty! Benny's walking over this way!

Perty was like an excited child.

Benny said,

- Hey guys, I love your group, I watched the rehearsal and enjoyed your harmonies. As you know, in Abba we also love harmonies. I was so impressed by you, and hope to see a lot more of you in Sweden.

With that, Perty, who was swooning to be in the presence of pop royalty, and blushing with excitement, turned to Benny and said (the sycophantic creep),

- Thank you Benny. That means more than the world, coming from you Benny.

And then, by way of trying to ingratiate himself still further, Perty added,

- You know, that musical you wrote, 'Time', was absolutely brilliant and I've lost count of the number of times I went to see it.

There was a weighty silence.

The problem was that Benny didn't write 'Time'. And musicians are particularly sensitive about being properly credited for their work.

A shadow crossed his face and he looked at Perty,

- I didn't write 'Time'.

(Of course, my idiot best friend meant 'Chess', which Benny *had* written but which not only had Perty never seen but had never heard of.)

Benny turned and walked away. I can't be certain, but I think I heard him mutter under his breath (in Swedish of course),

- Stupid bloody thick English wanker.

For Perty it was that John Cleese moment. He put his head in his hands and sank to the floor. It had been his once-in-a-lifetime opportunity to impress his hero and he had totally blown it.

What's really funny, and I think a little revealing, is that none of us *ever* lost our 'starstruckness' (I know that's not a real word, OK?). No matter how much success we had, whenever we worked with a famous performer or group we would come over all unnecessary and 'groupiefied' (I know that's not a real word either). Sometimes we would be topping the bill *above* our heroes and we would still be nudging each other and saying,

- Bloody hell! Can you believe this? Get *us*!

Some years later we were doing a TV show in Amsterdam and Anni-Frid Lyngstad was also on the show. Abba had split and she was now promoting her solo career. Perty was of course beside himself with excitement and was desperate to meet her, possibly to apologise for his cock-up with Benny, which of course he would have blamed on me anyway. We hung around the corridor outside her dressing room which was next to ours, under the pretence of vocally warming up for our camera rehearsal, but there was no sign of Anni. Our renditions became more and more strident, and we moved closer and closer to her door, but she did not emerge. Maybe Benny had warned her that, if she ever came across Wall Street Crash on her travels, she should give us a very wide berth, especially the tall good looking one, who was clearly not the sharpest tool in the box. With that we were called to the set to rehearse.

Perty was looking very glum.

- Hopefully she'll watch our rehearsal, be bowled over by our fab close harmony work, and insist on meeting us. (Incidentally, we were called a 'close harmony group' because, when we sang, people said, "Erm…. close!").

Onto the set we went.

The director said,

- For the moment, just do your songs so that the production team and the camera crew can check out the choreography and staging, then we'll do a camera script and have another rehearsal later before the live show.

All of this we did but, disappointingly, there was still no sign of Anni-Frid. Was she tired and resting in her dressing room? Was she in make-up? Was she rehearsing in another studio? OR, was she hiding from Wall Street Crash, and in particular, from my bezzy mate Perty, who didn't know 'Time' from 'Chess' or, to be honest, his arse from his elbow. We returned to our dressing room, and continued our onslaught by making an even bigger vocal demonstration outside Anni's room. It was just possible that she would throw open the door and exclaim,

- My God, I have never heard such incredible singing in my whole career.

Then, realising it was 'us of the fab harmonies', she would introduce herself and we would become lifelong friends…

Nothing! Notera! Zilch!

That evening we did the live show and were at our fabbest razor-sharp best, with rocking choreography, precision harmonies, and our trademark scintillating personalities at high octane. Anni was the next act on and was waiting at the side of the set (waiting, of course, to be introduced to the audience by the compère when we had finished our act). In the middle of our final song, as I was performing a sharp piece of dancing with Marge, I glanced stage right, knowing she must be watching. No, she was farting around with her hair in a makeup mirror. "Her loss", I petulantly thought, as Marge and I carried on being over-brilliant. OK then! At the after-show knees-up party Anni would be certain to rush over to us, gushy with admiration, and try to wheedle her way into *our* group, now that she no longer had one of her own. We hung around, and around. And *around* midnight it was clear that Anni was not coming, not now, not ever. Never. Upon reflection, taking everything into account…would we ever meet Anni-Frid? Would Benny ever forgive Perty? Well, maybe it's just a matter of Time…SORRY, a matter of Chess!

Scene Fifty-eight: Suspended Animation

Wall Street Crash were asked to do a New Year's Eve gig in St Moritz. It ended up being a really bizarre journey. We flew out from London, just the group with no musicians. We landed in Frankfurt where we picked up an orchestra of German musicians. We then boarded a coach and drove to Lichtenstein (which I had never heard of) and had a rehearsal with the orchestra. The next day we headed off to St Moritz for a one-night gig.

On the way we were caught in a huge snowstorm. We were all terrified. The driver was fantastic and we got there safely. We had another rehearsal in St Moritz and that night, New Year's Eve, we did the gig. Everything gelled like it sometimes does and it was brilliant. We had to get back to Lichtenstein the next day to drop the band off and we were then due to fly from Hamburg to Amsterdam. The driver came to the dressing room after the gig, looking rather concerned. He said that he was aware of our deadline but he thought we should know that the roads were treacherous. He said we could wait until the morning but it would be cutting it fine, or we could risk it. It was down to us. He would drive us, but it was our decision.

We discussed it with the orchestra. They also had a gig on the next night. We decided to go for it. Before we left we loaded the bus with lots of alcohol to lessen the pain. We were soon very jolly and all having a good old singsong with the orchestra. By about four o'clock in the morning we had fallen into a drunken stupor when the coach stopped very abruptly. This woke us all up.

- What's happening?
- Nobody move. Stay where you are.

The driver got out of the bus and came back a few moments later.

- Look, there's a car in front of us. There's been nothing on the road for the last three hours, but this car is hanging over the side of the cliff, suspended over a sheer vertical drop. It's only just happened. There are people in the car. They have climbed into the back seat and the car is balancing on the edge.

This seemed just like 'The Italian Job'.

The driver said we should try to pull the car away from the drop. There were a lot of us: a ten-piece orchestra, the five of us and the sound guy. So we all got out, still somewhat inebriated, and we practically lifted the car away from the cliff edge and onto the road. As we were doing this, parts of the cliff were coming away. There was no way anyone could have survived if the car had gone over. Our driver alerted the rescue services and we left them there to freeze to death. We tossed them a few blankets to assuage our consciences and hoped they could hang on long enough.

Seriously though, we were a bit shaken by the whole experience. It took another three and a half hours to get down those treacherous roads, with precipitous drops on either side, and on to Lichtenstein where we parted from the orchestra, and then to Hamburg.

We never knew if they survived and frankly we didn't care. For sure, if we had left them a couple of WSC CDs they would have thrown themselves into the abyss anyway.

Scene Fifty-nine: The Sauna the Better

Wall Street Crash were doing very well in Holland where we had a big following. Our audiences enjoyed the theatricality of our performances. This drove the record companies mad because we would record songs as singles and, as we all came from the theatre, the first thing we would think about was how to stage them. They would come along to see the show and say,

- Why do you record all of these commercial songs and then go onstage and turn them into three-act fucking dramas? It doesn't sell the records.
- Piss off, dear. We're from the theatre, we're *thespians* you know.

Our elaborate theatricality probably did us no good whatsoever, but it was who we were.

Anyway, we always had huge audiences in Holland. We used to fly back there often, sometimes two or three times a week. If we were working in Amsterdam we stayed at the Golden Tulip Hotel which was next to Schiphol Airport so that the air commute would be easier. It was a nice hotel and had a small gym in the basement. I used to go there to work out before we did our sound check. None of the others in the group was remotely interested in exercise, so I was always there on my own. For months I went to the gym and never saw another person. The sauna hadn't been working for all of that time. One day I went to reception and asked why that was. The answer was that it was a business hotel and there was no demand for the sauna but the receptionist said that, because we were there nearly every week, she would have it turned on if I called the day before we were due to arrive. So that is what happened. From then on I had my own private sauna.

One day I was lying there, butt naked, contemplating the world, when I heard a cacophony in Japanese. With that, the doors to the sauna swished open, and in came about fourteen gorgeous Japanese girls, completely naked. Being a 'sort-of' pop star, I didn't want to leap up and coyly grab my towel. I thought I should front this out, in more ways than one. So I gradually sat up and assumed an appropriately pop star demeanour, or whatever I thought might pass as very cool. They came and sat all around me, chatting incessantly: 私たちと一緒にサウナに座っている格好良いスタッドは誰ですか？ 彼と折り紙を作

りたい[22] This went on for about five minutes, with all of them jabbering on in Japanese when one girl turned to me and said,

- You here on vacation?
- No, no. I'm working.
- Ah-so, you working! What job you do?
- I am a singer with a band. We're doing a concert in Amsterdam tonight.

She turned to the other girls and a lively conversation ensued.

- My friends say, where you do concert tonight? Maybe we come along.
- Well, I can see if there are any tickets. I think it's sold out but I'll see what I can do. But tell me, what are you all doing here? I've been coming to this gym for ages and no one else has even come in before.
- We flight attendants on Japanese Airlines, and flight go technical so we have to land in Amsterdam. We always fly straight from Tokyo to London or New York but never come to Netherlands. But plane is mechakucha[23] so we here overnight so they fix plane. We would love to see concert, OK?
- I will have a word with the guys but, yes, I'm sure we can fit you in somewhere. You may have to stand on the side, but we'll get you in.
- Oh! Thank you (a rapid flurry of Japanese, almost certainly extolling my attributes).
- No problem. Tell me your name,
- My name Shinko. Shinko my name.
- OK Shinko, I will leave the address at reception. Come along at 7.30 and I will get you in to see the show.

With that, I thought that the time had come to stand up and walk past all of these gorgeous ladies. So, reminding myself of my 'sort of' pop star status, I stood up and walked out brazenly. I think they gasped, "Oh, oh, oh!" and a couple of them almost fainted - and not because of the heat of the sauna. (*In*

---

22 Who is the cool stud sitting in the sauna with us? I'd like to do some origami with him.

23 The F-word in Japanese (which of course I would never use, especially not in Japanese).

my dreams, that bit!) As Japan is a country dedicated to martial arts, maybe they had seen my judo commercial for Tunes (for which I got *repeat fees*, you know), but I don't remember receiving any repeat fees in yen.

When I went to the gig that night I said to our tour manager, Mark Endlich,

- Mark, this is a bit of a long shot but it's possible that fourteen or fifteen Japanese air stewardesses may turn up at 7.30. Is there any chance of getting them in?
- Well, we're sold out but let me have a word with Dickie.

Dickie was our sound engineer. The sound desk was always three quarters of the way down the auditorium so that he could hear the sound quality out front. The seats around the desk were always kept empty because the sight lines weren't very good.

Mark said,

- Maybe the girls can sit near Dickie. He'll love it. Let me find out.

He came back a few minutes later,

- All cool. I've had a word with Dickie. He loves the idea of having a bunch of Japanese flight attendants sitting near him so that he can show off.
- Fine, thanks. They probably won't turn up, but thanks anyway.

A bit later I was in the dressing room, putting on the usual vast amounts of makeup, when Mark came in.

- You won't believe this. They've all turned up, the Japanese girls. I've taken them in; they're sitting with Dickie and they can see quite well. Dickie is over the moon because he can spend the night flirting.

The gig went very well. Mark came backstage,

- The girls want to come back to thank you.
- Great, just let me have a shower and change.

When the girls came back they said how much they had enjoyed the show but, when I first came on, they didn't recognise me with my clothes on. It turned out that they had never been to Amsterdam and wanted to see the town. Ten of them were working flight attendants and the other four were passengering flight attendants (at least that was as much as I could decipher). I suggested to the band that we all go out together. They thought that was a great idea so off we trooped around Amsterdam with this gorgeous group of girls.

Amsterdam has places called coffee bars which are actually drug bars. You can't buy alcohol, but there is a menu for the various kinds of dope: 'Red Lebanese', 'Black Russian' and so on. You make your selection and order it just as you would in a coffee bar. They bring it to your table and you can test various brands. We invited the girls to one of these bars, explaining that they are famous in Holland.

- Oh yes! We like do that. What we do? We smoke marijuana?

So we took them to a coffee bar and they really got into it, puffing away on huge joints. Everyone got completely stoned, apart from me as my body is my temple. (Total bullshit, we were *all* off our trolleys.)

As all of us in the band were from London we used to talk to each other in Cockney rhyming slang without even thinking about it. One of the Japanese girls, who spoke very good English, said,

- Sometimes I don't understand *what* you are saying to each other.

We hadn't realised we were doing it as it had become second nature, especially if we didn't want people to know what we were talking about. So, we decided to give the girls a crash course. Apples and pears = stairs, frog and toad = road, cherry pips = lips, mince pies = eyes, etc, etc.

We explained that it was important only to use the first part of the rhyme, so: going down the frog and up the apples = down the road and up the stairs. They soon got the hang of it. It was hilarious hearing Cockney rhyming slang in a Japanese accent. So then we got a bit naughtier and taught them orchestra stalls = balls, and Khyber Pass = arse. They loved it! We assured them that if they ever had difficult Londoners on their flight they should tell them to "Stick their orchestras up their Khybers and behave themselves". It's entirely possible we got some of these girls from JAL sacked for inappropriate behaviour...Ah-so! We then went on a tour of the red light district, a trip along the canals, and we danced to a rock band in the open air in Dam Square where they were all body popping while singing "Stick your orchestras up your Khyber". At the end of the evening we stumbled into about eight taxis and collapsed into our (own!) rooms at the hotel. Early the next morning a note was slipped under my door. It read:

- 'Tech problems fixed. On our way to airport.
  Thank you all for the best day of our lives.'
  Love, your JAL birds, flying away on a quiche
  (*quiche lorraine = plane*).
  Sayonara! xxxxxxxxxx

Well, when you think about it, they saw a really good concert, learned filthy rhyming slang, visited the red light area, inhaled a few spliffs, danced in Dam Square, and saw a 'sort of' pop star bollock naked. Not a bad day and night out for anyone.

Scene Sixty: The Italian 'Award' Job

In 1983 Wall Street Crash had a huge surprise top ten hit in Italy: our cover version of the old Dusty Springfield hit 'You don't have to say you love me' which, as I mentioned earlier, we sang half in Italian and half in English. It was chosen as the theme song on the prime time Canale Cinque (Channel Five) TV show, 'Attenti a Noi Due', which went to air throughout the network at 8p.m. every Saturday evening. We filmed the song in Milan. The show was a massive hit and, luckily, so were we.

Suddenly we went from complete unknowns to one of the most famous groups in Italy. We appeared on every pop music TV show, were photographed endless times, received very flattering write-ups in every magazine, and performed gigs all over the country. It was a professional whirlwind.

The Silver Cat, the TV equivalent of the Brits, was the top music award in the country. The winner was chosen by public vote, 'Vota la Voce' (Vote the Voice). In 1983 we won the award for the best group, and Robert Palmer was top solo vocalist. There were many other awards for film scores and so on. The presentation show was to be held in Verona, in its famous Roman amphitheatre. On the day of the awards we were doing lots of TV promotion and were rushing from one studio to another at breakneck speed; we would dash into a studio, perform the song, leap into the transport, go to another studio, perform the song again, and so on all day long without a break. The time for the award presentation, which was going out live all over Italy, was getting closer and closer. We were on our way but we could tell that our driver was getting a bit edgy, so we asked him if everything was OK. In an inventive combination of English and Italian, he informed us,

- We molto retardo coz of uno fucking incidente in autostrada. Now we up cascado torrente (*shit creek*), senza uno paddle.
- Oh dear! What the hell are we gonna do Giovanni?
- Come il fuck do I know? Sono not fucking chiaroveggente.

We assumed this meant "clairvoyant"! Whatever it meant it didn't seem very reassuring. We were stuck in a fifteen-mile long traffic jam that was going nowhere fast (or slow), and we were due to perform our huge hit live to the whole of Italy in thirty minutes. Beam me up Scotty!

- Giovanni, I said, in a panic-stricken falsetto voice, drive up onto the hard shoulder, then motor as fast as you can. If we are stopped by the cops, the TV station will pay the fines (*and we will visit you in prison sometime in the next ten years*).

Giovanni nodded gleefully, metamorphosed into Lewis Hamilton, floored the accelerator and the limo turned into the car from 'Back to the Future'. Wooosh! We were burning rubber like crazy and all whooping and hollering Giovanni on,

- C'mon a fuckeen Giovanni, give it some fuckeen welly.

Next thing, blue lights were flashing all over the place and we were surrounded by Italian motorcycle police. We slowed from 170 mph to a screeching halt, and realised our lasagne was well and truly cooked. Bugger! So close yet so far away. Giovanni wound down his window and was offering his wrists to be cuffed when, Mother of all Italian Gods, the lead cop leaned towards the window and recognised Marge. Marge, never slow on the uptake, started flirting with him at warp factor fifty. Giovanni explained our fate to the now fully erect policeman, lots of shouting in Italian ensued, and suddenly all of the engines kicked into life and we were off, speeding along the hard shoulder with an eight-piece police motorcycle escort, flashing blue lights, sirens, the lot.

We made it to the centre of Verona with minutes to spare. At the amphitheatre they were waiting for us (the police had radioed ahead). We were whisked through the labyrinth of tunnels under the stage, directed towards a ten-foot square moveable platform and, as the intro to our song began, we were lifted up to be greeted by fifteen thousand screaming fans holding their lighter flames into the night sky and all singing along with us,

- ♪ Io che non vivo senza te

(The YouTube video shows how stunned we all were.)

We were presented with our awards. I don't think Marge let the motorcycle cop have his wicked way with her but, if she had, he would certainly have deserved it. What a fantastic fuckeen day.

Scene Sixty-one: Red Light Lady

The Wallies had done quite a few tours of Holland and were getting more and more popular there. We always stayed in very nice hotels. After a gig, we would come back on the coach and would invariably end up in the hotel room, open the minibar and watch TV. It was a novelty at first but after a while it became a bit of a downer. So we asked Gerry if we could rent an apartment or a house in Amsterdam for the next tour, which was due to last two months.

- Let me get back to you Dolly. (He always called everyone Dolly)

The next day he announced,

- I've done it. There's a hotel called the Mercury Hotel. It's a nice place on a canal and the hotel has apartments attached to it. You will each have your own one.

Marvellous! So, off we went to Holland and moved into our apartments. We bought flowers, even added our names to the doors and settled into our new home. On the first day I went to reception. There was a lovely girl there. Her name was Annameke.

- Hi, I'm Col. I'm with Wall Street Crash and we'll be here for two months. We will probably be getting mail while we are here. What's the situation?
- No problem. There are pigeon holes here at reception for the apartments.

We had been there a couple of weeks. At lunchtime we and the musicians would leave for the evening's gig on the 'magic bus' as we called it, the tour bus. Because we occasionally had to go quite a distance to a gig, the bus was well-equipped, with a kitchen, bunk beds and a TV room at the back. There would be lunch waiting for us on the bus, with tables set, a chef and a couple of waitresses on hand. It was a very civilised way to travel. The musicians spent most of their time in the TV room, watching 'funny' movies. Apart from our own pianist, drummer and bass guitar player we used Dutch musicians, the best in Holland, a great band. They could play brilliantly, stoned, very stoned or completely stoned - totally versatile.

We used to go on stage, do the gig, have a quick shower and get back onto the magic bus. Candles would be lit on the tables and we would set off home. The fans would run after the bus, like in one of those pop movies, crying out and screaming, while we were sitting at our tables having our first glass of wine and about to have dinner. If the travel time was an hour, it was perfect. We had time to have dinner, settle down, maybe watch some TV and have a bit of a sing song (I think we did some of our best vocal work on the bus but, when you're three parts pissed, I suppose anything sounds good) before returning to our apartments, and bed.

Most mornings, when I went down to the lobby, I would be greeted by Annameke. We got on very well. One Saturday night we did a big gig near the Belgian border arriving back at about 3a.m., when everyone went to bed. The next morning I woke up early for some reason. Everyone else was asleep so I decided to go for a run.

It was about 10a.m. by then, and I ended up in the red light area, which was close to our apartments (this wasn't intentional!). The girls were sitting in their windows, waiting for customers. I saw a girl waving at me and thought she was just waving to attract punters so, being courteous, I waved back. She carried on waving, and I carried on waving back. She was wearing the full kit, suspenders and the works. She beckoned me over to the window. Something was telling me that this wasn't the usual come-on so, rather sheepishly, I went over.

- Hi, Colin, how are you?

It was Annameke the receptionist from the hotel.

- Annameke! What are you doing here?

Stupid question, plonker, as it was perfectly obvious what she was doing there.

- Oh, I moonlight here to earn some extra money.
- If the hotel found out, wouldn't you get the sack?
- No, no, Holland is a very liberal country. Half the male staff come down here in the evenings to see the girls. It isn't a problem at all. Well, enjoy your run! Would you like to come in before you continue?
- No, no! No, no, darling, thank you *very* much. I'd better get on.

And that was that.

The next morning I came down to get on the magic bus.

- Good morning, Annameke.
- Good morning, Colin, three letters for you today, have a good gig.

It was as if our early morning encounter in the red light district had been the most natural thing in the world. And who's to say it wasn't?

Scene Sixty-two: A Dutch Treat with Mad Ron

Mad Ronald Sommer, WSC's Dutch record producer, was so called because... well, quite frankly...he was mad.. but mad in the most funny, talented, impossible way. Mad Ron was producing our album 'No Strings Attached' at his studio, Summerlance, in Zeist, just outside Amsterdam. He was assisted on the album by his co-producer 'What's my note?' Marcel Schimscheimer a musical genius and a stonking Bass guitarist. We originally intended to record the album at Wisselord Studios in Hillversum, which was used by all the top artists like Elton John. However, we had already worked with Ron on our single, 'Music Man', and we found Summerlance a more relaxing location so we suggested to Phonogram, our record label, that we would get faster and better results there.

Mad was not only the handsomest dude on the block, tall and with a shock of long black hair and a mid-Atlantic accent, but he was also the coolest. I well remember one evening taking a break in recording (which was rare in itself as Mad never wanted to stop recording for anything), and going to a nearby restaurant. In the car park was a very, very attractive girl who was having trouble reversing her sports car into an impossibly tight parking space. Wearing a beautiful full length black leather coat and knee length riding boots, his long black locks blowing in the evening breeze, Mad sauntered over to the panicking gorgeous creature, knocked on her window and asked if he could help. The vision of loveliness looked up at Ron and nearly fainted at the sight of this hunk of manhood and his smooth but raw charm.

- Yes please,

she simpered.

She slipped out of her car and Ron, like the superhero he is, eased in. He drove the car forward at eighty-five miles an hour then reversed it at ninety-five miles an hour straight into the space with less than a centimetre on either side (this is no exaggeration). Steve McQueen's driving skills in 'Bullitt' paled into insignificance. Had Steve witnessed this feat of off-the-scale driving, he would have willingly handed his 'king of cool' crown to Mad. Mad climbed out of the car (by way of the sun roof) as nimbly as he had entered it. I swear he had grown even taller and more handsome in the twenty-eight seconds it had taken him to park the Porsche. The stunning Dutch girl, now on the verge of climax, sighed,

- I don't know how to thank you (*but I bet she had at least one good idea*). May I buy you a drink?
- Thank you. You're very kind, but I'm about to have dinner with my friends. Nice meeting you.

He handed her the keys, gave her a last melting look, turned on his heels and walked like a god into the restaurant. She gazed after him with lust-filled longing while we trailed after him lamely, in awe of the sex-charged atmosphere he had created so effortlessly.

I felt sick with jealousy and bitterness. You may think me cruel, Dear Reader, but, in my heart of hearts and as much as I loved Mad, at that moment I was secretly hoping that maybe, just maybe, he suffered from some form of untreatable dysfunction of the intimate kind or, at the very least, was the owner of a tiny member. Even though we were 'sort of' pop stars we knew we were in the presence of a far greater being (pass the bucket!).

Mad had some quirky eccentricities. He would say, if we were looking a bit tired after singing for fourteen hours non-stop (not that he really gave a monkey's, as I don't think he had bothered himself with sleep since his third birthday),

- Hey guys, you tired? Need twenty winks?
- Ron, it's forty winks!
- Y'know, you guys're not professional!
- Mad! We've been in this bloody vocal booth for half a day without a break. Yeah let's stop and catch forty winks.
- Not professional!
- Mad can we just have a pee break? We haven't had one for nine hours.
- Y'know you guys're not professional. Colboy sing that harmony line two octaves higher.
- I can't sing that high, Mad! Maria Callas couldn't sing that high, Barry Gibb can't sing that high, Tiny Tim couldn't sing that high.
- Y'know, you're not professional!
- No! I haven't been castrated either. Yet!

It wasn't that Mad actually thought that we were unprofessional; he *actually* thought that we were the dog's bollocks. It was just part of Mad's 'wonderful madness'.

We were recording 'No Strings' while also doing a long tour of Holland so there was never any down time. Sometimes we would get back from a gig at 4.30a.m. and be singing in the studio at 8a.m.

It was rare not to be gigging on a Saturday night but on one miraculous weekend we didn't have a concert on Saturday and Mad was off recording with some other artistes and probably telling *them* that they weren't professional, which meant that we weren't recording on the Sunday either. Yippee! A whole weekend off. The rest of the Wallies had their other halves coming over for the weekend but Kathy, my girlfriend, couldn't join us because of work commitments. I didn't want to play gooseberry, so for that weekend I was going to be 'Colboy no mates'. OK! I'll go out on the razzle on my own. Batten down the hatches, Amsterdam, here I come!

After visiting a few bars, I was wandering down a side street adjacent to one of the canals when I heard the most amazing singing from a bar that was heaving with people, the overflow spilling out onto the street. Right! This is the place for me. I fought my way inside and propped myself up at the crowded bar, ordered myself a 'Duvel', one of the strongest beers in the world (three Duvels and you remain pissed for at least a month). I took a swig and turned around to face the tiny stage to discover who was singing. The amazing voice belonged to one René Froger. WOW! What a set of vocal cords. He had a massive range, incredible musicality and was so powerful I think you could have heard him in Buenos Aires, without a microphone. I was mesmerised. But what is this incredible talent doing on a stage the size of a postage stamp in a backstreet bar in Amsterdam? He should be headlining in Vegas. As I pondered this mystery I noticed that 'the voice' was looking at me and giving me the thumbs up. I looked over my shoulder in case I was mistaken, but no, he was definitely gesturing to me. I returned the thumbs up back, and poured some more Duvel down my throat. When he had finished his set he came straight over to me, shook my hand and introduced himself,

- Hi! I'm René Froger, and I'm a massive fan of Wall Street Crash. I've seen you in concert many times and I can't believe you're here, in my bar.

- Great to meet you René. Wow! So this is *your* bar?
- Well it's actually my dad's. He was a famous accordion player here in the Netherlands and when he retired he bought this place and named it the Accordion Bar.
- René, with the greatest respect to your dad's bar, and clearly the crowd love you, I can't believe a singer of your calibre is wasting his time up on that tiny stage singing to backing tracks. You should be in America! You should be everywhere.
- Colin I just can't seem to make a breakthrough. I don't have a record deal or an agent so I sing here, work behind the bar and live in hope. If you have any suggestions or can help in any way I would be very grateful. I'd love to chat later but I've got to do my next set now. The bar's heaving and we're short of staff so I'll have to cut my act short and get back behind the bar.
- Rene, don't cut your act. If you want me to, I'll work behind the bar. I've pulled plenty of pints working in pubs when showbiz work was a bit thin on the ground. Just show me how the till works and you get back on the stage and give it some welly. They love you here. Don't cut them short.
- Really?
- Really! Have a good one.

Thirty minutes later I was getting into my top Amsterdam barman stride. Suddenly I was Tom Cruise in the film 'Cocktail', juggling with the bottles, throwing them in the air and catching them behind my back, dropping them onto my foot, kicking them up, jumping, and catching them mid-air. My new adoring Dutch bar friends thought I was FAB! René was belting out the ballads and went straight into some heart thumping rock numbers. The bar was hot and so was I. Then lo and behold who should walk into *my* bar? The Wallies and their partners. I saw them before they saw me. When they finally struggled through the heaving throng of *my* two hundred new best friends to reach the bar, I popped up like a Jack-in-the-box from my behind-the-bar-position and asked,

- What can I get you folks?

They stared in stunned silence.

- Of all the gin joints in all the towns in all the world, you have to walk into mine.

Humphrey Bogart impressions were not my strong point but they got the gist. The last time they had seen me I was Colboy-no-mates. Now I was the Bar Room God of Amsterdam (modesty has never been my strong point).

- Bloody hell! What are you doing *here?*
- Oh you know...making a living.

René finished his brilliant set and I introduced him to the Wallies and their squeezes. He was in his element. More Duvels flowed and a great night was had by all.

And that's how René Froger came into my life. The next time we were in the studio I asked Mad if he had heard of the Accordion Bar. He said that he had and told me about René's famous dad. I mentioned René and his fantastic voice and Mad said that the next time he was in Amsterdam he would check him out. I thought no more about it, put my 'cans' (headphones) on my head and prepared to sing for the next eighteen hours hoping that Mad wouldn't ball me out for being unprofessional, well, at least not more than twenty times during the course of the next 36 hours.

After a few weeks gigging around Italy we returned to Mad's studio to finish off 'No Strings'. We walked into the control room and who was in the vocal booth recording his first single and album? You guessed it. Mr. René Froger. René went on to become, and to this day still is, one of the biggest stars of the Netherlands and became a household name all over Europe.

At this stage I have to say that I claim no credit for René's well deserved success. Even if I had not mentioned him to Mad, it would only have been a matter of time before he cracked it. A talent as big as that, with a bit of luck along the way, will always win through eventually.

Back in the UK I received a call from Mad.

- Colboy we need a new song for René to record. We want it to be like 'New York, New York' but about Amsterdam. If I send you the backing track, will you write the song?

And so I wrote 'Amsterdam (My Lady)'. I recorded a rough demo in my home studio and sent it back to Mad. It became the B side of his next single and one of the tracks on his platinum selling album.

On our next trip to Holland, Mad took us to René's sold-out concert. He got to the third number and said to the audience,

- Ladies and gentlemen In the audience tonight is a dear friend of mine. He wrote this next song for me and I would like to thank him from the bottom of my heart. Please put the spotlight on him. And give the biggest round of applause for my pal, Colin Copperfield.

The spotlight came on me, the whole audience applauded and cheered. I must confess I had a lump in my throat and slightly moist eyes. What a great moment. Thanks René.

As I mentioned before, René still has a cracking career. I would like to think that if ever my luck goes tits up, there will always be a job for me behind René's dad's bar in Amsterdam.

Scene Sixty-three: Right Song, Wrong Trousers

We ended every WSC show with a swing medley which had been brilliantly arranged by Keith Strachan. The theme of one particular medley was that I, as the bozo of the group, was always getting the song wrong, so Polly would chastise me and sing,

> - It's the wrong song, in the wrong place,
>   though your voice is charming,
>   not in this case, etc. ♪♫

Everyone loved WSC's cleverly constructed piece called 'It Don't Mean a Thing if it Ain't Got That Swing'. At the end, I would finally get it right and all the audience would cheer because the little guy, the underdog, had cracked it. It was great fun and always went down really well. We all wore white tails for this number and it was a very quick change to get into them. While Polly was singing the intro the rest of us would dash off both sides of the stage, where our costumes (or 'frocks' as we always called them) would be lined up ready for us to leap into. On tour our wardrobe department would set out our frocks before the show. One night in Amsterdam Polly went into his usual singing intro and we all rushed off-stage, Marge and me stage left, and Perty and Mandy stage right. As I scrambled into my trousers, I noticed that they felt a bit baggy and more than a bit long. The horror hit me like a cannonball. I had Perty's trousers, so he must have mine. He was on the other side of the stage and there was no time to run round and swap them over. (Wardrobe had taken our frocks to the cleaners and they had been put back on the wrong hangers.) Perty is 6' 2" and I'm 5' 6", Perty weighs 13 stone and I weigh 9 stone 7 wringing wet. We were fucked. Polly was coming to the end of his bit and we were about to get the big drum roll intro, our cue to run on and give it our all.

Polly, singing,

> - There's something else that makes the tune complete. ♪♫

Drums:

> Bash bash bash bash bash bash....

On we come. Perty is wearing my trousers which reach to just below his knees, the waist gaping open where he couldn't fasten it, and I am stumbling along in Perty's trousers which hang eighteen inches off the bottom of my feet, gripping the waist desperately with my spare hand in an attempt to keep them up. This medley lasts for approximately eight minutes and involves a lot of clever choreography and tricky microphone changes. Within ten seconds, the audience were rolling in the aisles; the whole show had turned into a circus clown performance with Perty running around like a blue-arsed fly with his pale legs and belly hanging out of my trousers (I have to say here, my bezzy mate has got lovely legs, and a very toned tum, but not in *my* trousers) and me tripping arse over tit, dropping my microphone, hauling Pert's strides up, just for them to fall down again. Mandy and Marge were doing their best to help us, but it was futile. We were doomed. You couldn't have written a better slapstick comedy routine. All we needed were red noses, and flowers on our lapels squirting water in each other's faces. By the time we had reached the end of the medley, the audience were sobbing with laughter. This *really* classy, sophisticated, vocal harmony, performance group was actually a touring comedy show.

That performance got more encores than any other show we performed. Hang on a minute, maybe that's the act we should always have done; maybe we would still be on tour now?

I used to make up an impromptu poem at the end of every show. This was the poem for that night:

- I've sung swing in Nairobi, I've sung swing in Gibraltar,
  I've sung swing making love on a bed filled with water,
  I've sung swing in cheap flats and in luxury houses.
  but I've never sung swing in someone else's trousers.

I don't think Sir John Betjeman would have felt his career was threatened by me, but the ad-lib poems always got a good response from the audience.

Scene Sixty-four: Tony Christie's Head

Tony Christie was and still is a fantastic singer. He has the vocal range and power of Tom Jones. Tony had a massive hit in 1971 with 'Is This the Way to Amarillo' (later a big hit video for Comic Relief in 2005, in which Peter Kay mimed to Tony's voice).

WSC were to appear on a German TV show with him, I think it was in Frankfurt. We arrived at the studio early and wandered onto the set to have a look around and to get the feel of the place. The backdrop of the set was a huge fifty-foot square photo of the Wallies and next to us the same size photo of Tony Christie. As we were standing admiring how fab we looked in such large scale Polly (he of the observant eye) said to me,

- Colboy, what do you notice about the Tony Christie photo?

I stared at it but couldn't see anything untoward; it was just a full length photo of Tony looking his usual handsome self, wearing black trousers and a black shirt.

- Nah! I give up mate, what is it?
- That photo is of Tony's head superimposed on your body
- Bloody hell, so it is. But why?

I mean, OK so I'd worked out a bit over the years and of course being a dancer my bod was in pretty good nick but, as far as I could remember so was Tony's. So why replace his body with mine? It was a mystery. We were all puzzling about this phenomenon when into the studio walked the man himself, with his *own* body attached to his *own* head, looking for all the world....well....normal. As he was walking toward us I said to the other Wallies but especially to Polly who, as we know, isn't the most retiring of blokes.

- Don't say anything to him.

Yeah! As if Polly was going to listen to me. Right off the bat, Polly welcomed the bodyless photo'd one,

- Hi Tony how's it going?

Not waiting for a reply.

- 'ere Tone, just a little quiz question for you, mate. What do you notice about your photo up there?

Tony was a little taken aback by this strange greeting and started to introduce himself to us. Polly was having none of it.

- No, seriously Tone, does anything strike you as odd about your photo?

Realising that Polly was seemingly a sandwich short of a picnic, Tony looked up at the mammoth photo hanging from the set. He perused it for a while then declared,

- Yeah! I sort of see what you mean but I can't put my finger on it. I've only just had these photos taken and I haven't had a chance to look at them yet.
- No. Exactly, mate. That's because it's your head, I think we can safely all agree on that but, by some quirk of magic, it's sitting on top of Colboy's body.

Tony looked at me, looked at the photo, looked at me, looked at the photo... we all looked at Tony, Tony looked at us and we all started killing ourselves laughing.

The director appeared on the set and all was revealed. The TV production office had asked Tony's management for a photo and they assumed it was a head and shoulders shot that was needed so that's what they sent. By the time it arrived it was too late to have a full body shot sent out so they looked at our shot, decided that I had the closest matching body and the editing scissors went into action.

Everyone saw the funny side of it and we desperately tried to persuade the director to have Tony sing ♪♫ 'I ain't got no body' ♪♫ on the show but of course that might have been too much of an in-joke.

It would be interesting to know if any eagle-eyed German viewers ever noticed the deliberate mistake.

Scene Sixty-five: Anyone for Shakespeare?

My old acting agent was Keith Whittle (known to one and all as Kitty, because he was as gay as a French horn). He said to me one day, before Wall Street Crash,

- It's all very well doing these musicals, dear, but you need to get some straight acting work under your belt. Coventry Rep are doing three productions. I've spoken to them. They have seen you in 'Superstar', and they would be very happy for you to play Judas in 'Godspell'. There's a Peter Shaffer play called 'The Bed Before Yesterday' in which there's quite a small part of a taxi driver. He's only in the first scene but it's a nice scene. And then they are doing 'Twelfth Night', and this is the one we want. We want to see some Shakespeare on your resumé dear. The audition is tomorrow at Cecil Sharp House in London, so go along and be bona dear.

So along I went. There were about five or six people sitting at a table, among them the director and the producer.

- Colin, thanks for coming along. We saw you in 'Jesus Christ Superstar' and we think you're great to play Judas in 'Godspell'. 'The Bed Before Yesterday' isn't a big part but it's a nice little part. Now, 'Twelfth Night'. Are you familiar with the play?
- Yes I am.

I didn't have a fucking clue what 'Twelfth Night' was about, or any other Shakespeare play for that matter. If I'd had half a brain, I would have studied it all through the night by candlelight. But, being a cocky plonker, I thought they would simply give me the script and I would be able to sight read it. But they hadn't done that.

- That's good Colin. Cast yourself.

I had no idea. I obviously looked a bit confused. I trawled the *shallows* of my Shakespearean repertoire, trying desperately to remember *anything* the Bard had written. Nope! I was going to be hoisted by my own cocky petard. Wait a minute! something flashed into my thick head. Let's give it a whirl,

- Puck?

They looked at me as if I was raving mad and thought I was joking. After a few polite embarrassed sniggers, they realised that not only was I *not* joking but that I was also the only actor in the history of the theatre who had never even given one of the greatest playwrights EVER, a passing glance. I know that they wanted to say,

- Thank you Colin. Leave your name and address in the waste paper basket on the way out.

But, with undeserved kindness, the director said,

- Thank you Colin. We'll be in touch,

Needless to say, there *was* no getting in touch. I didn't go to Coventry and didn't do 'Twelfth Night'. In fact, I never did do any Shakespeare. In my heart of hearts I must confess that Will was better off without me.

What a plonker.

Scene Sixty-six: Mick and Keith in Stoned Confusion

'Let the Good Stones Roll' was a musical based on the creation and life of the Rolling Stones. The action was set in a circus ring and I was playing the role of Keith Richards. There were only seven of us in the cast, the five Stones including Brian Jones, a ringmaster who was the narrator of the piece and Sara Coward who played all the female roles: Marianne Faithfull, Bianca Jagger etc. Although it was a musical there was a lot of dialogue which, in my opinion, is what let the show down. We played the Stones' songs live onstage and, after rehearsing for a month in London and then performing the show for a month in Newcastle at the Theatre Royal, we had reached a pretty high musical standard. Unfortunately, in spite of several rewrites, the script never seemed to hit the right mark. At the end of the Newcastle run the producer Charles Ross came up for the final show and announced,

> - Fantastic news everyone! We're taking the show into town and opening at the Ambassadors Theatre.

There was a stunned silence from all of us. Despite the valiant efforts of all concerned none of us thought it was up to West End standards. Someone, I can't remember who, spoke up but Charles was convinced that, with more rewrites, it would work. So to the Ambassadors we went in March, 1978. The two writers Raynor Borden and Steve Dawson worked their butts off re-writing, re-writing and then more re-writing with the result that the show became more and more confusing.

We were doing a run of previews before the opening night proper. I was applying my 'slap' (make up) for the matinée when Raynor came into my dressing room with the latest rewrites which were little more than random lines here and there. Most actors will agree that it is easier to remember big chunks of changes than it is to remember odd lines. Louis Selwyn who was playing Mick came in to me in a state of near panic, a state I was fast approaching myself, saying,

> - Have you seen the new rewrites? I haven't got a fucking clue what's going on any more. Have you?
> - No. (*I am rarely reduced to monosyllables*)

Louis and I had a long scene together in which we discussed being part of the immediate post-war generation. This scene had been changed so many times that we were both totally confused. Trying to stay calm I suggested,

- Let's just go on and wing it. We'll sort it out in between shows.

We got to the long WW2 scene, started the dialogue and quickly realised that neither of us had a clue where we were going with it. We were improvising like mad (thank God for all the improv I had done with Philip Hedley). Even so it wasn't long before the audience clocked that we were spouting absolute bollocks; their unease was manifested by a lot of coughing and seat squirming. (This phenomenon is a reliable indication that the audience wishes you would just fuck off, stop annoying them and let them get to the bar.) I realised that drastic action was needed before this scene entered the Guinness Book of Records for its sheer length and awfulness.

- Mick,

I said,

- Yeah Keith.
- Let's talk about it later.
- Good idea,

said Mick.

And, yielding to the audience's clearly-expressed wishes, we both fucked off, him stage left and me stage right. Our long overdue exit was greeted with the biggest applause of the afternoon.

'Let the Good Stones Roll' closed very shortly after it had opened. We felt for Raynor, Steve and Charles Ross. They could not have tried harder to make it work and it very nearly did but, sadly, not nearly enough. I bought one of the guitars I had played in the show and every now and then I knock out a medley of Stones hits just in case they 'rewrite' the show and want the old Keith back.

Scene Sixty-seven: Richard Beckinsale's Rubbish Motor

As was the norm after the shows on a Saturday night many of us would end up in Macready's Club where we would revel until the very, very early hours, the club being licenced to stay open until the last thespian had fallen out of the door. It was also the norm for anyone who wasn't thoroughly sloshed to give a shout when they were leaving in case someone who *was* sloshed lived in their neighbourhood and could be dropped off on the way.

Early one morning a few of us were still propping up the bar and no doubt drunkenly discussing who should be running the Royal Shakespeare Company, the National Theatre, and the Royal Opera house (of course the answer was...'any one of us'). This was the usual old bollocks we thesps would drone on about after far too much falling-down water had been consumed.

There came a shout from the top of the stairs,

- Anyone going Fulham way?

Fulham? I live in Fulham.

- Yes please. I'll be right up
- OK mate, I'll get my car and meet you outside.

I extracted myself from the drunken clutches of someone telling me that he was "the best fucking actor the world had ever seen". Pausing just long enough to confirm that it wasn't Larry Olivier I'd been boring shitless all night, I stumbled upstairs into the early morning half-light of the real world and waited for my mystery chauffeur to arrive. Three minutes later around the corner appeared a vision of four-wheeled beauty. Out of the morning mist, a white Silver Cloud Rolls Royce drew up next to me. At least I think it was a Silver Cloud but, having never got much beyond a Ford Cortina, how would I know?

- Hop in mate, just chuck all the shit onto the back seat.

I recognised the voice and peered into the car to see the unmistakable face of Richard Beckinsale. I had long admired Richard, first watching him in the TV series 'The Lovers' followed by, amongst others, 'Rising Damp' and 'Porridge', in which he starred alongside the amazing Ronnie Barker. I opened the gorgeous door of this dream car and was almost knocked off my feet by an avalanche of garbage. The shit that Richard had instructed me to throw onto the back seat was an overwhelming heap of fish and chip papers, pizza boxes some still containing half eaten pizza slices, hamburger boxes, empty bottles and tins of soft drinks and at least twenty empty crisp packets. I looked at Richard's face which didn't seem to have a trace of acne and said,

- Many thanks. I'm just off Fulham Broadway but drop me anywhere
  that's good for you.

On the journey home I was treated to a wealth of theatrical stories and anecdotes. He dropped me right to my doorstep then drove the classiest, most magnificent dustcart I have ever seen off down the Fulham road.

Richard was not long for this world. He passed away far too young, aged 31. A great actor and the loveliest, most down-to-earth guy you could ever wish to meet.

Scene Sixty-eight: What a Gas

I had just finished filming the first series of the TV show 'Oh Boy', performing as one of the 'cats', the in-shot backing singers. We sang backup for all the main performers: Joe Brown, Alvin Stardust, Shakin' Stevens and some young vocalists. One of these was a young boy straight out of school with no previous TV or stage experience and no idea how the biz worked. We all helped to show him the ropes and we enjoyed singing with him. On the last day he asked what we would all do now that this show was over, and what were our next singing jobs. We explained that we had agents who would try to get us work but that the nature of the business meant you could be unemployed for weeks, sometimes months or years and, if work was really thin on the ground, you might have to take any job you could find: waiting tables, telephone sales, cleaning, anything just to pay the rent. He was a little shocked by this as he thought we must all be working full time. We wished him well with his career and hoped that we would work together again in the future.

My agent Kitty Whittle sent me to a casting interview for a new commercial for North Thames Gas. I got the gig and a week later turned up for the night shoot in a back street in South London. There were twelve of us guys dressed in the uniforms of gas board maintenance engineers. We were supposed to be the 'North Thames Gas Male Voice Choir', singing Christmas carols outside houses to drum up work for the gas company.

We were filming at 3a.m.; it was winter, and freezing cold. The director explained the shot he wanted: we would all hum the Christmas carol 'Silent Night' looking up at a bedroom window. The lady of the house would be so impressed by our dulcet tones that she would open the window and throw mince pies down to us (and then, presumably, promptly order a new boiler). We had been hanging around for hours while the technicians sorted the sound, lighting etc. Even though we were given hot drinks and blankets it was still bloody freezing. We did a couple of rehearsals, humming our tune and the lady opening the window and, for rehearsal purposes, she mimed throwing the mince pies down to us. When he was happy with everything the director said,

   - OK everyone, it's very important we get this filmed in one take.

"Strange", I thought, as we always did multiple takes of everything: different angles and close ups. Anyway, one take was fine with me, then it would be home to a nice warm bed, job done, feet up.

- Ok, stand by everyone…..cameras rolling…and…..action!

We were humming our socks off. The window opened. The lady appeared……. and, in what felt like slow motion, threw a massive bucket of freezing cold water over all of us. Well, you can imagine the reaction from the choir! We gasped, screamed, shouted, swore. This was the shot the bastard wanted. There never were any mince pies, this was *the* commercial. He got his shot in one and apologised for the setup, and explained the reason for his deception,

- If you had known what was going to happen, you would have anticipated the water, and the reactions wouldn't have been as real.

The truth is…he was right, the fucker.

Now, let's get to the point of this story. Polly of WSC fame who was also one of the backup singers on 'Oh Boy', bumped into the young vocalist we had been mentoring a few months earlier. Polly asked how he was doing and he replied,

- Yeah I'm doing pretty well, I've got some more TV work and I've just started a band. But isn't it sad about Col?

Polly was a bit confused,

- What do you mean, sad about Col?
- Bless his heart. I know you were all telling me that things could be tough in this profession and that sometimes you had to take any work you could get. But the other night, I was watching the telly and a commercial came on. And there was Col. I thought you would have known, Polly. Col's working for North Thames Gas as a fitter!

If only all the ingénues of showbiz could stay so innocent.

Scene Sixty-nine: Royal ....Pardon?

My agent sent me for a TV commercial casting in the West End. It was in one of those huge swanky buildings with lots of offices and conference rooms. I arrived fifteen minutes early and went to the ground floor reception desk. There was a very young, very pretty, very flustered girl on the desk. I politely tried to introduce myself and explain why I was there. Phones were ringing on her desk and she was making a futile effort to work out which buttons to press to connect the callers.

PG (pretty girl), holding up a finger,

> - Sorry love. Give us a mo will ya. I'm a temp. The agency only sent me 'ere half an 'our ago. Driving me bleedin' mad all these phones. Dunno how the normal girl 'andles it. 'Ang on.

She answered the phone,

> - 'Allo. Clitheroe Swanky Braithwaite Foster and Cockbinder. Can I help you?
> Oh sod it. I've gone and disconnected 'im. Bugger!

Me:

> - Oh dear! No problem. I have a casting with Braithwaites at 10.30. Colin Copperfield?

PG, holding the phone the wrong way up, and speaking into the earpiece,

> - Yeah, I'm trying to connect you ain't I? Keep yer 'air on. Twat (*under breath*). Now he's bloody 'ung up on me.

Mmm! Right girl for the job?

Me:

> - Sorry! I can see you're up against it but I'm just a little worried about the time. I don't like to be late for these things.....

> - I'm doing me best luv. Yes, Clitheroe Swanky Braithwaite Foster and ... (holding hand over receiver) Go and sit over there luv, I'll sort you out in a minute... (and to the caller) Cockbinder.

Resigning myself to the situation and to the fact that this commercial was probably a dead loss, I sifted through the magazines on the coffee table and opened a well-worn 'Horse and Hound'.

- Clitoris, Wanky...oh, piss off.

PG slammed down the receiver and, with all seventeen phones ringing off the hook, she started to file her nails and plonked one stiletto-heeled foot on the desk.

At that moment, both of the glass entrance doors flew open and in walked an entourage of about fifteen people, with four bodyguards flanking the biggest black man I had ever seen. He was costumed from head to foot in brightly-coloured robes, topped by a huge tribal hat. The entourage approached the desk and the head honcho tapped the desk with his walking cane. PG removed the white stilettoed foot from the reception desk and looked up from filing her nails.

- The King of Tonga has a 10.30 meeting with Sir John Clitheroe. Inform him that we have arrived if you would be so kind.

PG, who clearly couldn't give a shit by this stage,

- Right! 'Ang on. I'll see if e's around.

She pressed a few buttons, randomly, and got lucky.

- Oh 'allo. I've got a bunch of people 'ere to see Sir John. What? Oh, I forgot. 'Ang on.

She turned to the brightly-costumed, very large, very regal-looking man and said,

- Sorry, luv. Who did ya say you was king of?

I realised that this was not my day, and exited onto Bond Street, smiling to myself and slightly in love with my elocution-challenged PG.

Scene Seventy: I've Got a Brand New Wall Street Crash Combine Harvester

Like all bands WSC always had a lot of kit to transport what with all the musical instruments and sound equipment, so we would arrange for a driver to meet us in the airport car park with a truck to take all the gear directly through customs to the group check-in. Our regular driver was a mountain of a man all of six feet seven with a strong Cornish accent. I was fascinated by his accent and would always perch myself in the front of the truck with him so we could have a natter. I would start off the conversation something like

- Terry, what did you do before you worked at Heathrow?
- Well oy'll tell thee. Oy waz in the parachute regiment see, coz oy loiked jumpin' out o' them there aeroplanes I did. It royt excited me that did.

And so on…. After a year of chatting to Terry nearly every week, one day he said to me,

- Oy've got summit oy'd like to ask ye.
- What's that then, Terry?
- Well oy knows oy picks yous up every week like, but oy don't knows that much bout music, like. So can oy ask you summit coz oy wants to tell moy wife. Now, Are you Wall Street Crash or The Wurzels?

Dear Reader, if you are far too young to know The Wurzels, they were a scrumpy and Western group who sang songs about farming and the countryside. A group less like WSC you could never imagine.

We invited Terry and his wife to a WSC concert in London. He came backstage after the gig and seemed a little disappointed.

- Did you enjoy it, Terry?

- Well oy liked some of it but yous never sung that song 'bout the combine harvester and that were one of moy favourites of yours.

Help!

Scene Seventy-one: Col's the Man for a Singing Telegram

Resting: that good old theatrical expression meaning "Nobody will give me a job even though I'm a better actor than Olivier, a better dancer than Astaire, a better singer than Pavarotti, a better writer of musicals than Sondheim and a better choreographer than Bert Flunchbucket. (You won't have heard of Bert, but he choreographed a marvellous line-dancing routine for my Uncle Harry's eightieth birthday barn dance at Pinner Working Men's Club last November.)

Singing telegrams originated in America and were very popular for many years. When the American company, Music World, started up in the UK, many resting performers answered the advertisement in the theatrical newspaper, 'The Stage' for:

OUTGOING PERFORMERS WITH STRONG VOICES AND FUN PERSONALITIES FOR SINGING TELEGRAM WORK IN LONDON. TIME OFF FOR AUDITIONS AND GOOD RATES OF PAY.

For my audition I sang the Tommy Steele song 'Flash Bang Wallop' which seemed to do the trick and I became the first boy to do a singing telegram in the UK. This is how it worked. Music World kitted us out with black tuxedos and black top hats. A potential client would call the office requesting, for example, a telegram for their son's twenty-first birthday. The office would correlate whatever information they could about the recipient: hobbies, nicknames, friends' names, profession, girlfriend, funny incidents, embarrassing incidents, pets' names - anything that would make an entertaining song. The office would write the song and then ring me with instructions:

Gram, 10p.m. Saturday, Gino's Italian restaurant Soho, contact at front door Gill Davies, sing the gram to the tune of 'I'm a Yankee Doodle Dandy'.

The lyrics would be read to me over the phone, I would note them down on a Music World celebration card, and I would be ready to rock.

At this stage the company had no idea if the idea would float in this country. They were concerned that the Brits might be too reserved for this sort of thing.

Far from it, they loved it, and sometimes I would be doing twenty telegrams a day, driving all over London.

Much later, when I was with the Wallies, we wrote a pilot for a TV sitcom called 'A Funny Way to Make a Living', based on my singing telegram experiences. The TV companies liked the idea and wanted us to expand on it, possibly for a TV series but, by that stage, the group had taken off and unfortunately we didn't have enough time to dedicate to it. When we came back to it a few years later the trend for singing telegrams had passed. It was a shame as it may have worked really well as a light entertainment show.

Showbiz is a fickle, baffling, frustrating profession. I had worked in the West End for six years straight then, suddenly, I couldn't get arrested. I was still doing good auditions, my singing, dancing and acting were sharp, yet I was somehow missing the mark. There seemed to be no rhyme or reason for it, but roles I could have done standing on my head were going to other people. Not to blow my own piccolo, but these were roles I was much more suited to, and some of the guys who got the parts actually agreed with me.

I auditioned for one musical which required doing the lot: singing, dancing, acting, juggling, gymnastics and comedy and, although I was better at some disciplines than others, I could do all of them to a pretty high standard. I saw several of my friends at the audition and they all said, "You're in mate! You're so right for this show". Every one of them got parts and I didn't. I wasn't bitter, upset or jealous, none of those things at all, just confused. But that's the name of the show business game. For certain in the biz the stars are sometimes aligned right for you and sometimes not. I don't think any of us can explain it, understand it, or know the answer to it. I guess it's just the nature of the game.

So, that might explain why, sporting my tuxedo, I was primed for the next gram/gig, ready to burst into any restaurant, club, office, factory, home, hotel, caravan, boat or private plane and treat the assembled company to some slack-arsed versification.

- Hi, I'm Colin from Music World, the singing telegram company, and I have a singing telegram for John Smith…. 2.3.4 ♪♪♪ to the tune of "Give My Regards to Broadway"

Here's our regards to, you John, coz it's your birthday,
Sandra and Billy and all of your friends would just like to say,
Though you have now reached forty, don't think your life will stall,
You're handsome and sexy and top of your game,
So come on John have a ball.
Remember when you were six, John, at Uncle Bill's party in Staines,
You drank all the booze that you could, John, and got pissed out of
your brains,
Your family were shocked and disgusted. They said you'd gone past
the brink,
But you didn't care, you just laughed like a drain,
And then threw up in the sink.........all together now.... ♪♪

Scene Seventy-two: A Touch of Frost

Remember David Frost? "Hello, good evening and welcome" ('That Was the Week that Was')?

Jilly rang.

> - Hi Col I've got a gram for you at (she mentioned a swish private London club - I can't remember the name). This Saturday, 11p.m. It's from David Frost to his girlfriend, Diahann Carroll.

Wow! I had always fancied her. Maybe, once she has heard me sing she'll give Dave the Spanish Archer (El Bow) and she and I will drive off into the sunset in my clapped out Hillman Minx. (Well, a fella can dream, can't he?)

The lyrics were all very lovey dovey, with the clear, but unspoken, agenda of a bit of leg over at the end of the evening. At the appointed time I met my contact man Rupert at the front entrance to the club and he briefed me on the modus operandi. He said there would be some birthday speeches and that he would cue me with three quick knocks on the door, behind which I would be lying in wait. I should then burst into the room in my usual jovial manner and deliver my song to Diahann.

The speeches were going on a bit and I was desperately in need of a pee. I listened at the door and it sounded as though the chap speaking was in for the long haul. I thought I had better do the deed while the going was good. Luckily I found a loo close by. I was just at that ecstatic moment of release when I heard a frantic shout.

> - Singer, singer where are you? Where the bloody hell are you?

You so know what's coming next don't you? I panicked and pulled my zip up so fast that ..... Ahhhhhhh!, fuuuuuuuuck!

> - Singer, quick ! They're waiting. Hurry, hurry.

Not only had I zipped my zinger, but I had also peed down my leg. In excruciating pain I pulled the zip back down. Ahhhhhhhh!, fuuuuuuuck! I pulled the lyrics out of my pocket and ran down the corridor. I leapt into the room sweating profusely, pee dribbling down my leg and a todger throbbing faster than a Suzuki 750 motorcycle engine at full revs. Am I a pro? Does the show always have to go on? Of course it bloody does!

- Hi I'm Colin from Music World the singing telegram company, and I...etc, etc.

I somehow managed to keep my voice within a normal vocal range rather than slipping into falsetto (the logical consequence of my injury).

Diahann (she who should have ridden off with me into the sunset) will never know of my agony as I sang to her. The gram went well and my contact man gave me a handsome tip (almost enough to pay for the plastic surgery on my ailing organ)...Job done, feet up.

The following night, in the Evening News there was a small write-up from one of the journalists. It went like this, verbatim:

Last night I was a guest at a birthday party in a private members' club in Mayfair. The evening was most memorable due to the unexpected appearance of a chap in top hat and full evening dress who sang a delightfully humorous birthday song for the hostess. I can only guess that his fantastic performance will strike fear into the hearts of tone deaf postmen everywhere.

Finally, I'd made it!

Scene Seventy-three: Hope you Get the Message, Dad

Most of my gigs were pretty straightforward but some were bizarre. One day the office rang saying they had a job for me on Father's Day in South Kensington but that I had to turn up on Sunday morning at 4a.m. The booking came from this chap's two sons who were living in America. I was living in Fulham so South Ken was only ten minutes away. I figured that I could sing the gram and be back in bed within thirty minutes *and* they had agreed to pay me three times the set rate. Great!

I thought the lyrics were borderline abusive but guessed that was just their family sense of humour so I didn't give it too much thought. Often the lyrics to the grams were politically incorrect, and sometimes disgusting, but they always got a good response and nobody seemed to take any offence in those days. I found the block of flats next to South Ken tube station and rehearsed the song in my car a couple of times. At 4a.m., tuxedo looking sharp, top hat at a jaunty angle and lyrics in my hand I gave a confident knock on the door.....
no response. Well, I thought, it is four in the morning and the poor bugger's probably fast asleep. I waited a minute or so and then gave a slightly louder knock. The door flew open and an irate, dishevelled man stood before me in his jimjams. I went into my well-rehearsed spiel,

> - Hi I'm Colin from Music World the singing telegram company and I have a singing telegram from your two sons in America.
> - Fuck off!

The door slammed in my face. It was 4.07a.m. I was standing in my penguin suit feeling like a complete prat. OK, so it may be a bit early for a jaunty little song but it is Father's Day and it has cost your sons a few bucks to do this, so maybe that was an ever so slightly over the top reaction. What to do? Like an idiot, I decided to try again. Maybe he was still pissed or drugged up from a pre-Father's Day party, maybe he was meditating and I had buggered up his yogic waves or maybe he had seen me playing Keith Richards in the musical 'Let the Good Stones Roll' and really didn't want to hear me sing anything ever again, under any circumstances. I braced myself .....I knocked....the door flew open.

- Hi I'm Colin from Mus…
- Listen you tosser. SEX AND TRAVEL!!!
- I don't understand.
- Translation? FUCK OFF!!

Well! This guy may have wanted many things in his life, but it was clear that he didn't want a singing telegram at 4a.m. I rolled up the lyrics, posted them through his letter box, and headed for home.

The phone rang at nine the same morning, interrupting an absurd dream about doing a singing telegram at 4a.m. and being told to fuck off.

- Hello Col it's Jilly (Music World). What happened?

I relayed the story.

- I'm so sorry Col. I just heard from the sons. They wanted to know what their father's reaction was because they hate his guts and haven't spoken to him for years. The whole thing was a sick joke. I'm so, so sorry.

Well at least it was nothing personal and I got three times the money without even having to sing a note. In fact it was one of the easiest grams I'd ever done; it was not completely unknown for me to have sung the gram and *then* been told to fuck off!..........

♪♪♪ Oh…there's no business like show business, like no business I know.

Scene Seventy-four: Scent of a Woman

Estée Lauder, the famous perfume designer, was retiring and going to live in America. This would have been in the mid-1970s.

Jilly rang.

- Hi Col I've got a very classy gram for you to do next Saturday, in the Grosvenor Hotel, Mayfair.

It was a pretty straightforward song and involved thanking Estée Lauder for the brilliant products she had created over so many years and wishing her well for her future life in America. I arrived at the required time and met my contact girl.

CG explained that the room had been set up in a strange way. There was very little room behind the stage so most of the guest speakers would simply come up from their tables rather than making their entrance through the curtains. Then, when they had done their bit, they would step off the stage and return to their table. However, I was asked to make a grand entrance through the curtains. There was a dance area just in front of the stage and Estée Lauder's table was situated on the edge of it. CG intimated that she didn't know how long the speeches would go on for and explained that, once I was behind the curtain, I wouldn't be able to get out until I had sung my song and exited through the audience. Oh dear! The willy-in-the-zip saga still loomed large in my memory. My instrument had only just returned to full working order. I explained my predicament to CG and, with impressive lateral thinking, she suggested that we find a vessel of some sort which I could use if things got desperate. She returned with a flower vase that was so enormous it would have taken a herd of elephants three months to get it half full. CG also said she would organise some sandwiches and drinks in case I was behind the curtain for a long time, adding that they would also be paying me for the whole evening and that a huge box of all Estée Lauder's products would be waiting for me at the hotel reception desk. Rockin'!

As the guests were due to arrive at 7.30, I was in my cubby hole by 7.15 with a book, a huge platter of sandwiches, cakes, nuts, crisps, water (still and sparkling), my emergency receptacle and, best of all, a magnum of Cristal champagne. CG popped her head in to say "Break a leg" and hoped I wouldn't have to hang around for too long.......Famous last words.

Eleven o'clock arrived and the speeches were still going on and on and on and on. The sandwiches and nuts were history and I had read my book and started again at the beginning. The cakes were all over my face and up my nose, the receptacle was fast approaching the three quarter mark, and I was bored shitless.

- Yes! And well I remember when Estée and I were developing our latest fragrance. It must have been in 1973 or was it '74? No, I remember now, it was the summer of '76…or was it the spring of '79?

Who gives a fuck? How much longer am I going to be incarcerated in this isolation unit? Maybe a glass of Cristal will ease the pain of boredom… Bad move! I eased the cork out of the bottle with barely a pop.

12.30 arrived. The receptacle was now full and so was I, full of eight glasses of Cristal and getting merrier by the minute.

- It must have been in the winter of '72 when we launched our most successful fragrance, or was it the autumn '75?.

OOO GIVE'Z ZA FUUCKK?

- And now, Estée and all of your wonderful family, friends and colleagues, we have a special farewell surprise for you all. Instead of a telegram to wish you good luck we have a singing telegram to wish you bon voyage. Ladies and gentlemen… a round of applause please for Colin.

Now, you lot are getting all excited and expecting me to say that, by this stage, I was comatose on the floor behind the curtain clutching the empty bottle of Cristal in one hand and the overflowing gargantuan receptacle in the other, that I staggered to my feet, fumbled my way through the curtain, fell arse over tit down the steps, crashed into Ms Lauder, causing the displacement of her decolletage, was arrested for being drunk and disorderly and spent the night in the cells at Brixton nick. Soz to disappoint but that very amusing scenario never unfolded. I may have been four or five sheets to the gale force wind but I was hot to trot. I was on the case.

The curtain opened and I leapt forth with all the gusto of a man fresh from serving fifteen years in Wandsworth prison. I was wired. I had enough pent-up energy to blow up the national grid. I was motoring, I was Charlie Chat. After five hours in penal confinement, listening to all those endless speeches, I knew more about Estée Lauder than she knew about herself. I was ad-libbing like crazy. This wasn't a singing telegram; this was a Las Vegas show and I was the star.

The song (when I eventually got to it) went exceptionally well and, as I squeezed through the tables, pausing only to shake the delighted Estée's hand and give her a presumptuous peck on the cheek, the applause was ringing in my ears. I collected my box of goodies from reception, explaining to the receptionist that I was "a bit pissed" (understatement) and that I would be back in the morning to collect my car from the car park. I exited onto Park Lane, hailed a black cab, and kipped all the way home.

Music World received great feedback about my performance, so a good time was had by all.

I am still working my way through the eighty three bottles of Modern Muse Le Rouge, Youth Dew, Modern Muse Nuit, Pleasures Bloom, Aliage, Amber Mystique, Azuré, Beyond Paradise, Estée and Intuition from my goody box. Yes, I know they are ladies' perfumes but, hey, I'm a theatrical don't ya know?

COVID 19:
The Theatres Go Dark

It is astounding that, throughout World War II, with bombs raining down on London nightly, the theatres went dark for only a few weeks. There were twenty-four plays and musicals on in the West End on the 7th of September 1940 at the start of the Blitz; one week later only two theatres were open. However, very soon, all of the theatres were back up and running and they stayed open for the duration of the war. Covid-19 managed to do what Adolf Hitler and his Luftwaffe failed to do: it decimated the world of show business: the theatres, clubs, cinemas and arenas are now 'dark'....

All dark ....except for one single incandescent bulb which is left energized and glowing in the dark on the stage of every theatre. It is known as the 'Ghost Light' and is mounted in a wire cage on a portable stand, centre stage. The origin and reason for this light has become part of theatre folklore.

The logical, and probably the correct reason, is for safety. It would be quite easy for someone unfamiliar with the topography of the theatre, perhaps a security person, to wander onto a darkened stage and fall into the orchestra pit. Of course it would be handy if said security person was armed with a big torch to swish around, thereby avoiding such a dunderhead calamity. There is a story of a burglar who wasn't armed with a swishing torch and who tripped on a darkened stage, broke his leg and later sued the theatre for damages.

There is another theory that the light is left on for the theatre ghosts - maybe so that they aren't too alarmed when they come across another spectral being. However, I would have thought that a fundamental qualification for becoming a ghost would be the ability to see in the dark.

Interestingly, the Palace Theatre in London keeps two seats in the balcony permanently bolted open to provide seating for the house ghosts. I have to say that, in the three years I performed in Jesus Christ Superstar at the Palace,

I saw not one single ghost, but it is quite possible that, when they heard me sing, they thought "Sod this for a game of haunting", and buggered off to do their ghosting down the road at the nearby Queens Theatre in Shaftesbury Avenue, to get a little peace and quiet and protect their ears. ...

However as you all well know, I'm a bit of a thespy sentimentalist and the theory that I favour is that the Ghost Light is left on to comfort the theatre and to reassure it that it will be open again soon. Ahhhhhh.[24]

During the war, the London Palladium narrowly missed destruction when it was hit by an unexploded German parachute mine. On 11th May, 1941, the bomb crashed through the roof and became lodged in the flys (the area above the stage used to fly in scenery). A Royal Navy bomb disposal team arrived but, when they touched the fuse locking ring in order to remove the fuse, the bomb started ticking again. The surrounding area was rapidly evacuated but mercifully the bomb didn't explode. Two members of the bomb disposal team returned, extracted the fuse and other dangerous components to render the bomb safe, and it was lowered down to the stage and disposed of. The men were deservedly decorated for their bravery. If only we could remove the fuse locking ring from Covid-19.

So many of my friends have had their professional lives crushed by Covid: dancers, actors, singers, directors, lighting technicians, sound engineers, the list is incredibly, sadly, devastatingly endless. A great friend who is a top flight session and theatre saxophonist has all but given up hope of earning a living any time soon and is now completing a painting and decorating course, just to survive. Others are working as delivery drivers or stacking shelves in supermarkets. These are talented musicians who, early in 2020, were playing in West End shows and recording top-selling records.

My dear closest friend Perty from The Wallies has 'almost' done one gig in the last twelve months. I say 'almost' because he was booked to perform his cabaret act in a marquee tent at a golf club but, thirty minutes before the show,

---

24 Speaking of theatre lights: the expression "In the limelight" has an interesting origin. The invention of limelight has been attributed both to Thomas Drummond, a Scottish army officer, and to Sir Goldsworthy Gurney, a doctor, scientist and inventor. After experimenting with different substances, Gurney discovered that a brilliant light was produced when a flame was directed onto a chunk of lime. The light was so bright that it could be seen almost a hundred miles away. It is believed that limelight was first used on stage in 1837. The actors who were the centre of attention on the stage were said to be standing in the limelight. This saying now applies to anyone who is the focal point of any situation.

a storm erupted and a massive gust of wind carried away the tent, and with it, his props, costumes and music. His amplifiers and speakers were flooded. "So what did you do?" I asked. What he did was conduct a Cockney singalong in the pouring rain for the three members of the audience who hadn't gone home. When he relayed the story we both fell into hysterical laughter….How on earth do you go from a Royal Command performance at the Palladium to singing "Knees Up Mother Brown" with an audience of three in a mud-soaked field in the middle of nowhere? At least he was paid, but I doubt that his fee covered the expense of replacing his show shoes.

By mid-June, 2021, about 60% of the population of the UK had been given at least one dose of the vaccine and we were all straining our weary lockdown eyes, trying to catch a glimpse of that very faint light at the end of this incredibly long dark tunnel. When we come out of the other side of this, what will the entertainment industry look like? (What will any industry look like? As this is the industry that has been my life for so long, please forgive me for concentrating on the one that I know and love.) Will we be comfortable surrounded by thousands of people at the 02 or any other large venue across the globe? Or sitting with a few hundred other people in one of our world's fantastic theatres? We are resilient people so I think and hope that we will. It will take time of course.

As always, some good things invariably come out of bad things, so maybe we will appreciate the theatre even more than we did before; maybe we'll applaud even louder; maybe we'll sing along and go for the high notes without giving a damn if we miss them; maybe we'll do the Mexican wave with even more gusto while holding onto the stranger's hand next to us more tightly and be glad to be able to do so; maybe, instead of rushing to our cars, trains, buses and cabs at the end of being entertained, we'll pause and smell the theatrical roses for a bit longer? As I've said before, "It's not how you start, it's how you finish." Adolph couldn't finish us and neither will Covid. WE ARE UNFINISHABLE!

Not the Final Curtain
(here's hoping)

My life still revolves around performing. As I mentioned at the beginning of this book I have just finished writing a musical called 'Paradise Lane' which is set in the East End. If the universe is smiling on me, it will soon be coming to a theatre near you. I write songs for other artists, which still gives me a huge buzz. I work as a dance teacher, specialising in tap, modern and ballet (my pink tutu still fits perfectly), and I look after my wonderful clients as a personal fitness trainer.

There is an old theatrical saying: "Always leave them wanting more". So, although I have quite a few more stories up my theatrical sleeve, maybe this is the right time to leave you wanting more.

If you've enjoyed this little trip *half* as much as I have, then I've enjoyed it *twice* as much as you. Bye for now.

Printed in Great Britain
by Amazon

78025761R00163